PRAISE FOR

THE
INDISPENSABLE
MILTON
FRIEDMAN

"Milton Friedman was the most authoritative exponent of the libertarian tradition in economics. He will be remembered as long as the subject endures, and this collection epitomizes the power of his mind and range of his mastery."

—**George Gilder,** *author of* Wealth and Poverty

"Milton Friedman was one of the most important scholars of the 20th century.... He perfected the art of making economics understandable to the ordinary, untrained individual. That's the true mark of a teacher."

—**Walter E. Williams,** *John M. Olin Distinguished Professor of Economics, George Mason University*

"In addition to being a great innovator in economic thought, Milton, assisted by his wife Rose, helped to create a warm fellowship for young new faculty.... Milton, along with Ted Schultz, George Stigler, Harry Johnson, Al Harberger, and Al Reese, created 'The Chicago School.'"

—**Robert Fogel,** *Nobel Laureate, Economic Sciences*

"Economists can succeed Milton Friedman, but nobody can replace him. As this collection of rare but brilliant essays confirms, he was one of a kind, and is greatly missed."

—**Mark Skousen,** *Editor,* Forecasts & Strategies

"This volume of essays from the corpus of Milton Friedman's work is not only welcome in light of the centennial of this brilliant intellectual's birth, but will clear the air of so many prevalent economic myths that continue to haunt us today."

—**Fr. Robert A. Sirico,** *author of* Defending the Free Market,
President, Acton Institute

"Milton Friedman was not only mentor to me but to young people all over the world. Together with Rose, his wife and collaborator of 68 years, they wrote many influential books dealing with the relationship between capitalism and freedom. Their last book, *Two Lucky People*, impacted the lives of so many. But, we are the lucky people to have known them personally. This collection of essays keeps the vision of this great man and woman alive. They were the quintessential team."

—**Sally Pipes,** *President and CEO, Pacific Research Institute*

"Keynes was wrong, and Friedman was right: political freedom and economic liberty are necessary allies in the expression of free minds and free markets, and the tyranny of control will always hamper prosperity. This extraordinary collection of essays illustrates the best of the Nobel laureate's thoughts on how economics affects the world we live in."

—**David Nott,** *President, Reason Foundation*

"Milton Friedman was probably the most important advocate of individual freedom in the United States in the second half of the 20th century. In particular, he was that rare individual: both a world-class scholar and a world-class communicator. He won a Nobel Prize for studies that revolutionized the science of economics. But the essays in this book are clear and accessible to any newspaper reader. They are a good sampling of the work of a man who said, 'Our central theme in public advocacy has been the promotion of human freedom.'"

—**David Boaz,** *Executive Vice President, Cato Institute*

THE INDISPENSABLE

MILTON FRIEDMAN

THE INDISPENSABLE MILTON FRIEDMAN

ESSAYS ON POLITICS AND ECONOMICS

EDITED BY Dr. Lanny Ebenstein

Cataloging-in-Publication data on file with the Library of Congress
ISBN 978-1-59698-808-8

For original publication information for individual essays, see pages 255–257.

Published in the United States by
Regnery Publishing, Inc.
One Massachusetts Avenue NW
Washington, DC 20001
www.Regnery.com

Manufactured in the United States of America
10 9 8 7 6 5 4 3 2 1

Books are available in quantity for promotional or premium use. Write to Director of Special Sales, Regnery Publishing, Inc., One Massachusetts Avenue NW, Washington, DC 20001, for information on discounts and terms or call (202) 216-0600.

Distributed to the trade by
Perseus Distribution
250 West 57th Street
New York, NY 10107

To Art Rupe

—L. E.

CONTENTS

INTRODUCTION

Milton Friedman would have turned one hundred years old on July 31, 2012. The son of Hungarian Jewish emigrants to the United States, he had both an immigrant's faith in the future of this country and an impressive intellectual understanding that America's future prosperity and freedom depended on her continued respect for private property and free enterprise. He believed the lessons of economics, history, and politics all showed that where private property was protected and free markets were allowed to flourish, prosperity and freedom followed.

Friedman received the Nobel Prize in Economic Sciences in 1976, and the ideas he put forward helped to guide policy-making in capitals across the globe. Particularly in the area of inflation, his consistent admonition that "inflation is always and everywhere a monetary phenomenon" has influenced the theory and practice of monetary policy for decades. But his influence in advancing free market policy initiatives was broad; as Daniel Patrick Moynihan once remarked: "If you were to ask me to name the most creative social-political thinker of our age I would not hesitate to say Milton Friedman."[1]

Among the issues that Friedman championed were floating international exchange rates, reducing increases in money supply to control inflation, an all-volunteer army, school vouchers, privatization of many government functions, a greatly reduced role for government, denationalization, lower taxes, a negative income tax, and drug legalization. He was perhaps most effective as a teacher.

In a 1996 interview, he commented that the "greatest problem facing our country is the breaking down into two classes, those who have and those who have not.... We really cannot remain a democratic, open society that is divided into two classes. In the long run, that's the greatest single danger. And the *only* way I see to resolve that problem is to improve the quality of education."[2] He lamented the influence of the welfare state in "creating a different kind of culture and a different kind of human being." He believed that if "people are born into a world in which there are very few welfare supports, in which the culture requires people to be responsible for themselves, there will be many fewer such [dependent] people than if they are born into a society in which it is taken for granted that the government will come in and help them out."[3]

The essays collected here are in two broad areas—politics and economics—and they are distinguished by several factors. For the most part, they have not been republished before, and some of them were originally published in journals with very small circulations. This is the first comprehensive collection of essays by Milton Friedman since his death in 2006, and these essays span his career. The earliest essay in this collection was originally published in 1950, the last a few months before he died. They cover the highlights of his career as a public intellectual, from defending the "freedom of individuals to control their own destinies" ("Liberalism, Old Style," 1955), to showing how the first step in fixing health care is realizing that "nobody spends somebody else's money as wisely or as frugally as he spends his own" ("How to Cure Health Care," 2001); from Friedman's most important lecture on monetary policy ("The Counter-Revolution in Monetary Theory," 1970), to his assessment that John Maynard Keynes was "truly a remarkable scientist, even if, to use the words that William Stanley Jevons applied to an earlier brilliant economist, David Ricardo, he 'shunted the car of economics on to a wrong line' for some decades" ("The Keynes Centenary," 1983).

I was privileged to know Milton Friedman as a source and subject for projects of mine. He had a terrific sense of humor, an unfailing memory, and a brilliantly insightful mind. I remember well the first time I interviewed him. I asked whether he minded if I taped the conversation. He responded: "What I say to one person, I say to everyone. I never say anything off the record."

A biographer of John Locke commented that Locke was so great that his biographer could not measure his greatness. It is hoped that the essays that follow will give the reader some measure of another great man, the Nobel Prize Laureate Milton Friedman.

NOTES

1.   Steven F. Hayward, *The Age of Reagan* (New York: Random House, 2001), p. 524.
2.   Michael Albert, *Parecon: Life After Capitalism* (London: Verso, 2003), p. 77.
3.   Milton Friedman, correspondence with Lanny Ebenstein, June 1, 2005.

PART ONE

POLITICS

NEO-LIBERALISM
AND ITS PROSPECTS

1951

In his magnificent book, *Law and Public Opinion*, A. V. Dicey distinguished between the trend of legislation on the one hand and the trend of opinion on the other. Legislation, he argued, is dominated by the underlying current of opinion, but only after a considerable lag. Men legislate on the basis of the philosophy they imbibed in their youth, so some twenty years or more may elapse between a change in the underlying current of opinion and the resultant alteration in public policy. Dicey sets 1870 to 1890 as the period in which public opinion in England turned away from individualism (Manchester liberalism) and toward collectivism; yet he points out that economic legislation was not strongly affected by the new trend of opinion until after the turn of the century.

In most of the world, legislation is still largely dominated by the trend of opinion toward collectivism that Dicey documented some forty-odd years ago. True, there have recently been a whole series of elections in which the Right has gained at the expense of the Left—in Australia, England, and the United States, and continental Europe. But even if a political trend to the right were to develop out of these small beginnings, which is by no means certain, it would probably mean simply collectivist legislation of a somewhat different kind to be administered by different people. The men of the conservative parties, no less than those of the left, have been affected by the underlying current of opinion. Men may deviate in emphasis from basic social values and beliefs but few can hold a thoroughly different philosophy, can fail to be infected by the intellectual air they breathe. By the standards of nineteenth century individualism, we are all of us collectivists in smaller or greater measure.

A number of small incidents will illustrate my point that a political trend to the right is by no means synonymous with a reversal of the trend toward collectivism. A few years ago, I happened to be in England when the Labour Government proposed a higher excise tax on tobacco as a means of curtailing tobacco imports. In reporting this decision, the government spokesman deplored the necessity of using a tax to curtail consumption and justified it on the grounds that direct rationing of tobacco products had been deemed too difficult administratively. Far from applauding the Labour Government for having decided to use the price system rather than direct controls, the Conservatives hastened to condemn the government for rationing "by the purse" instead of directly. More recently, in the United States, the president asked Congress for emergency economic powers to meet the problems raised by re-armament. He did not ask for powers to control prices and wages. The Congress insisted on giving him such powers as well, and many Republicans were among those who insisted he should have them. If I may speak of my own country again, the Republicans profess to be in favour of free enterprise and strongly opposed to a drift toward socialism. Yet their published program favours protective tariffs, agricultural subsidies and support of the prices of agricultural products as well as a number of other measures that can fairly be termed collectivist in their implications.

I do not mean to argue that it makes no difference which party is elected, which side gains votes. It clearly makes a difference of degree if not of kind and offers the opportunity to begin a drift in a new direction. My point is rather that the direction this drift takes will be determined not by the day-to-day shifts in political power or by the slogans of the parties or even their platforms but by the underlying current of opinion which may be already— if only we could penetrate its mysteries—determining a new direction for the future.

While the trend of legislation is still strongly toward collectivism, I have the feeling that this is no longer true of the underlying trend of opinion. Until a few years ago, there was a widespread—if naïve—faith among even the intellectual classes that nationalization would replace production for profit with production for use, whatever these catchwords may mean; that centralized planning would replace unplanned chaos with efficient coordination; that it was only necessary to give the State more power in order to solve this supposed paradox of poverty in the midst of plenty and to prevent the "selfish interests" from exploiting the working masses; and that because socialists favoured peace and international amity, socialism would in some unspecified way further these goals. The experience of the last few years has shaken if not shattered these naïve beliefs. It has become abundantly clear that nationalization solves no fundamental economic problems; that centralized economic planning is consistent with its own brand of chaos and disorganization; and that centralized planning may raise far greater barriers to free international intercourse than unregulated capitalism ever did. Equally important, the growing power of the State has brought widespread recognition of the extent to which centralized economic control is likely to endanger individual freedom and liberty.

If these judgments are correct, we are currently at one of these periods when what Dicey called the "cross-currents" of public opinion are at a maximum, a period at which underlying opinion is confused, vague and chaotic. The same beliefs are still largely held by the same people, but there is no longer the same unthinking acceptance of them. Stubbornness and unwillingness to relinquish a faith once blindly held are taking the place of fanaticism. The stage is set for the growth of a new current of opinion to replace the old, to provide the philosophy that will guide the legislators of the next generation even though it can hardly affect those of this one.

Ideas have little chance of making much headway against a strong tide; their opportunity comes when the tide has ceased running strong but has not yet turned. This is, if I am right, such a time, and it affords a rare opportunity to those of us who believe in liberalism to affect the new direction the tide takes. We have a new faith to offer; it behooves us to make it clear to one and all what that faith is.

The major fault of the collectivist philosophy that has dominated the western world is not in its objectives—collectivists have wanted to do good, to maintain and extend freedom and democracy, and at the same time to improve the material welfare of the great masses of the people. The fault has rather been in the means. Failure to recognize the difficulty of the economic problem of efficiently coordinating the activities of millions of people led to a readiness to discard the price system without an adequate substitute and to a belief that it would be easy to do much better by a central plan. Together with an overestimate of the extent of agreement on *detailed* objectives, it lead to a belief that one could achieve wide-spread agreement on a "plan" couched in precise terms and hence avoid those conflicts of interest that could be received only by coercion. The means collectivists seek to employ are fundamentally inconsistent with the ends they seek to attain. A state with power to do good by the same token is in a position to do harm; and there is much reason to believe that the power will sooner or later get into the hands of those who will use it for evil purposes.

The collectivist belief in the ability of direct action by the State to remedy all evils is itself, however, an understandable reaction to a basic error in nineteenth-century individualist philosophy. This philosophy assigned almost no role to the state other than the maintenance of order and the enforcement of contracts. It was a negative philosophy. The state could do only harm. Laissez-faire must be the rule. In taking this position, it underestimated the danger that private individuals could through agreement and combination usurp power and effectively limit the freedom of other individuals; it failed to see that there were some functions the price system could not perform and that unless these other functions were somehow provided for, the price system could not discharge effectively the tasks for which it is admirably fitted.

A new faith must avoid errors. It must give high place to a severe limitation on the power of the state to interfere in the detailed activities of individuals; at the same time; it must explicitly recognize that there are important positive functions that must be performed by the state. The doctrine sometimes called neo-liberalism which has been developing more or less simultaneously in many parts of the world and which in America is associated particularly with the name of Henry Simons is such a faith. No one can say that this doctrine will triumph. One can only say that it is in many ways ideally suited to fill the vacuum that seems to me to be developing in the beliefs of intellectual classes the world over.

Neo-liberalism would accept the nineteenth century liberal emphasis in the fundamental importance of the individual, but it would substitute for the nineteenth-century goal of laissez-faire as a means to this end, the goal of the competitive order. It would seek to use competition among producers to protect the consumer from exploitation, competition among employers to protect workers and owners of property and competition among consumers to protect the enterprises themselves. The state would police the system, establish conditions favorable to competition and prevent monopoly, provide a stable monetary framework, and relieve acute misery and distress. The citizens would be protected against the state by the existence of a free private market; and against one another by the preservation of competition.

The detailed program designed to implement this vision cannot be described in full here. But it may be well to expand a bit on the functions that would be exercised by the state, since this is the respect in which it differs most from both nineteenth century individualism and collectivism. The state would of course have the function of maintaining law and order and of engaging in "public works" of the classical variety. But beyond this it would have the function of providing a framework within which free competition could flourish and the price system operate effectively. This involves two major tasks: first, the preservation of freedom to establish enterprises in any field, to enter any profession or occupation; second, the provision of monetary stability.

The first would require the avoidance of state regulation of entry, the establishment of rules for the operation of business enterprises that would make it difficult or impossible for an enterprise to keep out competitors by any means other than selling a better product at a lower price, and the prohibition of combinations of enterprises or actions by enterprises in restraint of trade. American experience demonstrates, I think, that action along these lines could produce a high degree of competition without any extensive intervention by the state. There can be little doubt that the Sherman anti-trust laws, despite the lack of vigorous enforcement during most of their existence, are one of the major reasons for the far higher degree of competition in the United States than in Europe.

The provision of monetary stability would require a reform of the monetary and banking system to eliminate the private creation of money and to subject changes in the quantity of money to definite rules designed to promote stability. The provision of money, except for pure commodity money, cannot be left to competition and has always been recognized as an appropriate function of the state. Indeed, it is ironic and tragic that the consequences of the failure of government planning in this area—which, in my view, include both extreme inflations and deep depressions—should form so large a part of the alleged case against private enterprise, and be cited as reasons for giving government control over yet other areas.

Finally; the government would have the function of relieving misery and distress. Our humanitarian sentiments demand that some provision should be made for those who "draw blanks in the lottery of life." Our world has become too complicated and intertwined, and we have become too sensitive, to leave this function entirely to private charity or local responsibility. It is essential, however, that the performance of this function involve the minimum of interference with the market. There is justification for subsidizing people because they are poor, whether they are farmers or city-dwellers, young or old. There is no justification for subsidizing farmers as farmers rather than because they are poor. There is justification in trying to achieve a minimum income for all; there is no justification for setting a minimum wage and thereby increasing the number of people without income; there is no justification in trying to achieve a minimum consumption of bread separately, meat separately, and so on.

These are broad powers and important responsibilities that the neo-liberal would give to the state. But the essential point is that they are all powers that are limited in scope and capable of being exercised by general rules applying to all. They are designed to permit government by law rather than by administrative order. They leave scope for the exercise of individual initiative by millions of independent economic units. They leave to the unparalleled efficiency of the impersonal price system the coordination of the detailed economic activities of these units. And above all, by leaving the ownership and operation of economic resources predominantly in private hands, they preserve a maximum of individual freedom and liberty.

Even if I am right in my belief that the underlying trend of opinion toward collectivism has passed its peak and been reversed, we may yet be doomed to a long period of collectivism. The trend of legislation is still in that direction; and, unhappily, collectivism is likely to prove far more difficult to reverse or change fundamentally than laissez-faire; especially if it goes so far as to undermine the essentials of political democracy. And this trend, which would be present in any event, is certain to be radically accelerated by the cold war, let alone by the more dreadful alternative of a full-scale war. But if these obstacles can be overcome, neo-liberalism offers a real hope of a better future, a hope that is already a strong cross-current of opinion and that is capable of capturing the enthusiasm of men of good-will everywhere, and thereby becoming the major current of opinion.

LIBERALISM, OLD STYLE

1955

L iberalism, as it developed in the seventeenth and eighteenth centuries and flowered in the nineteenth, puts major emphasis on the freedom of individuals to control their own destinies. Individualism is its creed; collectivism and tyranny its enemy. The state exists to protect individuals from coercion by other individuals or groups and to widen the range within which individuals can exercise their freedom; it is purely instrumental and has no significance in and of itself. Society is a collection of individuals and the whole is no greater than the sum of its parts. The ultimate values are the values of the individuals who form the society; there are no super-individual values or ends. Nations may be convenient administrative units; nationalism is an alien creed.

In politics, liberalism expressed itself as a reaction against authoritarian regimes. Liberals favored limiting the rights of hereditary rulers, establishing democratic parliamentary institutions, extending the franchise, and guaranteeing civil rights. They favored such measures both for their own sake, as a direct expression of essential political freedoms, and as a means of facilitating the adoption of liberal economic measures.

In economic policy, liberalism expressed itself as a reaction against government intervention in economic affairs. Liberals favored free competition at home and free trade among nations. They regarded the organization of economic activity through free private enterprise operating in a competitive market as a direct expression of essential economic freedoms and as important also in facilitating the preservation of political liberty. They regarded free trade among nations as a means of eliminating conflicts that might otherwise produce war. Just as within a country, individuals following their own interests under the pressures of competition indirectly promote the interests of the whole; so, between countries, individuals following their own interests under conditions of free trade, indirectly promote the interests of the world as a whole. By providing free access to goods, services, and resources on the same terms to all, free trade would knit the world into a single economic community.

"Liberalism" has taken on a very different meaning in the twentieth century and particularly in the United States. This difference is least in the concrete political forms favored: both the nineteenth-century liberal and the twentieth-century liberal favor or profess to favor parliamentary forms, nearly universal adult franchise, and the protection of civil rights. But even in politics there are some not unimportant differences: in any issue involving a choice between centralization or decentralization of political responsibility, the nineteenth-century liberal will resolve any doubt in favor of strengthening the importance of local governments at the expense of the central government; for, to him, the main desideratum is to strengthen the defenses against arbitrary government and to protect individual freedom as much as possible; the twentieth-century liberal will resolve the same doubt in favor of increasing the power of the central government at the expense of local government; for, to him, the main desideratum is to strengthen the power of the government to do "good" "for" the people.

The difference is much sharper in economic policy where "liberalism" now stands for almost the opposite of its earlier meaning. Nineteenth century liberalism favors private enterprise and a minimum of government intervention. Twentieth century liberalism distrusts the market in all its manifestations and favors widespread government intervention in and control over, economic activity. Nineteenth century liberalism favors individualist means to foster its individualist objectives. Twentieth century liberalism favors collectivist means while professing individualist objectives. And its objectives are individualist in a different sense; its keynote is welfare, not freedom. As Schumpeter remarks, "as a supreme, if unintended, compliment, the enemies of the system of private enterprise have thought it wise to appropriate its label."[1] The rest of this article is devoted entirely to "liberalism" in its original meaning; and the term will be used throughout in that sense.

Political liberalism and economic liberalism derive from a single philosophy. Yet they have frequently led independent lives in application, which suggests that their relation to one another deserves examination in the realm of ideas as well. During the nineteenth century, many countries adopted large elements of economic liberalism, yet maintained political forms that were neither liberal nor developing at any rapid pace in a liberal direction. Russia and Japan are perhaps the outstanding examples. During the twentieth century, countries that have achieved and maintained most of the concrete elements of the liberal political program have been moving away from liberal and toward collectivist economic policies. Great Britain is the most striking example; certainly for the first half of this century, the general drift of British economic policies has been toward greater direct intervention and control by the state; this drift has been checked in the past few years but whether the check is more than transitory remains to be seen. Norway, Sweden, and, with a lag of several decades, the United States, exhibit much the same tendencies.

As already noted, liberal thinkers and writers in the nineteenth century regarded political reforms as in large part a means of achieving economic liberalism. The earlier political forms concentrated political power in the hands of groups whose special interests were opposed to such measures of economic liberalism as free trade. Let all the people have a vote, and there would be, so liberals like James Mill argued, no special interest. And since the general interest was simply the interest of all the individuals composing the society, and these in turn would be furthered most effectively by economic liberalism, democracy could be expected to rid itself of the dead hand of government and to give maximum scope to the invisible hand of self-interest.

In the twentieth century, a group of liberal thinkers, especially Henry Simons, Ludwig von Mises, and Friedrich von Hayek, have emphasized that this relation also runs in reverse: that economic liberalism is a means of achieving political freedom. Economic liberalism alone does not guarantee political freedom—witness the examples of Russia and Japan cited earlier. But economic liberalism is, it is argued, an indispensable prerequisite for political freedom. Historically, there are no countries that enjoyed any substantial measure of political freedom that did not also practice a substantial measure of economic liberalism. Analytically, the preservation of political freedom requires protection against the concentration of power; it requires the existence of largely independent loci of power. Political power by its nature tends to be concentrated; economic power can be highly deconcentrated if it is organized by means of an impersonal market; economic power can thus be an independent offset to political power. Let both economic and political power be in the same hands and the only protection of political freedom is the good will of those in power—a frail recourse particularly in view of the corrupting influence of power and the talents that make for political survival.

A few examples may clarify the asserted relation between economic and political freedom, though they cannot of course demonstrate it. A characteristic of a politically free society is that proponents of radical reform in the structure of the society are permitted to express their views and to seek to persuade their fellows. It is a testimonial to the freedom of the United States that socialist and communist magazines and papers are published. Suppose a change to a collectivist economic society with government control of the bulk of economic activity. How could the proponents of a return

to capitalism secure the resources with which to publish a magazine urging
their point of view? Through a government fund for dissidents? Through
the collection of small sums from millions of government employees? If
they had the resources in the form of funds, what guarantee could they have
that the government would sell them paper on the same terms as it does to
others? In an economically liberal society, it is possible to get the general
resources with which to spread dissenting views either by subsidies from a
small number of individuals or by selling a magazine or other publication
to many; and if there is a reasonable chance that enough people will want
to buy a magazine expressing the minority view to make it profitable, even
people who disagree fundamentally with the view will in their own self-
interest provide the resources to make its establishment possible. In effect,
there are thousands or millions of independent loci of power to decide
whether an idea is worth trying to promote, rather than the few or one in
a political structure. And given the general resources, there is no further
obstacle: in a thoroughly free market, the sellers of paper do not know
whether the paper is going to the *Daily Worker* or the *Foundation for Economic Education*. Perhaps some similar impersonal and effective guarantees
of freedom to promote dissenting views could be contrived for a collectivist society; certainly no proponents of such a society have yet suggested any
or even faced this problem squarely.

As another example, consider those individuals who have lost or
resigned government jobs in the United States in recent years because they
were or were accused of being Communists. Government employment in
our society is not a right and it is entirely appropriate that at least certain
governmental positions should not be open to actual or suspected Communists. It is easy also to see how strong public feeling can lead to a closing
of all government posts to Communists. Yet, the maintenance of political
freedom surely requires that people be free not only to believe in but also
to advocate Communism; those of us who abhor Communism do so in
part precisely because we know it would not grant us freedom to express
contrary views; our defense against Communism is to persuade our fellow

citizens of its evil, not to suppress its advocates. But if government employment were the only employment, nominal freedom to express extreme
views would be a mockery. The exercise of this freedom would be at a
prohibitive price—namely, giving op the possibility of earning a living. By
contrast, in the existing society, those who have left government employment have had a wide variety of other opportunities. The way a private
market economy protects these opportunities is revealed most clearly by
considering an individual who goes into farming and produces, say, wheat.
The purchasers of the wheat do not know whether it has been produced by
a Communist or a Fascist, a white man or a Negro; they could hardly dis-
criminate if they wanted to. The competitive market in this way separates
economic activity from intellectual or political activity and the more competitive the market, the more sharply it does so. It is a paradox that minor-
ities who have in this way the most to gain from a competitive society have
contributed unduly large numbers to the ranks of its opponents.

Many writers who emphasize the importance of economic liberalism
as a prerequisite for political freedom have interpreted tendencies toward
collectivism in recent decades as betokening a trend toward political "serfdom." They may yet be proved right. So far, however, the relation they stress
has manifested itself mostly in a very different way: namely, the collectivist
tendencies have been checked because they tended to interfere with civil
and political freedom; when the conflict has been reasonably clear, the collectivist policy has frequently given way. Perhaps the most striking example
is British experience with the compulsory allocation of labor. Socialist
economic thinking in the postwar period called for compulsory allocation
of labor to achieve "social priorities"; though some compulsory powers
were provided by law, they were never widely used; the powers themselves
were permitted to lapse; and the whole character of attempted economic
policy changed because compulsory allocation of labor so clearly interfered
with widely and deeply cherished civil rights.

We turn now to a more detailed examination of the content of liberalism, particularly economic liberalism, and of the role it assigns to the state.

This examination deals primarily with the principles that liberalism provides for judging social action. Any set of concrete proposals that these principles lead liberals to favor will vary with the particular circumstances of time and place, and consequently are less fundamental and invariant than the principles themselves. There is some possibility of being reasonably comprehensive with respect to principles; none, with respect to concrete proposals.

Principles for social action must be based on both ultimate values and a conception of the nature of man and the world. Liberalism takes freedom of the individual—really, of the family—as its ultimate value. It conceives of man as a responsible individual who is egocentric, in the sense not of being selfish or self-centered but rather of placing greater reliance on his own values than on those of his neighbors. It takes as the major problem of modern society the achievement of liberty and individual responsibility in a world that requires the co-ordination of many millions of people in production to make full use of modern knowledge and technology. The challenge is to reconcile individual freedom with widespread interdependence.

The liberal answer derives from the elementary—yet even today little understood—proposition that both sides to an economic transaction can benefit from it; that a gain to a purchaser need not be at the expense of a loss to the seller. If the transaction is voluntary and informed, both sides benefit; the buyer gets something he values more than whatever he gives up, and so does the seller. In consequence, voluntary exchange is a way to get cooperation among individuals without coercion. The reliance on voluntary exchange, which means on a free market mechanism, is thus central to the liberal creed.

The working model which embodies this vision of a society organized through voluntary exchange is a free private enterprise exchange economy. The elementary social unit—the family or household—is generally too small for efficient use of modern productive techniques. Accordingly, the productive unit takes the form of an enterprise which purchases productive services—labor, the use of capital, and so on—from households and other enterprises and sells the goods or services it produces to households and other enterprises. The introduction of such enterprises does not change the strictly voluntary and individual character of the cooperation, provided two conditions are satisfied: first, the enterprises are *private*, which means that the ultimate locus of authority and responsibility is an individual or a group of individuals; second, individuals are *free* to sell or not sell their services or to buy or not buy products from particular enterprises, which means, also, that they are *free* to establish new enterprises.

The final point deserves special emphasis in view of widespread misunderstanding of it. "Free" in the liberal conception of free enterprise means freedom to establish enterprises, not freedom of established enterprises to do whatever they want. This is one of those familiar cases in which absolute freedom is impossible because the freedom of some limits the freedom of others: the freedom of existing enterprises to do whatever they want, including combining to keep new entrants out or to fix prices and divide markets, may limit the freedom of others to establish new enterprises or to make the best bargain they can. When such a conflict arises, the liberal tradition regards freedom of entry and of competition as basic; it therefore justifies state action to preserve competition and to make selling a product of higher quality or at a lower price the only means whereby existing enterprises can prevent new enterprises from being established. The most difficult practical problem in this area and one on which liberals have spoken with many tongues is combinations among laborers—the trade union problem.

In the free enterprise exchange economy envisaged by liberalism, the primary role of government is to preserve the rules of the game by enforcing contracts, preventing coercion, providing a stable monetary framework, and, as just noted, keeping markets free. Beyond this there are only three major grounds on which government intervention is justified: (1) "natural monopoly" or similar market imperfections; (2) the existence of substantial "neighborhood effects"; (3) protection of children and other irresponsible individuals.

An exchange is "voluntary" only when essentially equivalent alternatives exist; when an individual can choose whether to buy from one enterprise or another, to work for one enterprise or another. Monopoly means the absence of alternatives and thus is incompatible with strictly voluntary exchange. Monopoly may arise from combinations among enterprises in circumstances where competition is entirely feasible, and, as already noted, liberal tradition justifies state intervention to preserve competition in such cases. But monopoly may also be "natural," as in the textbook examples of a single spring providing drinking water, or of a product subject to such large economies of scale that the most efficient productive unit is large enough to serve the whole market. The only available alternatives are then all bad: government regulation, government ownership, or private monopoly, and the problem is to choose the least of these evils. As might be expected, liberals have no clear-cut answer. Henry Simons, after observing in the United States the consequences of government regulation of such alleged natural monopolies as the railroads, concluded that government ownership was the least of the evils when monopoly was inevitable. Walter Eucken, after observing in Germany the consequences of government ownership, concluded that government control was the least of the evils. And some have argued that in a dynamic world private monopoly may well be, citing the case of the regulation of transportation in the United States as their prime example. The Interstate Commerce Commission was established to protect the public against the railroads when railroads probably did have a large element of natural monopoly. The development of highway and air transport has largely eliminated any natural monopoly element in railroads, yet instead of the abolition of the Interstate Commerce Commission, government control has been extended to these other transportation media. The ICC has become a means of protecting the railroads from the competition of trucks instead of the public from the absence of competition. Fortunately for the possibility of a liberal society, the area within which natural monopoly is a serious problem is exceedingly limited, so that no large amount of government intervention is called for on this score.

In practice, the claim of natural monopoly is more often an excuse for intervention desired on other grounds than a valid justification for intervention.

A different kind of threat to strictly voluntary exchange arises from the so-called "neighborhood effect." This occurs when the action of one individual imposes significant costs on other individuals for which it is not feasible to make him compensate them or yields significant gains to other individuals for which it is not feasible to make them compensate him. A simple example is that of an individual polluting a stream. He has in effect forced other individuals further down the stream to exchange good water for bad; they clearly would have been willing to do so for a price; but it is not feasible to make this exchange the subject of voluntary agreement. Another, rather different example, is education. The education of a child is regarded as benefiting not only the child and his parents but also other members of society, since some minimum level of education is a prerequisite for a stable and democratic society. Yet it is not feasible to identify the particular individuals benefited by the education of any particular child, much less the money value of the benefit, and so to charge for the services rendered. In consequence there is justification on liberal grounds for the state requiring some minimum amount of education for all children, even though this is above the amount parents would otherwise provide, and for meeting some of the cost of education from taxes imposed on all members of society.

Of course, all actions of an individual involve some "unborne costs" and "inappropriable benefits" to third parties. It is always a question of judgment whether these are sufficiently great in any particular case to justify state intervention; the state too will be plagued by the difficulties of identifying costs and benefits that prevent voluntary exchange and there are other costs of state action. The liberal philosophy thus gives no hard and fast line separating appropriate from inappropriate state action in this area. But it does emphasize that, in deciding any particular case, one general cost of state action—one general neighborhood effect, as it were—must always be taken into account; namely, that the extension of state action involves an encroachment on individual freedom. The liberal regards this as a count against any proposal for state action, though by no means a fatal obstacle to it, and hence requires a clear net balance of gains over other costs before regarding the state action as justified.

The third ground on which liberalism justifies state intervention derives from an ambiguity in the ultimate objective rather than from the difficulty of achieving fully voluntary exchange. The belief in freedom is for "responsible" individuals; and children and insane people cannot be regarded as "responsible." In general, this problem is avoided for children by treating the family as the basic unit of society and so regarding the parents as responsible for their children. In considerable measure, however, this procedure rests on expediency rather than principle. The problem of drawing a reasonable line between action justified on these paternalistic grounds and action that conflicts with the freedom of responsible individuals is clearly one to which no fully satisfactory—and certainly no simple—answer can be given.

A few additional examples may clarify the bearing of these principles in judging particular acts of social policy. Consider first a group of measures that clearly conflict with liberal principles: tariffs, direct controls of imports and exports, exchange control, general price controls. None of these can be justified on any of the grounds for state intervention that we have listed. Each represents an interference with the freedom of individuals to engage in any transactions that they want to, which do not have substantial effects on third parties, and thus involve a direct interference with essential freedoms. An extreme case which brings out this feature strikingly is the "tourist allowance" incorporated in the exchange control regulations of a number of countries; as the *Economist* puts it, "it sets a limit on the length of time that even the most economical British resident can choose to spend abroad without asking the permission of some bureaucrat." Finally, most of these measures prevent the market from operating effectively and thus threaten the heart of the liberal system. For example, if a legal maximum price is established below the level that would otherwise prevail, a "shortage" will inevitably follow (as in housing under rent control); some method other than the free market will have to be used to "ration" the available amount; and further government intervention replacing the market is set in train.

A second rather different example is medicine. As already noted, significant neighborhood effects justify substantial "public health" activities: maintaining the purity of water, assuring proper sewage disposal, controlling contagious diseases. There is little or no justification on these grounds for state intervention into private medicine—the care and treatment of individuals. Under liberal principles, this is a function the market can and should perform. To the argument of the proponent of socialized medicine that there is great uncertainty about possible medical bills, the liberal will reply that the market is perfectly capable of providing private insurance; if people don't want to pay the premium, that is their free choice. To the argument that people don't get as much medical service as is "good" for them, the liberal will reply that each man should judge for himself—not that he is necessarily the best judge but that he should make his own mistakes; insofar as we think he is making the wrong decision, there is no objection to telling him what we think and trying to persuade him, but there is no justification for making his decision.

A third example is public housing. It may be that certain types of housing, e.g., dense slum districts, impose higher costs of police and fire protection on the community. This literal "neighborhood effect," since its source can be identified, would justify higher taxes on such property than on others to meet these extra costs; it hardly justifies subsidies to housing. The main argument for public subsidy to housing is surely paternalistic: people "need" or "deserve" better housing, and it is appropriate to use public funds to provide housing. The liberal will object on two different levels. Given that some people are to be subsidized, why not give them the subsidy in general purchasing power and let them spend it as they will? Why say to them, we will give you a gift if you take it in the form of housing but not otherwise? Does this not involve an unnecessary restriction on their freedom? Second, he will question the redistribution of income itself that is involved in such a program—and, indeed, one advantage of making the subsidy explicit is that it would make clear what groups are being subsidized. Government relief of poverty, the liberal will support and welcome, primarily on the explicitly paternalistic ground of taking care of the irresponsible. But the more or less indiscriminate transfer of income involved in large scale public housing schemes, he will regard as undermining individual responsibility. The way to reduce inequality, he will urge, is not by the misleading palliative of sharing the wealth, but by improving the workings of the market, strengthening competition, and widening opportunities for individuals to make the most of their own qualities.

These two final examples illustrate how the central virtue of a liberal society is at the same time a major source of the objections to it: a liberal society gives people what they want instead of what a particular group thinks they ought to want or thinks is "good" for them; it makes it equally difficult for the benevolent and the malevolent to shape other people in their own image. At bottom of most arguments against the market is lack of belief in freedom—at least for other people—as an end.

Adam Smith provides an excellent summary of the preceding discussion of the role of the state in a liberal society: "Every man, as long as he does not violate the laws of justice, is left perfectly free to pursue his own interest his own way, and to bring both his industry and capital into competition with those of any other man, or order of men. The sovereign is completely discharged from a duty, in the attempting to perform which he must always be exposed to innumerable delusions, and for the proper performance of which no human wisdom or knowledge could ever be sufficient; the duty of superintending the industry of private people, and of directing it towards the employments most suitable to the interest of the society. According to the system of natural liberty, the sovereign has only three duties to attend to; three duties of great importance, indeed, but plain and intelligible to common understanding: first, the duty of protecting the society from the violence and invasion of other independent societies; secondly, the duty of protecting, as far as possible, every member of the society from the injustice or oppression of every other member of it, or the duty of establishing an exact administration of justice; and, thirdly, the duty of erecting and maintaining certain public works and certain public institutions, which it can never be for the interest of any individual, or small number of individuals, to erect and maintain; because the profit could never repay the expense to any individual or small number of individuals, though it may frequently do much more than repay it to a great society."[2]

NOTES

1.   Joseph A. Schumpeter, *History of Economic Analysis* (1954), p. 394.
2.   *The Wealth of Nations*, Book IV, Ch. IX (Cannan edition, Vol. II), pp. 184–185.

SCHOOLS
AT CHICAGO

1974

To economists the world over, "Chicago" designates not a city, not even a University, but a "school." The term is used sometimes as an epithet, sometimes as an accolade, but always with a fairly definite—though by no means single-valued—meaning. In discussions of economic policy, "Chicago" stands for belief in the efficacy of the free market as a means of organizing resources, for skepticism about government intervention into economic affairs, and for emphasis on the quantity of money as a key factor in producing inflation. In discussions of economic science, "Chicago" stands for an approach that takes seriously the use of economic theory as a tool for analyzing a startlingly wide range of concrete problems, rather than as an abstract mathematical structure of great beauty but little power; for an approach that insists on the empirical testing of theoretical generalizations and that rejects alike facts without theory and theory without facts.

These denotations of the Chicago school of economics are of long standing. They have prevailed for decades, with only minor though not negligible changes in meaning despite a complete change in the persons regarded as the "leaders" of the school. My personal experience with the Chicago school of economics began more than 40 years ago, as a graduate student, when Frank Knight, Jacob Viner, and Henry Simons were the acknowledged leaders of the Chicago school. Today, the Chicago school has an even broader base than it did then, numbering among its leaders not only some of us at the University but also economists at other institutions, some of whom have never been formally connected with the University. But all are students—direct or indirect—of Knight, Viner, and Simons, and, at a still longer remove, of Adam Smith—who but for the accident of having been born in the wrong century and the wrong country would undoubtedly have been a Distinguished Service Professor at The University of Chicago.

The mixture of irritation and pleasure that I have experienced at being alternately damned and applauded—and always, as I felt, misunderstood—as a member of the Chicago school has led me to become something of a collector of intellectual schools. One impression that I have formed from my casual collection is that The University of Chicago is a particularly fertile breeding ground for "schools"—though it clearly has no monopoly.

Already in 1903, William James greeted a book by John Dewey and several of his associates, *Studies in Logical Theory*, as "the signal of the birth of a 'Chicago school' of pragmatic philosophy."[1] Unfortunately, Dewey resigned his professorship at Chicago shortly thereafter, so that this Chicago school may not have had a long life.

In sociology, Albion Small—the initial head of the Department—laid the basis for the famous Chicago school of sociology led by W.I. Thomas, Robert Park, and Ernest Burgess—a school that reigned from 1920 to perhaps 1950. Morris Janowitz describes the central thrust of the Chicago school of sociology as consisting of emphasis "on empirical data and the need for integrating data into what they believed to be an appropriate theoretical framework"[2]—a description that applies equally to one aspect of the Chicago school of economics.

In political science, "the Chicago school . . . led by Charles E. Merriam and . . . Harold D. Lasswell," has been described as "diverse in its interests but united in its aim to explore new methods of studying political and administrative behavior"[3] again a description that could apply to economics and sociology.

Chicago pioneered in the social sciences and fostered active cooperation among them—most concretely by constructing a single social science building to house them all, so it is perhaps not surprising that "schools" should have flourished in the social sciences and should have had much in common. Witness the quotation from Lord Kelvin carved in stone on the Social Science Building: "When you cannot measure, your knowledge is meagre and unsatisfactory"—a quotation which Frank Knight one day contemplated at length and then muttered: "And if you cannot measure it, measure it anyhow."

However, schools have flourished at Chicago not only in the social sciences, but elsewhere as well.

In English, a Chicago school of criticism was initiated and led by Ronald Crane. In theology, the larger part of a history of The University of Chicago Divinity School by Charles H. Arnold is devoted to tracing the 60-year history of the "Chicago School of Theology." Members of this audience can, I am sure, add to that list, and I shall appreciate it very much if they do. Indeed, one reason I chose this topic for tonight's talk is in order to add to my collection in the most painless and efficient way.

There are, of course, Cambridge schools and Oxford schools and Viennese schools and Harvard schools and I have made no exhaustive survey of them all. So I cannot claim to have demonstrated that Chicago is exceptionally fertile as a producer of "schools." But I shall assume for the present that my impression to that effect is correct and turn to the main question I want to discuss: Why? What has there been about The University of Chicago that has given rise to schools?

When I asked one friend this question, his offhand remark was that perhaps Chicago's geographical isolation had led people at Chicago to become inbred and to develop homogeneous, if offbeat, views.

This answer, while a very natural one, misconceives the nature of schools and is besides demonstrably wrong as a description of fact. A "school" may be, but need not be, a "cult." None of the social science schools I have mentioned was a "cult." All of them were rather pioneer attempts to open up new directions of research and analysis, new ways of looking at phenomena. All of them numbered among their members persons working on a wide variety of topics and holding diverse views. All of them affected the course of scientific research in their disciplines and have been in considerable measure absorbed in those disciplines. Rather than being "crank" outsiders, their leaders were recognized and honored by their professional brethren, serving as presidents of their professional associations and editors of professional journals.

But while a "school" need not be a "cult," neither, to go to the other extreme, is it simply a designation of excellence. To take another example from the social sciences, anthropology has always been an excellent department at Chicago, widely recognized as one of the best in the world. It has had many outstanding and famous members, yet apparently there has never been a Chicago school of anthropology, in the sense of a distinctive approach pursued by a number of leading scholars and propagated by their students.

If Chicago's geographical location had an effect—as I shall argue later that it did—it was not by encouraging narrowness, homogeneity, and inbreeding. The fact is that none of the departments ever consisted primarily of members of the corresponding schools. In his discussion of the Chicago school of sociology, Morris Janowitz notes that "Albion Small . . . was eclectic in his interests and tastes," and that "there was a continual effort to have all aspects of sociology actively represented." Robert E.L. Faris, in his book on *Chicago Sociology*, states that "probably the most important factor in the growth at Chicago was the intelligent perception by Small, accepted

enthusiastically by his colleagues and successors, of the inhibiting consequences of doctrines, schools of thought, and authoritative leaders. . . . This
openness to influences from other traditions was also reflected in the decision to bring Ogburn to Chicago from Columbia, thus enriching the local
sociological content with the research-method emphasis that had been
developing at Columbia. In that period [1920s and 1930s] no Chicago-
trained sociologist was brought into the department at Columbia or Yale.
Brown first appointed a very young instructor from Chicago . . . in 1931. . . .
Mid-century approached before Harvard ventured to bring in a representative of the Chicago sociology"—and I may add that Harvard has still not
ventured to bring in a full-fledged representative of the Chicago school of
economics, though it has, in recent years, hired a number of Chicago Ph.D.s.[4]

In political science, every biographical reference to Charles E. Merriam
that I have seen has stressed his eclecticism, his tolerance of diversity, his
concern solely for quality. And a political science department that in our
days has simultaneously included Hans Morgenthau, David Easton, and
Leo Strauss among its leading members can hardly be described as narrow
and inbred.

In economics—where I am personally most aware of the charge of narrowness and parochialism—the situation is similar. The first head of the
Department of Economics was James Laurence Laughlin—whose portrait
hangs in Social Sciences 122 and who was characterized by a historian of
the Chicago school of economics as "one of the most conservative economists in the country."[5] Laughlin was a leading "hard-money" man of his
time, vigorously opposing the free-silver movement that reached its climax
with William Jennings Bryan's famous "Cross of Gold" speech in 1896.
(Incidentally, to display one of my few bits of local lore, that speech was
given, and Bryan subsequently nominated for the Presidency, in the neighborhood of The University of Chicago, roughly at what later became known
as "sin corner"—63rd and Cottage Grove. In 1896, there were open fields
there, and the El provided convenient transportation, so the Democratic
National Convention was held in large tents pitched for the purpose.)

To return to Laughlin, he publicly debated in Chicago with William H. Harvey, whose pamphlet entitled "Coin's Financial School" provided the most influential intellectual justification for the free-silver movement.

In these ways, Laughlin would be regarded by many as sharing some of the characteristics of the present Chicago school, though I hasten to add that in other respects, he differed drastically. In particular, he was a firm opponent of the quantity theory of money—largely because it had been used by the free-silver advocates to justify their proposals—and as long ago as 1910, he analyzed inflation as arising from the monopolistic practices of trade unions and large enterprises rather than from increases in the quantity of money—a decidedly non-Chicago position.

Despite his own strong views and active participation in political controversy, Laughlin sought out quality and diversity in the men he appointed to the faculty. As A.W. Coats remarks: "Laughlin was, indeed, a rigid thinker, an uncompromising and sometimes unfair polemicist, and an extreme conservative. Nevertheless, during his 24 years at Chicago his department became a leading center and breeding ground of economic heterodoxy. . . . Laughlin was an unrelenting individualist who genuinely respected the independence of his colleagues, and he was as outspoken in his resistance to Harper's encroachments upon his departmental independence as he was toward the encroachments of government upon individual freedom."[6]

At the very outset, Laughlin brought with him from Cornell to The University of Chicago Thorstein Veblen, whom Laughlin liked "precisely because Veblen was different in his background, in his point of view, and even in his personal characteristics." Veblen served as the first managing editor of the *Journal of Political Economy* and remained on the faculty until 1906, even though "Laughlin on occasion had difficulty in getting Veblen's contract renewed and in securing advances for him."[7] Similarly, one of the students of Robert Hoxie, who joined the faculty in 1906, wrote: "generally speaking, Hoxie and Laughlin were as far apart as West and East, but it speaks worlds for Laughlin's tolerance that he brought Hoxie to, and kept him in his Department."[8] Laughlin appointed such diverse persons as Wesley C. Mitchell, Alvin Johnson, Walton Hamilton, and John Maurice Clark—all moreover not after they had become famous but when they were in the early stages of their careers. Scientific excellence, not conformity, was clearly his major criterion. Of course, we have never been able to monopolize excellence—each of these four famous scholars served most of their careers at other institutions.

Laughlin's example has been followed to this day. When I was a student at Chicago, Paul Douglas, hardly a full-fledged member of the Chicago school in the policy sense, was a leading member of the department. The disputes between Douglas and Knight and between Knight and Viner formed an important part of our education. The department included also Harry Alvin Millis, Simeon Leland, and John U. Nef, to mention only some of the outstanding non-Chicago Chicagoans. Subsequently, the department appointed Oskar Lange, a proclaimed Socialist, later Poland's representative to the U.N., and still later a member of Poland's Communist government—but also an outstanding economic scholar.

In 1964, during the Johnson-Goldwater presidential elections, my friend and colleague George Stigler remarked that Chicago was one of the few major universities, if not the only one, that without difficulty could staff a highly qualified Council of Economic Advisers for both Johnson and Goldwater. Many another university could have staffed (and did) a Johnson Council. Two or three others could have staffed a Goldwater Council. But only Chicago—and less easily, Columbia—could readily have staffed both.

To cite one other statistic. The American Economic Association awards a John Bates Clark medal every second year to the economist under 40 "adjudged to have made a significant contribution to economic thought and knowledge." Since its inception, thirteen medals have been awarded. Nine of the thirteen recipients were either teaching at Chicago when they received the award, or had taught at Chicago before receiving the award. Of the remaining four, two had studied at Chicago, and the remaining two had received offers from Chicago.

Clearly, Chicago has not been an enclave outside the professional mainstream. On the contrary, I believe that no other major university has consistently had so wide a spectrum of views represented on its economic faculty as has Chicago. Chicago is noted for free market and anti-Keynesian views, not because they are the only ones represented at Chicago, but because Chicago is one of the few universities at which they are strongly and effectively represented, albeit, even here, by only a minority of the Department.

Not isolation and uniformity, but tolerance for diversity, stress on scientific quality as the decisive criterion for appointments, and success in identifying and attracting future leaders of their profession—these are the sources of the Chicago proclivity to generate "schools." But what in turn accounts for these characteristics? This is a topic for a specialist in the sociology of knowledge, not for a mere economist. Yet perhaps my personal involvement will excuse my presumption in venturing to suggest a possible answer.

Part of the explanation for Chicago's proclivity to generate schools was suggested to me by Edward Shils—who is a specialist in the sociology of knowledge. The University of Chicago, he pointed out, was the first major university, with the possible exception of Johns Hopkins, that was not established primarily as either a finishing school for the children of the upper classes, or as a seminary for training clerics. From the very beginning, Chicago was established as a center of learning, devoted to advancing and transmitting knowledge. Harper's vision led to the assembling at The University of Chicago of an exceptionally able and dedicated faculty—and for our purposes, the critical feature is that they were dedicated not to training gentlemen for gentlemanly pursuits, not to spreading particular religious or ethical or social doctrines, but to the objective pursuit of knowledge—to science in the broadest sense. It is crucial also that Harper chose them not only for their ability but also for their personal force and demonstrated executive ability.

The group of extraordinarily able men could write on a tabula rasa. There was no deadwood to be eliminated, no vested interests to be rooted out, intellectual or personal. The result was to establish from the outset a tradition of which we all remain the beneficiaries, these eight decades later, a tradition of objective scholarship for its own sake, of stress on the intellectual quality of people, with little regard for their personal idiosyncrasies or political views, and above all, of tolerance and respect for diversity.

To complete Shils' explanation, I believe that this tradition was able to flourish and to be successful at The University of Chicago largely because of our geographic location. Had the University been established in or near New York City under precisely the same auspices and the same initial personnel, I believe that the results would have been very different.

I have been led to this view largely by personal experience. In 1964—to the disgust and dismay of most of my academic friends—I served as an economic adviser to Barry Goldwater during his quest for the Presidency. That year also, I was a Visiting Professor at Columbia University. The two together gave me a rare entree into the New York intellectual community. I talked to and argued with groups from academia, from the media, from the financial community, from the foundation world, from you name it. I was appalled at what I found. There was an unbelievable degree of intellectual homogeneity, of acceptance of a standard set of views complete with cliché answers to every objection, of smug self-satisfaction at belonging to an in-group. The closest similar experience I have ever had was at Cambridge, England, and even that was a distant second.

The homogeneity and provincialism of the New York intellectual community made them pushovers in discussions about Goldwater's views. They had cliché answers but only to their self-created straw-men. To exaggerate only slightly, they had never talked to anyone who really believed, and had thought deeply about, views drastically different from their own. As a result, when they heard real arguments instead of caricatures, they had no answers, only amazement that such views could be expressed by someone who had the external characteristics of being a member of the intellectual community, and that such views could be defended with apparent cogency. Never have I been more impressed with the advice I once received: "You cannot be sure that you are right unless you understand the arguments against your views better than your opponents do."

To come back to our present topic, this kind of intellectual homogeneity is destructive of tolerance. It is no accident that in the New York—or more generally, the Eastern—environment, divergent views take the form of cults not schools. One of the great economists of all time, Ludwig von Mises, who recently died at an advanced age, was barely tolerated for years in a peripheral academic position at New York University. He was never accepted as being in the intellectual mainstream, even though he had a far greater influence than all but a handful of the more prestigious professors of economics at Columbia, Yale, Princeton, or Harvard. Mises had disciples but few students because of the overpowering and stultifying intellectual atmosphere of New York.

The great good fortune of our University was that it was not established on the East Coast. If it had been, it would very likely have become like all the other Eastern universities. May Johns Hopkins not be a case in point? A university that was unable to achieve its initial promise except in the area of medicine.

Fortunately, we were established in Chicago, a new, raw city, bursting with energy, far less sophisticated than New York, but for that very reason far more tolerant of diversity, of heterodox ideas. New York looked East, to the Old World. It sought above all to be recognized by that world and therefore imitated it and was hostile to any influences that might cause the Old World to look down its nose at the New.

Chicago, like other cities this side of the Appalachians, looked West, to the frontiers—though needless to say it had its share of mindless fawning on Europe, as witness Colonel McCormick's love-hate affair with England. But this did not prevent Chicago from being characterized by diversity in every dimension, by a willingness to experiment, to judge people by their performance rather than their origins, to judge ideas by their consequences rather than their antecedents.

To return to my personal experience, I could hold the views I did at Chicago, and even be an adviser to Goldwater, without losing the respect of either town or gown, but rather while still being accepted as a responsible member in good standing of the intellectual community. Had my career been in New York, and had I held the same views, I suspect that that would not have been possible. I would have been regarded as a "kook" and no doubt would have begun to act like one even earlier than I did.

If this amateur exercise in the sociology of knowledge has any validity, it has important implications for our University. First and foremost, if we are to preserve our heritage, we must continue to insist that intellectual quality and intellectual quality alone be the basis of appointments to the faculty—not political or social views, not personal attractiveness or sex or race, not grantsmanship, not even potential contribution to a balanced faculty. Balance and diversity have been and will continue to be valuable by-products of an undeviating emphasis on quality alone. They are not objectives to be sought directly.

Second, as we face severe financial pressure in the coming years, it is well to recall that the schools that developed at Chicago owed far more to a handful of geniuses than to the lavish expenditure of funds. The availability of funds certainly helped. But far more crucial was the success of the faculty in seeking out the young scholars who had within them the capacity to strike out in new directions and the willingness of the administration to back the faculty's judgment. These remain the key to success in surmounting our present problems. And identification of potential geniuses remains the one clement that only the faculty can provide. Trustees, alumni, and other friends of the University can prepare the seedbed for excellence; only we can furnish the seeds.

NOTES

1.   *International Encyclopedia of the Social Sciences*, Vol. 4, p. 155.

2.   Foreword to Robert E. L. Faris, *Chicago Sociology, 1920–1932* (Chicago: University of Chicago Press, 1970).

3.   *International Encyclopedia of the Social Sciences*, Vol. 8, p. 366.

4.   Quotations from Faris, *op. cit.*, pp. ix, 128, 130.

5.   A. W. Coats, "The Origins of the 'Chicago School(s)'?" *Journal of Political Economy*, Vol. LXXI (October 1963), pp. 487–493; quotation from p. 489.

6.   *Ibid.*, p. 491.

7.   Alfred Bornemann, *J. Laurence Laughlin* (Washington: American Council on Foreign Affairs, 1940), p. 28.

8.   *Ibid.*, p. 29.

ADAM SMITH'S RELEVANCE FOR 1976

"History never repeats itself." Yet "there is nothing new under the sun." 1976 is not 1776. Yet there are many resemblances that make Adam Smith far more immediately relevant today than he was at the Centennial of *The Wealth of Nations* in 1876. Today as in 1776,

> by restraining, either by high duties, or by absolute prohibitions, the importation of such goods from foreign countries as can be produced at home, the monopoly of the home market is more or less secured to the domestic industry employed in producing them (I, 418).

Today to a far greater extent than in 1776, restrictions on foreign trade are reinforced by detailed interventions into domestic trade. Today as then, government departs very far indeed from those elementary functions that Smith regarded as alone compatible with the "obvious and simple system of natural liberty."

Adam Smith was a radical and revolutionary in his time—just as those of us who today preach laissez faire are in our time. He was no apologist for merchants and manufacturers, or more generally other special interests, but regarded them as the great obstacles to laissez faire—just as we do today. He had no great confidence in his chances of success—any more than we have today. He wrote:

> To expect, indeed, that the freedom of trade should ever be entirely restored in Great Britain, is as absurd as to expect that an Oceana or Utopia should ever be established in it. Not only the prejudices of the public, but what is much more unconquerable, the private interests of many individuals, irresistibly oppose it. Were the officers of the army to oppose with the same zeal and unanimity any reduction in the number of forces, with which master manufacturers set themselves against every law that is likely to increase the number of their rivals in the home market; were the former to animate their soldiers, in the same manner as the latter enflame their workmen, to attack with violence and outrage the proposers of such regulation; to attempt to reduce the army would be as dangerous as it has now become to attempt to diminish in any respect the monopoly which our manufacturers have obtained against us. This monopoly has so much increased the number of some particular tribes of them, that, like an overgrown standing army, they have become formidable to the government, and upon many occasions intimidate the legislature. The member of parliament who supports every proposal for strengthening this monopoly, is sure to acquire not only the reputation of understanding trade, but great popularity and influence with an order of men whose numbers and wealth render them of great importance. If he opposes them, on the contrary, and still more if he has authority enough to be able to thwart them, neither the most acknowledged probity, nor the highest

rank, nor the greatest public services, can protect him from the most infamous abuse and detraction, from personal insults, nor sometimes from real danger, arising from the insolent outrage of furious and disappointed monopolists (I, 435–36).

We are in a similar state today—except that we must broaden the "tribes" of "monopolists" to include not only enterprises protected from competition but also trade unions, school teachers, welfare recipients, and so on and on.

Adam Smith's pessimism turned out to be only partly justified. In 1846, seventy years after *The Wealth of Nations* appeared, the repeal of the Corn Laws in the United Kingdom ushered in a close approximation to that freedom of trade that he regarded as a dream. On the other side of the Atlantic, a comparable degree of freedom of international trade was never achieved, but an equal degree of internal trade was.

In the past century, we have come full circle. Throughout the world, the area of free trade—international and domestic—has declined. One restraint has been piled on another. Even where trade is freest, as within the massive United States economy, government today plays a far larger role than ever it did in Adam Smith's time, let alone in the nineteenth century high tide of laissez faire.

Surely, the most cheerful message we could extract from Adam Smith in this year 1976 is that we too may turn out to be wrong when we too fear that "to expect . . . that the freedom of trade should ever be entirely restored" in the United States or Great Britain, "is as absurd as to expect that an Oceana or Utopia should be established in it."

I. SPECIFIC ISSUES

Adam Smith is relevant to 1976 not only in the general sense just outlined, reflecting the turn of the wheel that has brought us back to an "overgoverned society," in Walter Lippman's phrase, but also in respect to highly specific issues of policy. I shall illustrate the extraordinary contemporaneity of *The Wealth of Nations* by examples from my own country; but I have no doubt that equally striking examples could be adduced by my fellow members for their own more than thirty countries.

1. We have recently been edified by the latest exhausting series of presidential primaries and the electoral campaign. Is there a better description of the participants' qualities, with their characteristic and simplistic preoccupation with short term issues and tactics, than Adam Smith's reference to "that insidious and crafty animal, vulgarly called a statesman or politician, whose counsels are directed by the momentary fluctuations of affairs." (I, 432–33)

2. A major proposal of the Democratic party is the Humphrey-Hawkins Bill, which is designed to "establish a process of long-range economic planning," which sets "a long-term full-employment goal . . . at 3 percent adult unemployment, to be attained as promptly as possible, but within not more than 4 years after the date of the enactment of this Act", and which enacts elaborate governmental machinery for these purposes.

Of the reams of print that have been spilled pro and con about this bill and its immediate predecessor (the Humphrey-Javits Bill), none is more succinct and to the point than this comment by Adam Smith:

> The statesman, who should attempt to direct private people in what manner they ought to employ their capitals, would not only load himself with a most unnecessary attention, but assume an authority which could safely be trusted, not only to no single person, but to no council or senate whatever, and which would be nowhere so dangerous as in the hands of a man who had folly and presumption enough to fancy himself fit to exercise it (I, 421).

Has any contemporary political writer described Hubert Humphrey more accurately, or more devastatingly?

3. Or consider Adam Smith's comment on the proposal by presidential candidate Ronald Reagan to decentralize government by turning back functions and taxes from the federal government to the states and cities:

> The abuses which sometimes creep into the local and provincial administration of a local or provincial revenue, how enormous soever they may appear, are in reality, however, almost always very trifling, in comparison of those which commonly take place in the administration of the avenue of a great empire. They are, besides, much more easily corrected (II, 222).

4. Or weigh his comment on the effect of the growth of government intervention into business in the form of ICC, FCC, Amtrak, Con-rail, etcetera, etcetera:

> Though the profusion of government must, undoubtedly, have retarded the natural progress of [the United States]* towards wealth and improvement, it has not been able to stop it (I, 327).

> The uniform, constant, and uninterrupted effort of every man to better his condition, the principle from which public and national, as well as private opulence is originally derived, is frequently powerful enough to maintain the natural progress of things towards improvement, in spite both of the extravagance of government, and of the greatest errors of administration (I, 325).

---

* England in the original.

This comment is particularly relevant in light of the tendency for enemies of freedom to attribute all defects in the world to the market and all
advances to beneficent governmental intervention. As Smith stresses,
improvements have come in spite of, not because of, governmental intru-
sion into the market place.

5. John Kenneth Galbraith, who is currently doing a BBC television
series on economists through the ages, has a view very different from mine
of Adam Smith's relevance today. He writes that:

> a sharp and obvious distinction must be made between
> what was important in 1776 and what is important now.
> The first is very great; the second, save in the imagination
> of those who misuse Smith as a prophet of reaction, is
> much less so. . . . Smith is not a prophet for our time.

Perhaps this attitude is simply Galbraith's defensive reaction to Smith's
devastating 1776 review of Galbraith's 1958 *Affluent Society* with its stress
on the contrast between private affluence and public squalor, and its deni-
gration of "tail-fins" and other items of conspicuous consumption:

> It is the highest impertinence and presumption . . . in kings
> and ministers, to pretend to watch over the economy of
> private people, and to restrain their expense, either by
> sumptuary laws, or by prohibiting the importation of
> foreign luxuries. They are themselves always, and without
> exception, the greatest spendthrifts in the society. Let them
> look well after their own expense and they may safely trust
> private people with theirs. If their own extravagance does
> not ruin the state, that of their subjects never will (I, 328).

To which might be added Smith's devastating comment:

> There is no art which one government sooner learns of
> another, than that of draining money from the pockets of
> the people (II, 346).

6. As another example of Smith's relevance to specific issues, here is his comment on the widely proclaimed "social responsibility of business," and on those nauseating TV commercials that portray Exxon and its counterparts as in business primarily to preserve the environment:

> I have never known much good done by those who
> affected to trade for the public good.

He goes on to say, and here he was unduly optimistic,

> It is an effectation, indeed, not very common among merchants, and very few words need be employed in dissuading them from it (I, 421).

Unfortunately, as George Stigler has often deplored, Adam Smith showed an uncharacteristic reticence at this point and never told us what those "few words" are.

7. It pains me to conclude this list of Smith's relevance to specific issues of 1976—but candor compels it—with two cases in which Smith provides arguments for the interventionist and statist, one minor, the other extremely important.

The minor case is Smith's defense of a legal maximum interest rate—which in part provoked Jeremy Bentham's subsequent splendid pamphlet *In Defence Of Usury.*

Smith is, of course, realistic about the limitations of such legislation, noting that where "interest of money has been prohibited by law . . . [it] has been found from experience to increase the evil of usury" (I, 338).

Accordingly, he recommended that the legal maximum "rate ought always to be somewhat above the lowest market price, or the price which is commonly paid for the use of money by those who can give the most undoubted security" (I, 338). However, he goes on to say:

> the legal rate . . . ought not to be much above the lowest market rate. If the legal rate of interest in Great Britain, for example, was fixed so high as eight or ten percent, the greater part of the money which was to be lent, would be lent to prodigals and projectors who alone would be willing to give this high interest. Sober people, who will give for the use of money no more than a part of what they are likely to make by the use of it, would not venture into the competition. A great part of the capital of the country would thus be kept out of the hands which were most likely to make a profitable and advantageous use of it, and thrown into those which were most likely to waste and destroy it (I, 338).

This is a highly uncharacteristic passage. Where is that "highest impertinence and presumption" for which Smith elsewhere castigates ministers who "pretend to watch over the economy of private people"? Where is the faith earlier expressed in "the uniform, constant, and uninterrupted effort of every man to better his condition"? Where is the recognition that the usurer deserves the same description as he gives the smuggler:

> a person who, though no doubt highly blameable for violating the laws of his country, is frequently incapable of violating those of natural justice, and would have been, in every respect, an excellent citizen, had not the laws of his country made that a crime which nature never meant to be so (II, 381).

8. The major case in which Smith provided an argument that has since been used effectively by the statists and interventionists is in the key passage in which he describes the "three duties" that "the system of natural liberty leaves the sovereign." The first two are unexceptionable:

> first, ... protecting the society from the violence and inva-
> sion of other independent societies; secondly ... protect-
> ing, as far as possible, every member of the society from
> the injustice or oppression of every other member of it,
> or ... establishing an exact administration of justice.

The mischief is done by the third:

> the duty of erecting and maintaining certain public works
> and certain public institutions, which it can never be for
> the interest of any individual, or small number of indi-
> viduals, to erect and maintain; because the profit could
> never repay the expense to any individual or small number
> of individuals, though it may frequently do much more
> than repay it to a great society (II, 184–185).

The standard textbook case is the smoke nuisance: your chimney pours out smoke that dirties my collar; you are forcing me to trade a clean collar for a dirty one; I would be more than willing to do so at the right price; but the cost of engaging in such transactions is prohibitive; hence government regulations on smoke are recommended. Another standard case is the lighthouse—one that Smith would doubtless have accepted. The trouble is that there is no transaction between individuals that does not affect third parties to some extent, however trivial, so there is literally no governmental intervention for which a case cannot be offered along these lines.

This third duty, which calls for relatively extended consideration, is mischievous because on the one hand, properly interpreted, it does specify a valid function of government; on the other hand, it can be used to justify a completely unlimited extension of government. The valid element is the argument for government intervention from third party effects—or "external economies and diseconomies" in the technical lingo that has developed. If a person's actions impose costs or confer benefits on others for which it is not feasible for him to compensate or charge them, then strictly voluntary exchange is not feasible; the third party effects are involuntary exchanges imposed on other persons.

Smith's own statement of the "duty" is one-sided in two different respects. First, he considers only external economies not external diseconomies. The currently popular pollution and environmental arguments can therefore not readily be included under his words, though his central point applies to them. Second, and far more important in my view, his statement does not allow for the external effects of the governmental actions in undertaking this duty, though as we shall see, his discussion of particular government activities does do so. The major consideration that gives rise to significant third party effects of private actions is the difficulty of identifying the external costs or benefits; if identification were relatively easy, it would be possible to subject them to voluntary exchange. But this same consideration hinders government actions, making it hard to evaluate the net effects of external costs and benefits and hard to avoid superimposing an additional set of external costs and benefits in taking supposedly corrective government action. In addition, governmental actions have further external effects, via its method of finance and via the danger to freedom from the expansion of government.

Perhaps the major intellectual fallacy in this area in the past century has been the double standard applied to the market and to political action. A market "defect"—whether through an absence of competition or external effects (equivalent, as recent literature has made clear, to transaction costs)—has been regarded as immediate justification for government intervention. But the political mechanism has its "defects" too. It is fallacious to compare the actual market with the "ideal" political structure. One should either compare the real with the real or the ideal with the ideal. Unfortunately, Smith's wording lends itself readily to this fallacy.

Smith himself spelled out at considerable length the "public works" and "public institutions" he included in his third duty. They were first of all, those required to perform the first two duties of providing for defense and a system of justice. Second came those required "for facilitating the commerce of the society," in which he included as "necessary for facilitating commerce in general," "good roads, bridges, navigable canals, harbours, etc." (II, 215) Though he recommended that the expense for these should so far as possible be defrayed by "tolls and other particular charges" (II, 215), he did not regard the feasibility of so financing them as eliminating the argument for governmental rather than private construction. If a bridge or navigable canal is to be financed by specific charges, why cannot it be a private enterprise? Smith considers the question explicitly, notes that "canals are better in the hands of private persons than of commissioners" (II, 216–17) but yet concluded, on what seem to me insufficient grounds, that "the tolls for the maintenance of a high road, cannot with any safety be made the property of private persons" (II, 217). Smith proceeded from those works and institutions for facilitating commerce in general to those for "facilitating particular branches of commerce" (II, 223). Here his main concern was with provision for protecting foreign trade, particularly with "barbarous" nations. But as he expanded his analysis, the section turns into his famous attack on joint-stock companies.

The final major category of institutions which Smith included in his third duty were "the institutions for the education of youth" (II, 244). Here again, he favored financing them largely by specific fees. Despite Smith's acceptance of the appropriateness of governmental establishment and maintenance of such institutions, he devotes most of his discussion to a scathing attack on the effects of governmental or church control of institutions of learning—and his comments have a direct relevance today. He observes:

> Those parts of education . . . for teaching of which there are no public institutions, are generally the best taught. When a young man goes to a fencing or a dancing school, he does not indeed always learn to fence or to dance very well; but he seldom fails of learning to fence or to dance (II, 253–54).

Today, try talking French with a graduate of a public high school—or of a Berlitz school.

> Were there no public institutions for education, no system, no science would be taught for which there was not some demand; or which the circumstances of the times did not render it either necessary, or convenient, or at least fashionable to learn (II, 266).

Despite his initial assertion that the erection of institutions for the education of the youth is included in the third duty, these considerations lead him to ask "Ought the public, therefore, to give no attention . . . to the education of the people?" and to answer rather equivocally, "In some cases, it ought, in others it need not" (II, 267). . . . "In a civilised and commercial society the education of the common people requires . . . the attention of the public more than that of people of some rank and fortune" (II, 269). He concludes:

> For a very small expense, the public can facilitate, can encourage, and can even impose upon almost the whole body of the people, the necessity of acquiring those most essential parts of education [to read, write, and account]. The public can facilitate this acquisition by establishing in every parish or district a little school, where children may be taught for a reward so moderate, that even a common labourer may afford it; the master being partly, but not wholly paid by the public; because, if he was

wholly, or even principally paid by it, he would soon learn to neglect his business (II, 270).

As this brief summary suggests, Smith himself did not regard his third duty as providing extensive scope for governmental activity. I do not criticize him for not recognizing its potential for abuse. Though his prescience leads us to analyze *The Wealth of Nations* as if it were a contemporary publication, he did not have our experience but had to rely on his own. To illustrate in a trivial way, could anyone write today as he did then, "The post office . . . has been successfully managed by, I believe, every sort of government"? (II, 303)

But since he wrote, there is hardly an activity which has not been regarded as suitable for governmental intervention on Smith's ground. It is easy to assert, as Smith himself does again and again, that there are "external effects" which make something or other in the "public interest" even though not in the "interest of any individual or small number of individuals." There are no widely accepted objective criteria by which to evaluate such claims, to measure the magnitude of any external effects, to identify the external effects of the governmental actions, and to set them against the external effects of leaving matters in private hands. Superficially scientific cost-benefit analysis erected on Smith's basis has proved a veritable Trojan horse.

II. GENERAL ISSUES

Beyond the particular issues just discussed, Smith's great importance for 1976, and his great achievement—as Hayek and others have so eloquently pointed out—is the doctrine of an "invisible hand," his vision of the way in which the voluntary actions of millions of individuals can be coordinated through a price system without central direction:

> As every individual, therefore, endeavours as much as he can both
> to employ his capital in the support of domestic industry, and so
> to direct that industry that its produce may be of the greatest

value; every individual necessarily labours to render the annual revenue of the society as great as he can. He generally, indeed, neither intends to promote the public interest, nor knows how much he is promoting it . . . he intends only his own gain, and he is in this, as in many other cases, led by an invisible hand to promote an end which was no part of his intention. Nor is it always the worse for the society that it was no part of it. By pursuing his own interest he frequently promotes that of the society more effectually than when he really intends to promote it (I, 421).

This is a highly sophisticated and subtle insight. The market, with each individual going his own way, with no central authority setting social priorities, avoiding duplication, and coordinating activities, looks like chaos to the naked eye. Yet through Smith's eyes we see that it is a finely ordered and delicately tuned system, one which arises out of man's actions, yet is not deliberately created by man. It is a system which enables the dispersed knowledge and skill of millions of people to be coordinated for a common purpose. Men in Malaya who produce rubber, in Mexico who produce graphite, in the state of Washington who produce timber, and countless others, cooperate in the production of an ordinary rubber-topped lead pencil—to use Leonard Read's vivid image—though there is no world government to which they all submit, no common language in which they could converse, and no knowledge of the purpose for which they cooperate.

Smith is often interpreted—and criticized—as the high priest of egotism and selfishness. That is very far from being the case. He was, first of all, a scientist who, driven by a sense of "wonder," excited by "incoherencies" in the processes of the economy, sought "some chain of intermediate events, which, by connecting them with something that has gone before, may render the whole course of the universe consistent and of a piece."* The subtle analysis of the price system was the result.

---

* Quoted words from Smith's *History of Astronomy*, as quoted by W. P. D. Wightman, "Adam Smith and the History of Ideas," *Essays on Adam Smith*, edited by Andrew S. Skinner and Thomas Wilson (Clarendon Press, Oxford, 1975), p. 50.

But second, on the moral level, Smith regarded sympathy as a human characteristic, but one that was itself rare and required to be economized. He would have argued that the invisible hand was far more effective than the visible hand of government in mobilizing not only material resources for immediate self-seeking ends but also sympathy for unselfish charitable ends. And the nineteenth century is a dramatic vindication. In both the United States and the United Kingdom, that century comes about as close to Smith's system of natural liberty as it is reasonable to hope to achieve. And in both countries that century saw the greatest outpouring of elee-mosynary and publicly directed activity that the world has ever seen. It was, in the United States, a century that produced a proliferation of private colleges and universities, of foreign missions, of nonprofit community hospitals, of the Society for the Prevention of Cruelty to Animals, of the nongovernment "public" library, of the Rockefeller and Carnegie Founda-tions, and so on and on. In Britain, the overwhelming bulk of hospital beds today are in the hospitals constructed in the nineteenth century through voluntary activity.

Though Smith fully develops the self-regulating market mechanism only in *The Wealth of Nations*, already in the *Theory of Moral Sentiments*, he is fully aware of the difference between an imposed order and what he would have called a natural order. In what is my own favorite Smith quota-tion he gives a devastating critique of the modern well-intentioned inter-ventionist who wants to attack major social problems via the political mechanism. Smith's name for him was "The man of system."

> The man of system ... seems to imagine that he can arrange the different members of a great society with as much ease as the hand arranges the different pieces upon a chessboard; he does not consider that the pieces upon the chessboard have no other principle of motion besides that which the hand impresses upon them; but that, in the great chessboard of human society, every single piece has a principle of motion of its own, altogether dif-ferent from that which the legislature might choose to impress

upon it. If those two principles coincide and act in the same direction, the game of human society will go on easily and harmoniously, and is very likely to be happy and successful. If they are opposite or different, the game will go on miserably, and the society must be at all times in the highest degree of disorder.*

The failure to understand this profound observation has produced an invisible hand in politics that is the precise reverse of the invisible hand in the market. In politics, men who intend only to promote the public interest, as they conceive it, are "led by an invisible hand to promote an end which was no part of" their intention. They become the front-men for special interests they would never knowingly serve. They end up sacrificing the public interest to the social interest, the interest of the consumers to that of the producers, of the masses who never go to college to that of those who attend college, of the poor working class saddled with employment taxes to the middle class who get disproportionate benefits from social security, and so down the line.

The invisible hand in politics is as potent a force for harm as the invisible hand in economics is for good. At the moment, unfortunately, it seems to have the upper hand. But the outlook is not entirely bleak. The far greater capacity of the many millions of ordinary men to find ways around government regulations than of the fewer millions of bureaucrats to plug the leaks, provides some measure of freedom. The inefficiency of government arouses the resentment of the citizen, offers the hope of a tax revolt, and encourages a widespread anti-Washington sentiment. Perhaps it is not entirely chimerical to hope that our corn laws too will one day be overturned.

---

* *Theory of Moral Sentiments*, Arlington House reprint with introduction by E. G. West, pp. 342–43.

INTRODUCTION TO REPUBLICATION OF THE *NEW INDIVIDUALIST REVIEW*

1981

When the *New Individualist Review* was founded, belief in "free, private enterprise, and in the imposition of the strictest limits to the power of government" and in "a commitment to human liberty"—to quote from the editorial introducing volume 1, number 1 (April 1961)—was at a low ebb even in the countries of the so-called free world. Yet, at the same time, there were many signs of an intellectual reaction against collectivist views, of a resurgence of interest in the philosophy of classical liberalism.

Two organizations in particular served to channel and direct this resurgence: the Mont Pelerin Society, founded in 1947 primarily as a result of the initiative of Friedrich Hayek, whose book *The Road to Serfdom* did so much to spark the resurgence; and the Intercollegiate Society of Individualists, founded in 1953 by Frank Chodorov, a freelance writer and journalist and a dedicated opponent of collectivism.

The Mont Pelerin Society brought together relatively mature intellectuals—economists, historians, journalists, businessmen—who had kept the faith and had not succumbed to the temper of the times. Its members were representatives of a small minority, but one that had more than its share of independence, integrity, selflessness, and breadth of vision. The Intercollegiate Society of Individualists (ISI) operated at the other end of the age scale. It promoted the establishment of chapters among undergraduate and graduate students on college campuses throughout the country. The members of these chapters too were a minority, but also one that had more than its share of independence, integrity, selflessness, and breadth of vision.

As the *New Individualist Review*'s introductory editorial of 1961 put it,

> Two or three decades ago, individualism was held in contempt by American intellectuals, and a decade ago they regarded it as at least mildly eccentric. We certainly do not deny that the majority of today's intellectuals are still guided by the ideas which grew up in the 1930s. But the slogans which the New Deal shouted, and the stereotypes which it propagated, while perhaps fresh and exciting then, have lost their appeal to the generation which has emerged in recent years, one which sees no reason to consider our march toward the Total State to be as "inevitable as a law of nature."
>
> . . . An increasing number of students in the past decades have recognized the inadequacies of the orthodox response to most of the present-day social and economic challenges. The party of liberty is steadily gaining adherents among students.

The University of Chicago played a key role in the preservation of liberalism and the resurgence of "the party of liberty." It was one of the few major universities in the world at which there persisted throughout the thirties and forties a strong liberal tradition, conveyed and maintained by eminent and respected members of the academic community like Frank H. Knight, Jacob Viner, Henry Simons, and others of their colleagues in the economics department, in other social science departments, in the Business School, and in the humanities. The university was by no means monolithic. Indeed, it had the general reputation of being a radical left-wing institution. Its student body and faculty had its share of Communist Party members, fellow travelers, and socialists. What distinguished it from most other institutions was that it also had a strong, cohesive, and intellectually respectable group of defenders of a free society.

After the war Hayek moved from the London School of Economics to the University of Chicago, where he became a professor in a newly formed Committee on Social Thought. Of the founding members of the Mont Pelerin Society, four were from the University of Chicago, more than from any other institution.

Both the time and the place were ripe for the emergence of the *New Individualist Review*. The time was ripe because the reaction against collectivism, and the resurgence of belief in individualism, had gone far enough to provide a sufficiently large and sophisticated audience—and pool of potential contributors—for a publication which aimed at a high intellectual level and proclaimed that "the viewpoints presented will generally be libertarian or conservative, but we will consider for publication any essay which indicates a reasoned concern for freedom, and a thoughtful valuation of its importance." The time was ripe also because the libertarian resurgence was still in an early enough stage that there were few periodical publications dealing with intellectual issues and offering a forum for their serious discussion. *National Review, Human Events*, and *The Freeman* were in existence but they were directed at an audience of concerned and interested citizens of all professions and viewpoints, and served a different purpose, being devoted largely to reporting developments in the world of affairs or to commenting on and analyzing current issues primarily from a traditionally conservative—as opposed to libertarian—perspective.

The place was ripe because at the time the University of Chicago was almost surely the only academic institution at which there was a sufficient concentration of students not only committed to the values of a free society but also engaged in serious scholarly study of the intellectual and historical underpinnings of a free society. In particular, Hayek had attracted a group of able, dedicated, and like-minded students to the Committee on Social Thought. They formed the core group responsible for the *New Individualist Review,* reinforced by students in economics, business, and other areas who shared the value commitment although they were more technically and professionally oriented in their studies. Faculty support was also present and important. However, it cannot be too strongly emphasized that the *New Individualist Review* was throughout—in its conception, editing, and management—a student venture.

The ISI assisted at the birth of the *New Individualist Review.* The first three issues were described as being published by "the University of Chicago chapter of the Intercollegiate Society of Individualists"; thereafter as being published by the *New Individualist Review.* The first eleven issues carried full-page advertisements for the ISI—presumably the form that financial assistance took. In addition, Don Lipsett, the midwestern representative of the ISI, who was primarily responsible for founding the Chicago chapter, advised and assisted on business matters.

The initial editorial board consisted of editor-in-chief Ralph Raico; associate editors John McCarthy, Robert Schuettinger, John Weicher; and book review editor Ronald Hamowy. Each of these contributed an article to the first issue. Three were students in the Committee on Social Thought, one a student in the history department, one in the economics department. Raico served as editor-in-chief, alone or along with Schuettinger or Hamowy, for all but the final two issues. Joe M. Cobb served in that capacity for the final two issues and has been guardian of the tradition ever since.

The editorial advisory board initially consisted of myself from the economics department, F. A. Hayek from the Committee on Social Thought, and Richard M. Weaver from the English department. Aside from occasionally contributing articles, our role was strictly advisory and little advice was required. The students who undertook the project were not only dedicated; they were also extraordinarily able and talented, and that continued to be the case with the students who joined or replaced the founders. Most of them remain active and effective defenders of a free society, and have achieved careers that fulfill their initial promise. Few phenomena have so reinforced my own personal belief in the validity of the philosophy of freedom as the high quality, both intellectual and personal, of the young men and women who were attracted to the "party of liberty"—to use the *New Individualist Review*'s parlance—when it had all the appearance of being a lost cause.

The *Review* quickly established itself as the outstanding publication in the libertarian cause. Although every contributor to its first issue was from the University of Chicago (one faculty member, five students), by the second issue, two out of five were from outside the university, and in the third, five out of seven. As every reader of this volume will find for himself, the quality of the *Review* was consistently high. The contributions were directed at important and controversial issues; they were reasoned and thoughtful without being arid; they touched on both basic philosophical issues and important practical problems; they were, as the initial editorial promised, "generally . . . libertarian or conservative" but not narrowly parochial, and ranged over a wide variety of points of view.

The subsequent history of the *Review* and its ultimate termination were partly typical of student ventures—ups and downs as the student body changed and the number of persons interested in its subject matter and willing to devote the time to its publication fluctuated. But two other events played a role—one local, the other national.

The local event was Friedrich Hayek's retirement from the University of Chicago and his relocation to Freiburg, Germany. His students had formed the core of the initial founders and had remained an important component of the editorial staff throughout.

The national event was the Vietnam War. In the early 1960s there was, as the introductory editorial said, a rising tide of support among the young for the party of liberty, for the principles of free, private enterprise, and a strictly limited government. I believe that tide would have continued to rise if the passions of the young had not been diverted by the Vietnam War and above all by conscription. The antiwar, anti-draft movement gained the support of young men and women of the left, the center, and the right; it absorbed their energies and their enthusiasm. The battle on the campuses deteriorated to an elemental level, as the very basic principles of civil discourse and reasoned, open-minded discussion came under attack. Little energy or possibility was left for more sophisticated examination of basic intellectual issues.

One of the final issues of the *Review* reflected one facet of this development: the spring 1967 issue devoted to a symposium on conscription. And even that was partly derivative from a conference on the draft held at the University of Chicago in December 1966.

Once the Vietnam War ended and the draft was replaced by an all-volunteer military, the former intellectual tide in favor of the party of liberty resumed, reinforced indeed by the antigovernment attitudes generated by the war and the draft. The result has been a veritable outpouring of publications, articles, and books devoted to examining and discussing the kinds of issues to which the *New Individualist Review* was devoted.

It is therefore highly appropriate that the progenitor of these publications be reprinted now. Most of the articles remain timely and relevant. More important, perhaps, this student venture, despite its narrow base and its limited resources, sets an intellectual standard that has not yet, I believe, been matched by any of the more recent publications in the same philosophical tradition.

THE TIDE IN THE AFFAIRS OF MEN

BY MILTON FRIEDMAN AND ROSE D. FRIEDMAN

1988

There is a tide in the affairs of men,
Which, taken at the flood, leads on to fortune;
Omitted, all the voyage of their life
Is bound in shallows and in miseries.
—*Shakespeare*, Julius Caesar

Shakespeare's image is an apt text for our essay. There are powerful tides in the affairs of men, interpreted as the collective entity we call society, just as in the affairs of individuals. The tides in the affairs of society are slow to become apparent, as one tide begins to overrun its predecessor. Each tide lasts a long time—decades, not hours—once it begins to flood and leaves its mark on its successor even after it recedes.

How tides begin in the minds of men, spread to the conduct of public policy, often generate their own reversal, and are succeeded by another tide—all this is a vast topic insufficiently explored by historians, economists, and other social scientists.[1]

The aim of this brief essay is modest: to present a hypothesis that has become increasingly plausible to us over the years, to illustrate it with experience over the past three centuries, and to discuss some of its implications. The hypothesis is that a major change in social and economic policy is preceded by a shift in the climate of intellectual *opinion*, itself generated, at least in part, by contemporaneous social, political, and economic circumstances. This shift may begin in one country but, if it proves lasting, ultimately spreads worldwide. At first it will have little effect on social and economic policy. After a lag, sometimes of decades, an intellectual tide "taken at its flood" will spread at first gradually, then more rapidly, to the public at large and through the public's pressure on government will affect the course of economic, social, and political policy. As the tide in *events* reaches its flood, the intellectual tide starts to ebb, offset by what A. V. Dicey calls counter-currents of opinion. The counter-currents typically represent a reaction to the practical consequences attributed to the earlier intellectual tide. Promise tends to be utopian. Performance never is and therefore disappoints. The initial protagonists of the intellectual tide die out and the intellectual quality of their followers and supporters inevitably declines. It takes intellectual independence and courage to start a counter-current to dominant opinion. It takes far less of either to climb on a bandwagon. The venturesome, independent, and courageous young seek new fields to conquer and that calls for exploring the new and untried. The counter-currents that gather force set in motion the next tidal wave, and the process is repeated.

Needless to say, this sketch is oversimplified and excessively formalized. In particular it omits any discussion of the subtle mutual interaction between intellectual opinion, public opinion, and the course of events. Gradual changes in policy and institutional arrangements are always going on. Major changes seldom occur, however, except at times of crisis, when, to use Richard Weaver's evocative phrase, "ideas have consequences." The intellectual tide is spread to the public by all manner of intellectual retailers—teachers and preachers, journalists in print and on television, pundits and politicians. The public begins to react to the crisis according to the options that intellectuals have explored, options that effectively limit the alternatives open to the powers that be. In almost every tide a crisis can be identified as the catalyst for a major change in the direction of policy.

We shall illustrate the relevance of our hypothesis with the two latest completed tides as well as the tide that, as we put it in the title of the final chapter of *Free to Choose*, is turning.[2]

THE RISE OF LAISSEZ-FAIRE (THE ADAM SMITH TIDE)

The first tide we discuss begins in the eighteenth century in Scotland with a reaction against mercantilism expressed in the writings of David Hume, Adam Smith's *Theory of Moral Sentiments* (1759), and above all Smith's *The Wealth of Nations* (1776).

The Wealth of Nations is widely and correctly regarded as the foundation stone of modern scientific economics. Its normative thrust and its influence on the wider intellectual world are of greater interest for our present purpose. Its rapid success in influencing the intellectual community doubtless reflected the seeds planted by Hume and others—the intellectual countercurrents to the mercantilist tide—as well as the early stages of the Industrial Revolution.

On the other side of the Atlantic 1776 also saw the proclamation of the Declaration of Independence—in many ways the political twin of Smith's economics. Smith's work quickly became common currency to the Founding Fathers. Alexander Hamilton documented that phenomenon in a backhanded way in his 1791 *Report on Manufactures*. He quoted Smith extensively and praised him profusely while at the same time devoting the substance of his report to arguing that Smith's doctrines did not apply to the United States, which needed not free international trade but the protection of infant industries by tariffs—an example of the homage that vice, even intellectual vice, pays to virtue.

Smith had no illusions about the impact of his intellectual ideas on public policy: "To expect that the freedom of trade should ever be entirely restored in Great Britain, is as absurd as to expect that an Oceana or Utopia should ever be established in it. Not only the prejudices of the public, but what is much more unconquerable, the private interests of many individuals, irresistibly oppose it."[3]

His prediction proved false. By the early nineteenth century, the ideas of laissez-faire, of the operation of the invisible hand, of the undesirability of government intervention into economic matters, had swept first the intellectual world and then public policy. Bentham, Ricardo, James Mill, and John Stuart Mill were actively engaged in spreading these ideas and promoting them politically. Maria Edgeworth was writing novels based on Ricardian economics. Cobden and Bright were campaigning for the repeal of the Corn Laws. Reinforced by pressures arising out of the Industrial Revolution, these ideas were beginning to affect public policy, though the process was delayed by the Napoleonic Wars with the accompanying high government spending and restrictions on international trade. Yet the wars also furnished the needed catalytic crisis.

The repeal of the Corn Laws in 1846 is generally regarded as the final triumph of Smith after a seventy-year delay. In fact some reductions in trade barriers had started much earlier, and many nonagricultural items continued to be protected by tariffs until 1874. Thereafter only revenue tariffs remained on such items as spirits, wine, beer, and tobacco, countervailed by excise duties on competing domestic products. So it took nearly a century for the completing of one response to Adam Smith.

The other countries of Europe and the United States did not follow the British lead by establishing complete free trade in goods. During most of the nineteenth century, however, U.S. duties on imports were primarily for revenue, though protection did play a significant role, as rancorous political debates, particularly between the North and the South, testify. Except for a few years after the War of 1812, customs provided between 90 and 100 percent of total Federal revenues up to the Civil War. And except for a few years during and after that war, customs provided half or more of federal revenues until the Spanish-American War at the end of the century.

Nontariff barriers such as quotas were nonexistent. Movement of people and capital was hardly impeded at all. The United States in particular had completely free immigration. In Europe before World War I "the inhabitant of London," in John Maynard Keynes's eloquent words, "could secure . . . cheap and comfortable means of transit to any country or climate without passport or other formality . . . and could . . . proceed abroad to foreign quarters, without knowledge of the religion, language, or customs . . . and would consider himself greatly aggrieved and much surprised at the least interference."[4]

Hamilton's success in achieving protectionist legislation in the United States reflects the absence of effective ideological commitment by policy makers to avoiding intervention by government into economic activity, despite the intellectual tide set in motion by Adam Smith, the French physiocrats, and their later followers. However, strong belief in states' rights meant that states, not the federal government, played the major role. Many states established state banks, built canals, and engaged in other commercial enterprises. The catalytic crisis that produced a drastic change was the panic of 1837, in the course of which many, perhaps most, government enterprises went bankrupt. That panic served the same role in discrediting government enterprise as the Great Depression did nearly a century later in discrediting private enterprise.

In the aftermath the ideas of Adam Smith offered both an explanation and an obvious alternative option; tariffs aside, near complete laissez-faire and nonintervention reigned into the next century.

Measuring the role of government in the economy is not easy. One readily available, though admittedly imperfect, measure is the ratio of government spending to national income. At the height of laissez-faire, peacetime government spending was less than 10 percent of national income in both the United States and Great Britain. Two-thirds of U.S. spending was by state and local governments, with about half for education; federal spending was generally less than 3 percent of national income, with half of that for the military.

A striking example of the worldwide impact of the Adam Smith tide—this time in practice, not in ideas—is provided by post-Meiji Japan. For centuries prior to the Meiji Restoration in 1867, Japan had been almost completely isolated from the Western world. The new rulers had no ideological understanding, let alone commitment, to laissez-faire. On the contrary, they attached little value to individual freedom, either political or economic. Their overriding objective was simply to strengthen the power and glory of their country.

Nevertheless, when the Meiji rulers burst into a Western world in which laissez-faire Britain was the dominant economy, they simply took for granted that Britain's policy was the one to emulate. They did not by any means extend complete economic and political freedom to their citizens, but they did go a long way, with dramatic and highly favorable results.[5]

The absence of a widespread ideological underpinning for these policies helps explain their lack of robustness. After World War I Japan succumbed to centralized control by a military dictatorship—a policy that led to economic stagnation, military adventurism, and finally Japan's entry into World War II on the side of the Nazis.

On the broader scale the tide that swept the nineteenth century brought greater political as well as economic freedom: widening rights and a higher standard of living for individuals accompanied increased international trade and human contact. It was heralded as a century of peace—but that is somewhat overstated. The tide did not prevent the U.S. Civil War, the Crimean War, the Franco-Prussian War, or other local conflicts. But there was no major widespread conflict between 1815 and 1914 comparable either to the Napoleonic Wars of the preceding years or to the world wars of the later years.

Despite occasional financial panics and crises, Britain and the United States experienced remarkable economic growth during the nineteenth century. The United States in particular became a mecca for the poor of all lands. All this was associated with—and many, including us, would say it was a result of—the increasing adoption of laissez-faire as the guiding principle of government policy.

THE RISE OF THE WELFARE STATE (THE FABIAN TIDE)

This remarkable progress did not prevent the intellectual tide from turning away from individualism and toward collectivism. Indeed, it doubtless contributed to that result. According to Dicey, "from 1848 onwards an alteration becomes perceptible in the intellectual and moral atmosphere of England."[6] The flood stage, when collectivism began to dominate intellectual opinion, came some decades later. The founding of the Fabian Society, dedicated to the gradual establishment of socialism, by George Bernard Shaw, Sidney Webb, and others in 1883 is perhaps as good a dividing date as any for Britain. A comparable date for the United States is 1885, when the American Economic Association was founded by a group of young economists who had returned from study in Germany imbued with socialist ideas, which they hoped to spread through the association—a hope that was largely frustrated when the association shortly adopted a policy of "nonpartisanship and avoidance of official commitments on practical economic questions and political issues."[7] Confirming evidence is provided by the publication in 1888 of Edward Bellamy's socialist utopian romance, *Looking Backwards*, which sold over a million copies.

How can we explain this shift in the intellectual tide when the growing pains of laissez-faire policies had long been overcome and impressive positive gains had been achieved? Dicey gives one indirect answer:

> The beneficial effect of State intervention, especially in the form of legislation, is direct, immediate, and so to speak, visible, whilst its evil effects are gradual and indirect, and lie out of sight . . . few are those who realize the undeniable truth that State help kills self-help. Hence the majority of mankind must almost of

necessity look with undue favor upon governmental intervention. This natural bias can be counteracted only by the existence
..., as in England between 1830 and 1860, of a presumption or
prejudice in favor of individual liberty—that is, of *laissez-faire*.
The mere decline, therefore, of faith in self-help . . . is of itself
sufficient to account for the growth of legislation tending
toward socialism.[8]

A more direct answer is that two effects of the success of laissez-faire fostered a reaction. First, success made residual evils stand out all the more
sharply, both encouraging reformers to press for governmental solutions
and making the public more sympathetic to their appeals. Second, it became
more reasonable to anticipate that government would be effective in attack-
ing the residual evils. A severely limited government has few favors to give;
hence there is little incentive to corrupt government officials, and government service has few attractions for persons concerned primarily with
personal enrichment. Government was engaged primarily in enforcing laws
against murder, theft, and the like and in providing municipal services such
as local police and fire protection—activities that engendered almost unan-
imous citizen support. For these and other reasons, Britain, which went
furthest toward complete laissez-faire, became legendary in the late nineteenth and early twentieth century for its incorruptible civil service and
law-abiding citizenry—precisely the reverse of its reputation a century
earlier. In the United States neither the quality of the civil service nor respect
for the law ever reached the heights they did in Britain, but both improved
over the course of the century.

Whatever the reasons, Fabian socialism became the dominant intellectual current in Britain, driving out, at the one extreme, radical Marxism,
and at the other, laissez-faire. Gradually that intellectual current came to
dominate first public opinion and then government policy. World War I
hastened the process, but it was already well under way before the war, as
is demonstrated by Dicey's prescient remarks in his 1914 preface to the
second edition of *Law and Public Opinion*:

By 1900, the doctrine of *laissez-faire*, in spite of the large element of truth which it contains, had more or less lost its hold upon the English people . . . It also was in 1900 apparent to any impartial observer that the feelings or the opinions which had given strength to collectivism would continue to tell as strongly upon the legislation of the twentieth century as they already told upon the later legislation of the nineteenth century . . . and this conclusion would naturally have been confirmed by the fact that in the sphere of finance there had occurred a revival of belief in protective tariffs, then known by the name of a demand for "fair trade" [echoes of 1987!].

Dicey lists "the laws which most directly illustrate the progress of collectivism," from the beginning of the twentieth century, starting with the Old Age Pension Act of 1908. In respect of a later act (the Mental Deficiency Act, 1913), he remarks that it "is the first step along a path on which no sane man can decline to enter, but which, if too far pursued, will bring statesmen across difficulties hard to meet without considerable interference with individual liberty."[9]

Clearly the seeds had been sown from which Britain's full-fledged welfare state grew, at first slowly in the interwar period and then with a final burst after World War II, marked perhaps by the adoption of the National Health Service and the panoply of measures recommended in the Beveridge report.

In the United States the development was similar, though somewhat delayed. After the popular success of Bellamy's utopian fantasy came the era of the muckrakers, led by Lincoln Steffens, Ray Stannard Baker, and Ida M. Tarbell, with their exposures of alleged corruption and malfeasance in municipal government, labor, and trusts. Upton Sinclair used the novel to promote socialist ideas, his most successful being *The Jungle* (1906), which resulted from an assignment by a socialist newspaper to investigate conditions in the Chicago stockyards. Sinclair wrote the novel to create sympathy for the workers, but it did far more to arouse indignation at the unsanitary conditions under which meat was processed. On a different level Louis Dembitz Brandeis criticized the financial community. His volume of essays, *Other People's Money and How the Bankers Use It* (1914), has been described as "a frontal assault on monopoly and interlocking directorates."[10]

"The Populist party, through which William Jennings Bryan rose to" the nomination for the presidency on the Democratic ticket in 1896, "called not merely for regulation of the railroads but for outright government ownership and operation."[11] The Interstate Commerce Commission, created in 1887, was shortly followed by the 1890 Sherman Antitrust Act and later by the 1906 Food and Drug Act, for which Sinclair's novel served as the catalyst. The modern welfare state was well on its way. World War I greatly expanded the role of government, notably by the takeover of the railroads. The postwar period brought something of a reaction, with the major exception of Prohibition.

As late as 1929 Federal spending amounted to only 3.2 percent of the national income; one-third of this was spent on the military, including veterans' benefits, and one-half on the military plus interest on the public debt. State and local spending was nearly three times as large—9 percent of national income—with more than half on education and highways. Spending by federal, state, and local governments on what today is described as income support, Social Security, and welfare totaled less than 1 percent of national income.

The world of ideas was different. By 1929 socialism was the dominant ideology on the nation's campuses. The *New Republic* and *The Nation* were the intellectuals' favorite journals of opinion and Norman Thomas their political hero. The impact of opinion on the world of practice, however, had so far been modest. The critical catalyst for a major change was, of course, the Great Depression, which rightly or wrongly shattered the public's confidence in private enterprise, leading it to regard government involvement as the only effective recourse in time of trouble and to treat government as a potential benefactor rather than simply a policeman and umpire.

The effect was dramatic. Federal government spending grew to roughly 30 percent of national income by the 1980s, or to nearly tenfold its 1929 level. State and local spending also grew, though far less dramatically, so that by the 1980s total government spending was over 40 percent of national income. And spending understates the role government came to play. Many intrusions into people's lives involve little or no spending: tariffs and quotas, price and wage controls, ceilings on interest rates, local ceilings on rents, zoning requirements, building codes, and so on.

The delayed impact of the intellectual climate of the 1920s illustrates one aspect of the influence of intellectual opinion—producing options for adoption when the time is ripe. Despite Norman Thomas's popularity on the campus, he received less than 1 percent of the popular vote for president in 1928 and only 2 percent in 1932. Nonetheless, we concluded that "the Socialist party was the most influential political party in the United States in the first decades of the twentieth century ... [A]lmost every economic plank in its 1928 presidential platform has by now [1980] been enacted into law."[12]

Like the earlier tide, the Fabian tide was worldwide. It contributed no less to the success of the Russian and Chinese communist revolutions than to the welfare state in Britain and the New Deal in the United States. And it largely explains the adoption of centralized planning in India and other British and European former colonies when they achieved independence. A major exception was Hong Kong, one of the few British colonial possessions that remained under the control of the Colonial Office. It never departed from the Adam Smith tide and as a result was a precursor to the next tide.

THE RESURGENCE OF FREE MARKETS (THE HAYEK TIDE)

As in the preceding wave, the world of ideas started to change direction just as the tide in the world of practice was cresting.[13] Throughout the ascendancy of socialist ideas there had, of course, been counter-currents—kept alive in Britain by G. K. Chesterton, Lionel Robbins, Friedrich Hayek, and some of their colleagues at the London School of Economics; in Austria by Ludwig von Mises and his disciples; and in the United States by Albert Jay Nock, H. L. Mencken, and other popular writers; Henry Simons, Frank Knight, and Jacob Viner at the University of Chicago; and Gottfried Haberler and Joseph Schumpeter at Harvard—to mention only a few.

Hayek's *Road to Serfdom*, a surprise best-seller in Britain and in the United States in 1944, was probably the first real inroad in the dominant intellectual view. Yet the impact of the free-market counter-current on the dominant tide of intellectual opinion, though perceptible to those directly involved, was at first minute. Even for those of us who were actively promoting free markets in the 1950s and 1960s it is difficult to recall how strong and pervasive was the intellectual climate of the times.

The tale of two books by the present authors, both directed at the general public and both promoting the same policies, provides striking evidence of the change in the climate of opinion. The first, *Capitalism and Freedom*, published in 1962 and destined to sell more than 400,000 copies in the next eighteen years, was not reviewed at the time in a single popular American periodical—not in the *New York Times*, the *Chicago Tribune*, *Newsweek*, *Time*, you name it. The second, *Free to Choose*, published in 1980, was reviewed by every major publication (by some more than once), became the year's best-selling nonfiction book in the United States, and received worldwide attention.

Further evidence of the change in the intellectual climate is the proliferation of think tanks promoting the ideas of limited government and reliance on free markets. In a recent talk Ed Feulner, president of the Heritage Foundation, could mention only four that existed three decades ago: the Hoover Institution, still here today; the Intercollegiate Society of Individualists, which has changed its name but kept the initials; an embryonic American Enterprise Institute; and the Center for Strategic and

International Studies. He should also have included Leonard Read's Foundation for Economic Education (FEE).

By contrast, Feulner noted a long list of additional institutions currently devoted to developing and spreading the idea of limited government and free markets, plus a host of others trying to translate ideas into action. The same contrast is true of publications. FEE's *Freeman* was the only one he or we can think of that was promoting the ideas of freedom thirty to forty years ago. Today numerous publications promote these ideas, though with great differences in specific areas: *The Freeman, National Review, Human Events, The American Spectator, Policy Review,* and *Reason.* Even the *New Republic* and *The Nation* are no longer the undeviating proponents of socialist orthodoxy that they were three decades ago.

Why this great shift in public attitudes? The persuasive power of such books as Friedrich Hayek's *Road to Serfdom,* Ayn Rand's *Fountainhead* and *Atlas Shrugged,* our own *Capitalism and Freedom,* and numerous others led people to think about the problem in a different way and to become aware that government failure was as real as market failure. Nevertheless, we conjecture that the extraordinary force of experience was the major reason for the change.

Experience turned the great hopes that the collectivists and socialists had placed in Russia and China to ashes. Indeed, the only hope in those countries comes from recent moves toward the free market. Similarly experience dampened, to put it mildly, the extravagant hopes placed in Fabian socialism and the welfare state in Britain and in the New Deal in the United States. One major government program after another, each started with the best of intentions, resulted in more problems than solutions.

Few today still regard nationalization of enterprises as a way to promote more efficient production. Few still believe that every social problem can be solved by throwing government (that is, taxpayer) money at it. In these areas liberal ideas—in the original nineteenth-century meaning of liberal— have won the battle. The neoconservatives are correct in defining themselves as (modern) liberals mugged by reality. They still retain many of their earlier values but have been driven to recognize that they cannot achieve them through government.

In this country the Vietnam War helped to undermine belief in the beneficence of government. And most of all, as Dicey predicted nearly seventy-five years ago, the rising burden of taxation caused the general public to react against the growth of government and its spreading influence.[14]

In both the United States and Britain respect for the law declined in the twentieth century under the impact of the widening scope of government, strongly reinforced in the United States by Prohibition. The growing range of favors governments could give led to a steady increase in what economists have come to call rent-seeking and what the public refers to as special-interest lobbying.

Worldwide the contrast between the stagnation of those poorer countries that engaged in central planning (India, the former African colonies, Central American countries) and the rapid progress of the few that followed a largely free-market policy (notably the Four Tigers of the Far East: Hong Kong, Singapore, Taiwan, and South Korea) strongly reinforced the experience of the advanced countries of the West.

Ideas played a significant part, as in earlier episodes, less by persuading the public than by keeping options open, providing alternative policies to adopt when changes had to be made.

As in the two earlier waves, practice has lagged far behind ideas, so that both Britain and the United States are further from the ideal of a free society than they were thirty to forty years ago in almost every dimension. In 1950 spending by U.S. federal, state, and local governments was 25 percent of national income; in 1985 it was 44 percent. In the past thirty years a host of new government agencies has been created: a Department of Education, a National Endowment for the Arts and another for the humanities, EPA, OSHA, and so on. Civil servants in these and many additional agencies decide for us what is in our best interest.

Nonetheless, practice has started to change. The catalytic crisis sparking the change was, we believe, the worldwide wave of inflation during the 1970s, originating in excessively expansive monetary growth in the United States in the 1960s. The episode was catalytic in two respects: first, stagflation destroyed the credibility of Keynesian monetary and fiscal policy and hence of the government's capacity to fine-tune the economy; second, it brought into play Dicey's "weight of taxation" through bracket creep and the implicit repudiation of government debt.

Already in the 1970s military conscription was terminated, airlines deregulated, and regulation Q, which limited the interest rates that banks could pay on deposits, eliminated. In 1982 the Civil Aeronautics Board that regulated the airlines was eliminated. Though government spending as a fraction of national income has continued to rise, the rate of increase has slowed. No major new spending programs have been passed since 1981. The increase in nonmilitary government spending has been predominantly the effect of earlier programs.

As in earlier waves, the tides of both opinion and practice have swept worldwide. Britain went further in the direction of collectivism than the United States and still remains more collectivist—with both a higher ratio of government spending to national income and far more extensive nationalization of industry. Yet Britain has made more progress under Margaret Thatcher than the United States has under Ronald Reagan.

Equally impressive are changes in the communist world. Even there it was impossible to repress all counter-currents, as Solzhenitsyn, Sakharov, and many other brave men and women so eloquently testify. But beyond the counter-currents, the economic reforms in Hungary, Solidarity in Poland, the widened resort to markets in China, the current reformist talk in the Soviet Union—these owe as much to the force of events and the options kept open by intellectual ideas as do the election of Margaret Thatcher and Ronald Reagan in the West. True, it is doubtful that such reforms will be permitted to go far enough to threaten the power of the current political elite. But that does not lessen their value as testimony to the power of ideas.

One interesting and instructive phenomenon is that freeing the market has been equally or more vigorously pursued under ostensibly left-wing governments as under ostensibly right-wing governments. Communist countries aside, one striking example is the U-turn in French policy effected by Mitterrand, a lifelong socialist. In Australia a Labour government replaced a conservative government and then moved sharply to widen the role of the market. New Zealand, under a Labour government headed by David Lange, first elected in 1984 and reelected in 1987, has gone further than any other country in dismantling government controls and economic intervention.

By contrast, Germany, though it owed its dramatic post–World War II recovery to the free-market policies of Ludwig Erhard, has steadily moved away from those policies first under a Social Democratic government and, more recently, under conservative governments. Can the explanation for this aberration be that the dramatic move to free-market policies was primarily the result of one man's (Erhard's) actions and not of a change in public opinion?

All in all the force of ideas, propelled by the pressure of events, is clearly no respecter of geography or ideology or party label.

CONCLUSION

We have surveyed briefly two completed pairs of tides in the climate of opinion and the "affairs of men" and one pair still in progress. Each tide lasted between fifty and 100 years. First came the tide in the climate of public opinion: toward free markets and laissez-faire from, say, 1776 to 1883 in Britain, 1776 to 1885 in the United States; toward collectivism from 1883 to 1950 in Britain, from 1885 to 1970 in the United States. Some decades later came the tide in the "affairs of men": toward laissez-faire from, say, 1820 to 1900 in Britain, 1840 to 1930 in the United States; toward collectivism from, say, 1900 to 1978 in Britain, 1930 to 1980 in the United States. Needless to say, these are only the roughest of dates. They could easily be set a decade or so earlier or later.

Two new pairs of tides are now in their rising phases: in public opinion, toward renewed reliance on markets and more limited government, beginning in about 1950 in Britain and 1970 in the United States; in public policy, beginning in 1978 in Britain and 1980 in the United States, and even more recently in other countries.

If the completed tides are any guide, the current wave in opinion is approaching middle age and in public policy is still in its infancy. Both are therefore still rising and the flood stage, certainly in affairs, is yet to come.

For those who believe in a free society and a narrowly limited role for government, that is reason for optimism. But it is not a reason for complacency. Nothing is inevitable about the course of history—however it may appear in retrospect. "Because we live in a largely free society, we tend to forget how limited is the span of time and the part of the globe for which there has ever been anything like political freedom: the typical state of mankind is tyranny, servitude, and misery."[15]

The encouraging tide in affairs that is in its infancy can still be aborted, can be overwhelmed by a renewed tide of collectivism. The expanded role of government even in Western societies that pride themselves in being part of the free world has created many vested interests that will strongly resist the loss of privileges that they have come to regard as their right. Everyone is capable of believing that what is good for oneself is good for the country and therefore of justifying a special exception to a general rule that we all profess to favor.

Yet the lesson of the two earlier waves is clear: once a tide in opinion or in affairs is strongly set, it tends to overwhelm counter-currents and to keep going for a long time in the same direction. The tides are capable of ignoring geography, political labels, and other hindrances to their continuance. Yet it is also worth recalling that their very success tends to create conditions that may ultimately reverse them.

NOTES

1.   A British constitutional-law scholar has written the most insightful book on the subject: A. V. Dicey, *Lectures on the Relation Between Law and Public Opinion in England During the Nineteenth Century,* 2d ed. (London: Macmillan, 1914).

2.   Milton Friedman and Rose D. Friedman, *Free to Choose* (New York and London: Harcourt Brace Jovanovich, 1980), p. 283.

3.   Adam Smith, *The Wealth of Nations,* Cannan 5th ed. (London: Methuen, 1930), bk. 4, chap. 2, p. 435.

4.   J. M. Keynes, *Economic Consequences of the Peace* (London: Macmillan, 1919), pp. 6, 7, 9.

5.   See Friedman and Friedman, *Free to Choose,* pp. 59, 61–62.

6.   Dicey, *Law and Public Opinion,* p. 245.

7.   A. W. Coats, "The American Economics Association and the Economics Profession," *Journal of Economic Literature* 23 (December 1985): 1702.

8.   Dicey, *Law and Public Opinion,* pp. 257–58.

9.   *Ibid.,* pp. xxxi, xxxii, xxxiii, li.

10.   *Encyclopaedia Britannica,* 1970 ed., s.v. "Brandeis, Louis Dembitz."

11.   Friedman and Friedman, *Free to Choose,* p. 196.

12.   *Ibid.,* pp. 286, 287.

13.   This section is based partly on Milton Friedman, "Where Are We on the Road to Liberty?" *Reason* 19, no. 2 (June 1987): pp. 31–33.

14.   "[I]f the progress of socialistic legislation be arrested, the check will be due, not so much to the influence of any thinker as to some patent fact which shall command public attention; such, for instance, as that increase in the weight of taxation which is apparently the usual, if not the invariable, concomitant of a socialistic policy" (Dicey, *Law and Public Opinion,* p. 302n).

15.   Milton Friedman, with the assistance of Rose D. Friedman, *Capitalism and Freedom* (Chicago: University of Chicago Press, 1962), p. 9.

AN OPEN LETTER
TO BILL BENNETT*

1989

Dear Bill:

In Oliver Cromwell's eloquent words, "I beseech you, in the bowels of Christ, think it possible you may be mistaken" about the course you and President Bush urge us to adopt to fight drugs. The path you propose of more police, more jails, use of the military in foreign countries, harsh penalties for drug users, and a whole panoply of repressive measures can only make a bad situation worse. The drug war cannot be won by those tactics without undermining the human liberty and individual freedom that you and I cherish.

You are not mistaken in believing that drugs are a scourge that is devastating our society. You are not mistaken in believing that drugs are tearing asunder our social fabric, ruining the lives of many young people, and imposing heavy costs on some of the most disadvantaged among us. You

---

* William J. Bennett served as the Director of the White House's Office of National Drug Control Policy from March 1989 to November 1990.

are not mistaken in believing that the majority of the public share your concerns. In short, you are not mistaken in the end you seek to achieve.

Your mistake is failing to recognize that the very measures you favor are a major source of the devils you deplore. Of course the problem is demand, it is demand that must operate through repressed and illegal channels. Illegality creates obscene profits that finance the murderous tactics of the drug lords; illegality leads to the corruption of law enforcement officials; illegality monopolizes the efforts of honest law forces so that they are starved for resources to fight the simpler crimes of robbery, theft, and assault.

Drugs are a tragedy for addicts. But criminalizing their use converts that tragedy into a disaster for society, for users and non-users alike. Our experience with the prohibition of drugs is a replay of our experience with the prohibition of alcoholic beverages.

I append excerpts from a column* that I wrote in 1972 on "Prohibition and Drugs." The major problem then was heroin from Marseilles; today, it is cocaine from Latin America. Today, also, the problem is far more serious than it was seventeen years ago: more addicts, more innocent victims, more drug pushers, more law enforcement officials; more money spent to enforce prohibition, more money spent to circumvent prohibition.

Had drugs been decriminalized seventeen years ago, "crack" would never have been invented (it was invented because the high cost of illegal drugs make it profitable to provide a cheaper version) and there would today be far fewer addicts. The lives of thousands, perhaps hundreds of thousands of innocent victims would have been saved, and not only in the United States. The ghettos of our major cities would not be drug-and-crime-infested no-man's lands. Fewer people would be in jails, and fewer jails would have been built.

Colombia, Bolivia, and Peru would not be suffering from narco-terror, and we would not be distorting our foreign policy because of narco-terror.

---

* See Milton Friedman and Thomas S. Szasz, *On Liberty and Drugs: Essays on the Free Market and Prohibition* (Washington, DC: Drug Policy Foundation Press, 1992).

Hell would not, in the words with which Billy Sunday welcomed Prohibition, "be forever for rent," but it would be a lot emptier.

Decriminalizing drugs is even more urgent now than in 1972, but we must recognize that the harm done in the interim cannot be wiped out, certainly not immediately. Postponing decriminalization will only make matters worse, and make the problem appear even more intractable.

Alcohol and tobacco cause many more deaths in users than do [illegal] drugs. Decriminalization would not prevent us from treating drugs as we now treat alcohol and tobacco: prohibiting sales of drugs to minors, outlawing the advertising of drugs, and similar measures. Such measures could be enforced, while outright prohibition cannot be. Moreover, if even a small fraction of the money we now spend on trying to enforce drug prohibition were devoted to treatment and rehabilitation, in an atmosphere of compassion not punishment, the reduction in drug usage and in the harm done to the users could be dramatic.

This plea comes from the bottom of my heart. Every friend of freedom, and I know you are one, must be as revolted as I am by the prospect of turning the United States into an armed camp, by the vision of jails filled with casual drug users and of an army of enforcers empowered to invade the liberty of citizens on slight evidence. A country in which shooting down unidentified planes "on suspicion" can be seriously considered as a drug war tactic is not the kind of United States that either you or I want to hand on to future generations.

Milton Friedman

HOW TO CURE HEALTH CARE

2001

Since the end of World War II, the provision of medical care in the United States and other advanced countries has displayed three major features: first, rapid advance in the science of medicine; second, large increases in spending, both in terms of inflation-adjusted dollars per person and the fraction of national income spent on medical care; and third, rising dissatisfaction with the delivery of medical care, on the part of both consumers of medical care and physicians and other suppliers of medical care.

Rapid technological advance has occurred repeatedly since the industrial revolution—in agriculture, steam engine, railroad, telephone, electricity, automobile, radio, television, and, most recently, computers and telecommunication. The other two features seem unique to medicine. It is true that spending initially increased after nonmedical technical advances, but the fraction of national income spent did not increase dramatically after the initial phase of widespread acceptance. On the contrary, technological development lowered cost, so that the fraction of national income spent on food, transportation, communication, and much more has gone down, releasing resources to produce new products or services. Similarly, there seems no counterpart in these other areas to the rising dissatisfaction with the delivery of medical care.

I. INTERNATIONAL COMPARISON

These developments in medicine have been worldwide. By their very nature, scientific advances know no geographical boundaries. Data on spending are readily available for twenty-nine Organization for Economic Cooperation and Development (OECD) countries. In every one, medical spending has gone up both in inflation-adjusted dollars per person and as a fraction of national income. Data are available for both 1960 and 1997 for twenty-one countries. In thirteen, spending more than doubled as a fraction of gross domestic product. The smallest increase was 67 percent, the largest, 378 percent. In 1997, sixteen of the twenty-nine OECD countries spent between 7 percent and 9 percent of gross domestic product on medical care. The United States spent 14 percent, the highest of any OECD country. Germany was a distant second at 11 percent; Turkey was the lowest at 4 percent.

A key difference between medical care and the other technological revolutions is the role of government. In other technological revolutions, the initiative, financing, production, and distribution were primarily private, though government sometimes played a supporting or regulatory role. In medical care, government has come to play a leading role in financing, producing, and delivering medical service. Direct government spending on health exceeds 75 percent of total health spending for fifteen OECD countries. The United States is next to the lowest of the twenty-nine countries, at 46 percent. In addition, some governments indirectly subsidize medical care through favorable tax treatment. For the United States, such subsidization raises the fraction of health spending financed directly or indirectly by government to over 50 percent.

What are countries getting for the money they are spending on medical care? What is the relation between input and output? Spending on medical care provides a reasonably good measure of input, but, unfortunately, there is no remotely satisfactory objective measure of output. For the hospital segment, number of beds occupied may at first seem like an objective measure. However, improvements in medicine have included a reduction in the length of hospital stay required for various medical procedures or illnesses. So, fewer patient days may be a sign of greater, not lesser, output. The desired output of medical care is "good health." But how can we quantify "good health," and equally important, allow for the role that factors other than medical care—such as plentiful food, pure water, and protective clothing—play in producing "good health"?

The least objectionable measure I have been able to find is expected length of life at birth or at various later ages, though that too is a far from unambiguous measure of the output attributable to spending on medical care. The remarkable increase in life span in advanced countries during the past century reflects much more than spending on medical care proper. Moreover, it does not allow for changes in the quality of life—attempted measurement of which is still in its infancy.

Figure 1 (see Appendix, pp. 23–30)* shows the relation in 1996 for the twenty-nine OECD countries between the percentage of the gross domestic product spent on medical care and the expected length of life at birth for females.[1] The relation is clearly positive, though very loose.[2] The United States and Germany are clear outliers, ranking first and second in spending but twentieth and seventeenth in length of life. As another indication of looseness, nine countries spent between 7 and 8 percent of GDP on medicine. The group includes Japan, which has the highest expected length of life (83.6 years), and the Czech Republic, fourth from the bottom (77.3 years). Clearly, many factors other than spending on medical care affect expected length of life.

---

* Please see original essay for referenced figures. See p. 256 for original publication information.

Exploring that relation more fully, however worthwhile a project, is not the purpose of this article, which is to examine the situation in the United States. I have presented the data on the OECD countries primarily to document the two (related?) respects in which the United States is an outlier: We spend a higher percentage of national income on medical care (and more per capita) than any other OECD country, and government finances a smaller fraction of that spending than all except Korea.

II. WHY THIRD-PARTY PAYMENT?

Two simple observations are key to explaining both the high level of spending on medical care and the dissatisfaction with that spending. The first is that most payments to physicians or hospitals or other caregivers for medical care are made not by the patient but by a third party—an insurance company or employer or governmental body. The second is that nobody spends somebody else's money as wisely or as frugally as he spends his own. These statements apply equally to other OECD countries. They do not by themselves explain why the United States spends so much more than other countries.

No third party is involved when we shop at a supermarket. We pay the supermarket clerk directly. The same for gasoline for our car, clothes for our back, and so on down the line. Why, by contrast, are most medical payments made by third parties? The answer for the United States begins with the fact that medical-care expenditures are exempt from the income tax if, and only if, medical care is provided by the employer. If an employee pays directly for medical care, the expenditure comes out of the employee's income after income tax. If the employer pays for the employee's medical care, the expenditure is treated as a tax-deductible expense for the employer and is not included as part of the employee's income subject to income tax. That strong incentive explains why most consumers get their medical care through their employer or their spouse's or their parents' employer. In the next place, the enactment of Medicare and Medicaid in 1965 made the government a third-party payer for persons and medical care covered by those measures.

We have become so accustomed to employer-provided medical care that we regard it as part of the natural order. Yet it is thoroughly illogical. Why single out medical care? Food is more essential to life than medical care. Why not exempt the cost of food from taxes if provided by the employer? Why not return to the much-reviled company store when workers were in effect paid in kind rather than in cash?

The revival of the company store for medicine has less to do with logic than pure chance. It is a wonderful example of how one bad government policy leads to another. During World War II, the government financed much wartime spending by printing money while, at the same time, imposing wage and price controls. The resulting repressed inflation produced shortages of many goods and services, including labor. Firms competing to acquire labor at government-controlled wages started to offer medical care as a fringe benefit. That benefit proved particularly attractive to workers and spread rapidly.

Initially, employers did not report the value of a fringe benefit to the Internal Revenue Service as part of their workers' wages. It took some time before the IRS realized what was going on. When it did, it issued regulations requiring employers to include the value of medical care as part of reported employees' wages. By this time, workers had become accustomed to the tax exemption of that particular fringe benefit and made a big fuss. Congress responded by legislating that medical care provided by employers should be tax-exempt.

III. EFFECT OF THIRD-PARTY PAYMENT ON MEDICAL COSTS

The tax exemption of employer-provided medical care has two different effects, both of which raise health costs. First, it leads employees to rely on their employer, rather than themselves, to make arrangements for medical care. Yet employees are likely to do a better job of monitoring medical-care providers, because it is in their own interest, than is the employer or the insurance company or companies designated by the employer. Second, it leads employees to take a larger fraction of their total remuneration in the form of medical care than they would if spending on medical care had the same tax status as other expenditures.

If the tax exemption were removed, employees could bargain with their employers for a higher take-home pay in lieu of medical care and provide for their own medical care either by dealing directly with medical-care providers or by purchasing medical insurance. Removal of the tax exemption would enable governments to reduce the tax rate on income while raising the same total revenue. This hidden subsidy for medical care, currently more than $100 billion a year, is not included in reported figures on government health spending.

Extending the tax exemption to all medical care—as in the current limited provision for medical savings accounts and the proposals to make such accounts more widely available—would reduce reliance on third-party payment. But, by extending the hidden subsidy to all medical-care expenditures, it would increase the tendency of employees to take a larger portion of their remuneration in the form of medical care. (I will more fully discuss medical savings accounts in the conclusion.)

Enactment of Medicare and Medicaid provided a direct subsidy for medical care. The cost grew much more rapidly than originally estimated— as the cost of all handouts invariably do. Legislation cannot repeal the non-legislated law of demand and supply. The lower the price, the greater the quantity demanded; at a zero price, the quantity demanded becomes infinite. Some method of rationing must be substituted for price and that invariably means administrative rationing.

Figure 2 provides an estimate of the effect on medical costs of tax exemption and the subsequent enactment of Medicare and Medicaid. The top line in the chart is actual per capita spending on medical care expressed in constant 1992 prices, to allow for the effect of inflation. Spending multiplied more than twenty-three-fold from 1919 to 1997, going from $155 per capita to $3,625. The bottom line shows what would have happened to per capita spending if it had continued to rise at the same rate as it did from 1919 to 1940 (3.1 percent per year). On that assumption, per capita spending would have risen to $1,751, instead of $3,625 by 1997, or less than half as much.[3,4]

To estimate the separate effects of tax exemption and of Medicare and Medicaid, the second line shows what would have happened to spending if, after Medicare and Medicaid were enacted, spending had continued to rise at the same rate as it did from 1946 to 1965 (4 percent per year). The segment between the two bottom lines shows the effect of tax exemption; the segment between the two top lines shows the effect of the enactment of Medicare and Medicaid. *According to these estimates, tax exemption accounts for 57 percent of the increase in cost; Medicare and Medicaid, 43 percent.*

Figure 3 presents a different breakdown of the cost of medical care: between the part paid directly by the government and the part paid privately. As the figure shows, the government share has been growing over the whole period. Government's share went from one-eighth of the total in 1919 to nearly a quarter in 1946 to a quarter in 1965 to nearly half in 1997. The rise in the government's share has been accompanied by centralization of spending—from primarily by state and local governments to primarily by the federal government. We are headed toward completely socialized medicine and are already halfway there, if in addition to direct costs, we include indirect tax subsidies.

Expressed as a fraction of national income, spending on medical care went from 3 percent of the national income in 1919 to 4.5 percent in 1946, to 7 percent in 1965 to a mind-boggling 17 percent in 1997.[5] No other country in the world approaches that level of spending as a fraction of national income no matter how its medical care is organized. The change in the role of medical care in the U.S. economy is truly breathtaking. To illustrate, in 1946, seven times as much was spent on food, beverages, and tobacco as on medical care; in 1996, fifty years later, more was spent on medical care than on food, beverages, and tobacco. In 1946, twice as much was spent on transportation as on medical care; in 1996, one-and-a-half times as much was spent on medical care as on transportation.

IV. THE CHANGING MEANING OF INSURANCE

Employer financing of medical care has caused the term "insurance" to acquire a rather different meaning in medicine than in most other contexts. We generally rely on insurance to protect us against events that are highly unlikely to occur but involve large losses if they do occur—major catastrophes, not minor regularly recurring expenses. We insure our houses against loss from fire, not against the cost of having to cut the lawn. We insure our cars against liability to others or major damage, not against having to pay for gasoline. Yet in medicine, it has become common to rely on insurance to pay for regular medical examinations and often for prescriptions.

This is partly a question of the size of the deductible and the co-payment, but it goes beyond that. "Without medical insurance" and "without access to medical care" have come to be treated as nearly synonymous. Moreover, the states and the federal government have increasingly specified the coverage of insurance for medical care to a detail not common in other areas. The effect has been to raise the cost of insurance and to limit the options open to individuals. Many, if not most, of the "medically uninsured" are persons who for one reason or another do not have access to employer-provided medical care and are not willing to pay the cost of the only kinds of insurance contracts available to them.

If tax exemption for employer-provided medical care and Medicare and Medicaid had never been enacted, the insurance market for medical care would probably have developed as other insurance markets have. The typical form of medical insurance would have been catastrophic insurance—i.e., insurance with a very high deductible.

V. BUREAUCRATIZATION AND GAMMON'S LAW

Third-party payment has required the bureaucratization of medical care and, in the process, has changed the character of the relation between physicians or other caregivers and patients. A medical transaction is not simply between a caregiver and a patient; it has to be approved as "covered" by a bureaucrat and the appropriate payment authorized. The patient, the recipient of the medical care, has little or no incentive to be concerned about the cost—since it's somebody else's money. The caregiver has become, in effect, an employee of the insurance company or, in the case of Medicare and Medicaid, the government. The patient is no longer the one, and the only one, the caregiver has to serve. An inescapable result is that the interest of the patient is often in direct conflict with the interest of the caregiver's ultimate employer. That has been manifest in public dissatisfaction with the increasingly impersonal character of medical care.

Some years ago, the British physician Max Gammon, after an extensive study of the British system of socialized medicine, formulated what he called "the theory of bureaucratic displacement. In *Health and Security*, he observed that in "a bureaucratic system . . . *increase in expenditure* will be matched by *fall in production*. . . . Such systems will act rather like 'black holes,' in the economic universe, simultaneously sucking in resources, and shrinking in terms of 'emitted production.'" Gammon's observations for the British system have their exact parallel in the partly socialized U.S. medical system. Here too input has been going up sharply relative to output. This tendency can be documented particularly clearly for hospitals, thanks to the availability of high quality data for a long period.

Before 1940, output, as measured by number of patient days per 1,000 population (equal to the number of occupied beds per 1,000 population) and input, as measured by cost per 1,000 population, both rose (input somewhat more than output presumably because of the introduction of more sophisticated and expensive treatments). The number of occupied beds per resident of the United States rose from 1929 to 1940 at the rate of 2.4 percent per year; the cost of hospital care per resident, adjusted for inflation, at 5 percent per year; and the cost per patient day, adjusted for inflation, at 2 percent per year.

The situation changed drastically after the war, as Figure 4 and the top part of Table 1 show. From 1946 to 1996, the number of beds per 1,000 population fell by more than 60 percent; the fraction of beds occupied, by more than 20 percent. In sharp contrast, input skyrocketed. Hospital personnel per occupied bed multiplied nine-fold, and cost per patient day, adjusted for inflation, an astounding forty-fold, from $30 in 1946 to $1,200 in 1996 (at 1992 prices). A major engine of these changes was the enactment of Medicare and Medicaid in 1965. A mild rise in input was turned into a meteoric rise; a mild fall in output, into a rapid decline. The forty-fold increase in the cost per patient day was converted into a thirteen-fold increase in hospital cost per resident of the United States by the sharp decline in output. Hospital days per person per year were cut by two-thirds, from three days in 1946 to an average of less than a day by 1996.

Taken by itself, the decline in hospital days is evidence of progress in medical science. A healthy population needs less hospitalization, and advances in science and medical technology have reduced the length of hospital stays and increased outpatient surgery. Progress in medical science may well explain most of the decline in output; it does not explain much, if any, of the rise in input per unit of output. True, medical machines have become more complex. However, in other areas where there has been great technical progress—whether it be agriculture or telephones or steel or automobiles or aviation or, most recently, computers and the Internet—progress has led to a reduction, not an increase, in cost per unit of output. Why is medicine an exception? Gammon's law, not medical miracles, was clearly at work. The provision of medical care as an untaxed fringe benefit by employers, and then the federal government's assumption of responsibility for hospital and medical care of the elderly and the poor, provided a fresh pool of money. And there was no shortage of takers. Growing costs, in turn, led to more regulation of hospitals and medical care, further increasing administrative costs, and leading to the bureaucratization that is so prominent a feature of medical care today.

Medicine is not the only area where this pattern has prevailed. Aside from defense and medicine, schooling is the only other major area of our society that is largely financed and administered by government, and here too Gammon's law has clearly operated. Input per unit of output, however measured, has clearly been going up; output, especially if measured in terms of quality, has been going down, and dissatisfaction, as in medicine, is growing. The same may well be true also in defense. However, measuring output independently of input is even more baffling for defense than for medicine.

To return to medicine, hospital cost has risen as a percentage of total medical cost from 24 percent in 1946 to 32 percent half a century later. The cost of physician services is currently the second largest component of total medical cost. It too has risen sharply, though less sharply than hospital costs. In 1946, the cost of physician services exceeded the cost of hospital services. According to the estimates in Table 1, the cost of physician services has multiplied four-fold since 1946, the major rise coming after the adoption of Medicare and Medicaid in 1965.

Figure 5 shows what has happened to the number of physicians and their income. The number almost doubled, and the income per physician almost tripled over the half-century from 1946 to 1996. Both reflect the increase in funds available to finance medical care and the third-party character of payment. The demand for physician services went up, and income had to go up to attract additional physicians. Paradoxically, the attempt by third-party payers—particularly the federal government— to keep costs down has been at least partly self-defeating, because it took the form of imposing onerous rules and regulations on physicians. The resultant bureaucratization of medical practice has made the practice of medicine less attractive as an occupation to most actual and potential physicians, which increased the necessary rise in incomes. It has also reduced their productivity.

VI. MEDICAL-CARE OUTPUT

So much for input. What about output? What have we gotten in return for quadrupling the share of the nation's income spent on medical care?

I have already referred to one component of output—days of hospital care per person per year. That has gone down from three days in 1946 to less than one in 1996. Insofar as the reduction reflects the improvements in medicine, it clearly is a good thing. However, it also reflects the pressure to keep hospital stays short in order to keep down cost. That this is not a good thing is clear from protests by patients, widespread enough to have led Congress to mandate minimum stays for some medical procedures.

The output of the medical-care industry that we are interested in is its contribution to better health. How can we measure better health in a reasonably objective way that is not greatly influenced by other factors? For example, if medical care enables people to live longer and healthier lives, we might expect that the fraction of persons aged sixty-five to seventy who continue to work would go up. In fact, of course, the fraction has gone down drastically—thanks to higher incomes reinforced by financial incentives from Social Security. With the same "if" we might expect the fraction of the population classified as disabled to go down, but that fraction has gone up, again not for reasons of health but because of government social security programs. And so I have found with one initially plausible measure after another—all of them are too contaminated by other factors to reflect the output of the medical-care industry.

As noted earlier, the least bad measure that I have been able to come up with is length of life, though that too is seriously contaminated by other factors—improvements in diet, housing, clothing, and so on generated by greater affluence, better garbage collection and disposal, the provision of purer water, and other governmental public-health measures. Wars, epidemics, and natural and man-made disasters have played a part. Even more important, the quality of life is as meaningful as the length of life. Perhaps the extensive research on aging currently underway will lead to a better measure than length of life.

Figures 6 and 7 present two different sets of data on expected length of life: Figure 6, expected length of life at birth; Figure 7, remaining length of life at age 65. Both cover the whole century, from 1900 to 1997, the last year for which I was able to get data. For Figure 6 the data are annual; for Figure 7, decennial until recent years. The two tell very different, but equally remarkable, stories.

Expected longevity went from forty-seven years in 1900 to 68 years in 1950, a truly remarkable rise that proceeded at a fairly steady rate, averaging four-tenths of a year per year. Public-health activities, such as those leading to cleaner water and air and better control of epidemics, played a major role in lengthening life, no doubt; but so too did improvements in medical practice and hospital care, particularly those leading to a sharp reduction in infant and maternal mortality. Whatever its source, *the increase in longevity did not have any systematic relation to spending on medical care as a fraction of income.* We have reasonably accurate data on spending only from 1929 on; crude data from 1919 on. Except for the deep depression years of 1932 and 1933, national health spending never exceeded 5 percent of national income, and from 1919 to 1948, varied between 3 and 5 percent, primarily as a result of wider swings in national income than in health spending.

The most striking feature of Figure 6 is the sharp slowdown in the increase in longevity after 1950. From 1950 on, longevity grew at less than half the rate that it grew from 1900 to 1950—averaging less than two-tenths of a year per year compared to the earlier four-tenths.[6] In the first fifty years of the century, the life span increased by twenty-one years; in the next forty-seven years, by eight years. As in the first fifty years, the increase proceeded at a surprisingly steady pace. I have no good explanation for the shift from one trend to the other. I conjecture that it reflects the exhaustion by the end of World War II of the possibility of further major improvements from public-health activity. I leave it to scholars more knowledgeable about medicine than I to give a more satisfactory answer.

The later trend was accompanied, as the earlier one was not, by a major increase in spending as a fraction of national income. However, I attribute that increase in spending to the changes in the economic organization of medical care discussed earlier. I doubt that it is related as either cause or effect to the slowdown in the growth of longevity.

Data are much less readily available for longevity at age 65 than at birth, so I have resorted to the use of decennial estimates except for the most recent year. Figure 7 is almost the mirror image of Figure 6—that is, the same picture reversed. Instead of first rising rapidly and then slowly, longevity at age sixty-five at first rose slowly and then rapidly. Until 1940, longevity rose at an average of only .025 years per year. Remaining years of life went from twelve—or to age seventy-seven—in 1900 to thirteen— or age seventy-eight—in 1940. Then there was a sharp acceleration, and in the next fifty-seven years, remaining years of life went up by an additional five years to eighteen—or age eighty-three, rising at the average rate of .085 years per year. Understandably, both the earlier and the later rates of growth in longevity at age sixty-five are much smaller than the comparable figures for longevity at birth. The remarkable phenomenon is the shift in trend around 1940, and the steadiness of the trend both before and after 1940.

Data for later years of life suggests that the steadiness of the trend in longevity at age sixty-five is not likely to continue. At these later ages, there has been a distinct slowing of increases in longevity since about 1980. At age eighty-five, remaining years of life for females has not changed in the seventeen years from 1980 to 1997. It was 6.4 years in both 1980 and 1997.[7]

What caused the change in the trend at age sixty-five, and why was that change in the opposite direction from the change in the trend at birth, and why did it occur about ten years earlier? Could it have been the emergence of penicillin and sulfa at around 1940 that explains the dating of the shift? No doubt many other advances in medicine, from the handling of blood pressure to the perfecting of open-heart surgery, the improved treatment of cancer, and the better understanding of diet were of special importance for preventing death at later ages. I am incompetent to judge these matters and their relative importance. But I have no doubt that one economic change also played an important role. That was the sharp improvement in the economic status of the elderly brought about by government transfer programs, notably Social Security. From being among the poorest groups in society, the elderly have become among the most affluent in the post-World War II period.

However interesting these speculations may be, they are a long way from providing an answer to the question with which we started this section, namely, "What have we gotten in return for quadrupling the share of the nation's income spent on medical care?" The slowdown in the increase of longevity at birth started before tax exemption and Medicare had any effect on spending. Similarly, the acceleration in the increase in longevity at age sixty-five started twenty-five years before Medicare was enacted and showed no speedup thereafter. Perhaps better measures of the health of the population and various subgroups will show a relation to total spending. But on the evidence to date, it is hard to see that we have gotten much for that spending other than bureaucratization and widespread dissatisfaction with the economic organization of medical care.

VII. THE UNITED STATES VS. OTHER COUNTRIES

Our steady movement toward reliance on third-party payment no doubt explains the extraordinary rise in spending on medical care in the United States. However, other advanced countries also rely on third-party payment, many or most of them to an even greater extent than we do. What explains our higher level of spending?

I must confess that despite much thought and scouring of the literature, I have no satisfactory answer. One clue is my estimate that if the pre-World War II system had continued—that is, if tax exemption and Medicare and Medicaid had never been enacted—expenditures on medical care would have amounted to less than half its current level, which would have put us near the bottom of the OECD list rather than at the top.

In terms of holding down cost, one-payer directly administered government systems, such as exist in Canada and Great Britain, have a real advantage over our mixed system. As the direct purchaser of all or nearly all medical services, they are in a monopoly position in hiring physicians and can hold down their remuneration, so that physicians earn much less in those countries than in the United States. In addition, they can ration care more directly—at the cost of long waiting lists and much dissatisfaction.[8]

In addition, once the whole population is covered, there is little political incentive to increase spending on medical care. In an insightful analysis of political entrepreneurship, W. Allen Wallis noted that

> one of the ways politicians compete for votes is by offering to have the government provide new services. For an offer of a new service to have substantial electoral impact, the service ordinarily must be one that a large number of voters is familiar with, and in fact already use. The most effective innovations for a political entrepreneur to offer, therefore, are those whose effect is to transfer from individuals to the government the costs of services which are already in existence, not to alter appreciably the amount of the service reaching the people.[9]

Medicare, Medicaid, the political stress on the "uninsured," and the current political pressure for government financing of prescriptions all exemplify this phenomenon. Once the bulk of costs have been taken over by government, as they have in most of the other OECD countries, the political entrepreneur has no additional groups to attract, and attention turns to holding down costs.

An additional factor is the tax treatment of private expenditures on medical care. In most countries, any private expenditure comes out of after-tax income. It does in the United States also, unless the medical care is provided by the employer. For this reason, the bulk of medical care is provided through employers, and private expenditures on medical care are decidedly higher than they would be if medical care, like food, clothing, and other consumer goods, had to be financed out of post-tax income. It is consistent with this view that Germany, the country second to the United States in the fraction of income spent on medical care, has a system in which the employer plays a central role in the provision of medical care and in which, so far as I have been able to determine, half of the cost comes out of pre-tax income, half out of post-tax income.

Our mixed system has many advantages in accessibility and quality of medical care, but it has produced a higher level of cost than would result from either wholly individual choice or wholly collective choice.

VIII. MEDICAL SAVINGS ACCOUNTS AND BEYOND

The high cost and inequitable character of our medical-care system is the direct result of our steady movement toward reliance on third-party payment. A cure requires reversing course, reprivatizing medical care by eliminating most third-party payment, and restoring the role of insurance to providing protection against major medical catastrophes.

The ideal way to do that would be to reverse past actions: repeal the tax exemption of employer-provided medical care; terminate Medicare and Medicaid; deregulate most insurance; and restrict the role of the government, preferably state and local rather than federal, to financing care for the hard cases. However, the vested interests that have grown up around the existing system, and the tyranny of the status quo, clearly make that solution not feasible politically. Yet it is worth stating the ideal as a guide to judging whether proposed incremental changes are in the right direction.

Most changes made in the final decade of the twentieth century have been in the wrong direction. Despite rejection of the sweeping socialization of medicine proposed by Hillary Clinton, subsequent incremental changes have expanded the role of government, increased regulation of medical practice, and further constrained the terms of medical insurance, thereby raising its cost and increasing the fraction of individuals who choose or are forced to go without insurance.

There is one exception, which, though minor in current scope, is pregnant of future possibilities. The Kassebaum-Kennedy bill, passed in 1996 after lengthy and acrimonious debate, included a narrowly limited four-year pilot program authorizing medical savings accounts. A medical savings account enables individuals to deposit tax-free funds in an account usable only for medical expense, provided they have a high-deductible insurance policy that limits the maximum out-of-pocket expense. As noted earlier, it eliminates third-party payment except for major medical expenses and is thus a movement very much in the right direction. By extending tax exemption to all medical expenses whether paid by the employer or not, it eliminates the present bias in favor of employer-provided medical care. That too is a move in the right direction. However, the extension of tax exemption increases the bias in favor of medical care compared to other household expenditures. This effect would tend to increase the implicit government subsidy for medical care, which would be a step in the wrong direction.[10] But, on balance, given how large a fraction of current medical expenditures are exempt, it seems likely that the net effect of widely available and flexible medical savings accounts would be very much in the right direction.

However, the current pilot program is neither widely available nor flexible. The act limits the number of medical savings accounts to no more than 750,000 policies, available only to the self-employed who are uninsured and employees at firms with fifty or fewer employees. Moreover, the act specifies the precise terms of the medical savings account and the associated insurance. Finally, at the end of four years (the year 2000) Congress will have to vote to continue or change the program. (Those who signed up in the first four years would be entitled to continue their accounts even if Congress terminates the program.) A number of representatives and senators have indicated their intention to introduce bills to extend and widen the availability of medical savings accounts.

Prior to this pilot project, a number of large companies (e.g., Quaker Oats, Forbes, Golden Rule Insurance Co.) had offered their employees the choice of a medical savings account instead of the usual low-deductible employer-provided insurance policy. In each case, the employer purchased a high-deductible major medical insurance policy for the employee and deposited a stated sum, generally about half of the deductible, in a medical savings account for the employee. That sum could be used by the employee for medical care. Any part not used during the year was the property of the employee and had to be included in taxable income. Despite this loss of tax exemption, this alternative has generally been very popular with both employers and employees. It has reduced costs for the employer and empowered the employee, eliminating much third-party payment.

Medical savings accounts offer one way to resolve the growing financial and administrative problems of Medicare and Medicaid. Each current participant could be given the alternative of continuing with present arrangements or receiving a high-deductible major medical insurance policy and a specified deposit in a medical savings account. New entrants would be required to accept the alternative. Many details would have to be worked out: the size of the deductible and the deposit in the medical savings account, the size of any co-payment, and whether additional medical spending would be tax-exempt. Yet it seems clear from private experience that a program along these lines would be less expensive and bureaucratic than the current system, and more satisfactory to the participants. In effect, it would be a way to voucherize Medicare and Medicaid. It would enable participants to spend their own money on themselves for routine medical care and medical problems, rather than having to go through HMOs and insurance companies, while at the same time providing protection against medical catastrophes.

An interesting and instructive experiment with medical savings accounts has recently taken place in South Africa, as explained by Shaun Matisonn of the National Center for Policy Analysis:

For most of the last decade [the nineties]—under the leadership of Nelson Mandela—South Africa enjoyed what was probably the freest market for health insurance anywhere in the world....

South Africa's insurance regulations were and are sufficiently flexible to allow the type of innovation and experimentation that American law stifles.... The result has been remarkable.... In just five years, MSA plans captured half the market, proving that they are popular and meet consumer needs as well as or better than rival products. South Africa's experience with MSAs shows that MSA holders save money, spending less on discretionary items in a way that does not increase the cost of inpatient care. Contrary to allegations by some critics, the South African experience also shows that MSAs attract individuals of all different ages and different degrees of health.

A more radical reform would, first, end both Medicare and Medicaid, at least for new entrants, and replace them by providing every family in the United States with catastrophic insurance—i.e., a major medical policy with a high deductible. Second, it would end tax exemption of employer-provided medical care. And third, it would remove the restrictive regulations that are now imposed on medical insurance—hard to justify with universal catastrophic insurance.

This reform would solve the problem of the currently medically uninsured, eliminate most of the bureaucratic structure, free medical practitioners from an increasingly heavy burden of paperwork and regulation, and lead many employers and employees to convert employer-provided medical care into a higher cash wage. The taxpayer would save money because total government costs would plummet. The family would be relieved of one of its major concerns—the possibility of being impoverished by a major medical catastrophe—and most could readily finance the remaining medical costs. Families would once again have an incentive to monitor the providers of medical care and to establish the kind of personal relations with them that were once customary. The demonstrated efficiency of private enterprise would have a chance to improve the quality and lower the cost of medical care. The first question asked of a patient entering a hospital might once again become "What's wrong?" and not "What's your insurance?"

While so radical a reform is almost surely not politically feasible at the moment, it may become so as dissatisfaction with the current arrangements continue to grow. And again, it gives a standard—if less than an ideal one—against which to judge incremental changes.

NOTES

1.   Females only are included to remove one source of irrelevant difference among countries. In general, females tend to have a longer expected length of life than males, and countries differ in the ratio of males to females. The correlation of expected length of life with per capita spending on medical care in dollars is almost the same as with percent of GDP spent on medical care.

2.   The correlation is partly spurious because percent spent tends to be positively correlated with real GDP, and real GDP is positively correlated with length of life for given percent spent. However, the partial correlation of percent spent with length of life is statistically significant and higher than the partial correlation of real GDP with length of life.

3.   In an extensive study, the Rand Corporation compared the effect of different health-insurance plans, varying from one with no deductible and no co-payment—that is, free medical care—to one with 95 percent co-payment, very close to complete private responsibility. In his summary of the results, Joseph Newhouse concluded that, "had there been no MDE [maximum deductible expense], demand on the 95 percent coinsurance plan would have been a little over half as large as on the free care plan," and an accompanying table gives 55 percent as the actual fraction.

The 1997 value of the extrapolated trend from 1919–1940 is 48 percent of actual expenditures in 1997, remarkably close to Newhouse's 55 percent, based on a completely independent set of data. See Joseph P. Newhouse, *Free for All? Lessons from Rand Health Insurance Experiment* (Harvard University Press, 1993), p. 458.

4.   Had this been the total expenditure in 1996, the United States would have ranked twenty-first, rather than first, among the 29 OECD countries in fraction of income spent on medical care.

5.   The figure of 14 percent referred to earlier was from OECD data; it referred to 1996 rather than 1997 and to percent of gross domestic product, not national income.

6.   I have used data for the population as a whole, although data are also available by sex and race. There are minor differences between the sexes and between the races, but the broad picture is essentially the same for all, so I have not thought it worthwhile to present more detailed data, as I did in *Input and Output in Medical Care* (Stanford: Hoover Institution Press, 1992).

7.   I am indebted to James Fries, a leading expert on aging, for calling this phenomenon to my attention. The data cited are from Metropolitan Life Insurance *Statistical Bulletin*, Oct.-Dec., 1998.

8.   See Cynthia Ramsay and Michael Walker, *Critical Issues Bulletin: Waiting Your Turn*, 7th edition (Vancouver, B.C., Canada: Fraser Institute, 1997).

9.   W. Allen Wallis, *An Overgoverned Society* (Free Press, 1976), p. 256.

10.   Whether medical savings accounts increase or decrease the government subsidy to medical care, including the hidden tax subsidy of tax exemption, depends on whether they raise or lower total medical expenditures exempted from tax. First party payment works toward reducing such expenditures by giving consumers an incentive to economize and by reducing administrative costs. The availability of tax exemption to a wider class of medical expenses has the opposite effect. Such experience as we have with medical savings accounts or their equivalent suggests that the first effect is highly significant and is likely to overwhelm the second. However, this issue deserves more systematic investigation.

FORTIETH ANNIVERSARY PREFACE TO *CAPITALISM AND FREEDOM*

2002

I n my preface to the 1982 edition of this book, I documented a dramatic shift in the climate of opinion, manifested in the difference between the way this book was treated when it was first published in 1962, and the way my wife's and my subsequent book, *Free to Choose*, presenting the same philosophy, was treated when it was published in 1980. That change in the climate of opinion developed while and partly because the role of government was exploding under the influence of initial welfare state and Keynesian views. In 1956, when I gave the lectures that my wife helped shape into this book, government spending in the United States—federal, state, and local—was equal to 26 percent of national income. Most of this spending was on defense. Non-defense spending was 12 percent of national income. Twenty-five years later, when the 1982 edition of this book was published, total spending had risen to 39 percent of national income and non-defense spending had more than doubled, amounting to 31 percent of national income.

That change in the climate of opinion had its effect. It paved the way for the election of Margaret Thatcher in Britain and Ronald Reagan in the United States. They were able to curb Leviathan, though not to cut it down. Total government spending in the United States did decline slightly, from 39 percent of national income in 1982 to 36 percent in 2000, but that was almost all due to a reduction in spending for defense. Non-defense spending fluctuated around a roughly constant level: 31 percent in 1982, 30 percent in 2000.

The climate of opinion received a further boost in the same direction when the Berlin Wall fell in 1989 and the Soviet Union collapsed in 1992. That brought to a dramatic end an experiment of some seventy years between two alternative ways of organizing an economy: top-down versus bottom-up; central planning and control versus private markets; more colloquially, socialism versus capitalism. The result of that experiment had been foreshadowed by a number of similar experiments on a smaller scale: Hong Kong and Taiwan versus mainland China; West Germany versus East Germany; South Korea versus North Korea. But it took the drama of the Berlin Wall and the collapse of the Soviet Union to make it part of conventional wisdom, so that it is now taken for granted that central planning is indeed *The Road to Serfdom*, as Friedrich A. Hayek titled his brilliant 1944 polemic.

What is true for the United States and Great Britain is equally true for the other Western advanced countries. In country after country, the initial postwar decades witnessed exploding socialism, followed by creeping or stagnant socialism. And in all these countries the pressure today is toward giving markets a greater role and government a smaller one. I interpret the situation as reflecting the long lag between opinion and practice. The rapid socialization of the post–World War II decades reflected the prewar shift of opinion toward collectivism; the creeping or stagnant socialism of the past few decades reflects the early effects of the postwar change of opinion; future desocialization will reflect the mature effects of the change in opinion reinforced by the collapse of the Soviet Union.

The change in opinion has had an even more dramatic effect on the formerly underdeveloped world. That has been true even in China, the largest remaining explicitly communist state. The introduction of market reforms by Deng Xiaoping in the late seventies, in effect privatizing agriculture, dramatically increased output and led to the introduction of additional market elements into a communist command society. The limited increase in economic freedom has changed the face of China, strikingly confirming our faith in the power of free markets. China is still very far from being a free society, but there is no doubt that the residents of China are freer and more prosperous than they were under Mao—freer in every dimension except the political. And there are even the first small signs of some increase in political freedom, manifested in the election of some officials in a growing number of villages. China has far to go, but it has been moving in the right direction.

In the immediate post–World War II period, the standard doctrine was that development of the third world required central planning plus massive foreign aid. The failure of that formula wherever it was tried, as was pointed out so effectively by Peter Bauer and others, and the dramatic success of the market-oriented policies of the East Asia tigers—Hong Kong, Singapore, Taiwan, South Korea—has produced a very different doctrine for development. By now, many countries in Latin America and Asia, and even a few in Africa have adopted a market-oriented approach and a smaller role for government. Many of the former Soviet satellites have done the same. In all those cases, in accordance with the theme of this book, increases in economic freedom have gone hand in hand with increases in political and civil freedom and have led to increased prosperity; competitive capitalism and freedom have been inseparable.

A final personal note: It is a rare privilege for an author to be able to evaluate his own work forty years after it first appeared. I appreciate very much having the chance to do so. I am enormously gratified by how well the book has withstood time and how pertinent it remains to today's problems. If there is one major change I would make, it would be to replace the dichotomy of economic freedom and political freedom with the trichotomy of economic freedom, civil freedom, and political freedom. After I finished the book, Hong Kong, before it was returned to China, persuaded me that while economic freedom is a necessary condition for civil and political freedom, political freedom, desirable though it may be, is not a necessary condition for economic and civil freedom. Along these lines, the one major defect in the book seems to me an inadequate treatment of the role of political freedom, which under some circumstances promotes economic and civic freedom, and under others, inhibits economic and civic freedom.

MY FIVE FAVORITE LIBERTARIAN BOOKS

2002

I am one of the many millions of beneficiaries of Andrew Carnegie's public libraries. The one in the small town in which I grew up (Rahway, New Jersey) fed my early interest in books, providing a range of reading matter that was available in no other way, since there were few books at home. That started me on a lifelong addiction, and, as financial conditions permitted, to homes filled with books.

I have been asked what was my first introduction to libertarian thought. I find that hard to answer, involving as it does looking back nearly three-quarters of a century. But if I had to make a guess, I would conjecture that it was John Stuart Mill's *Essay on Liberty*, which I must have read in my first or second year of college.

Herewith are my five favorite libertarian books.

ADAM SMITH'S
THE WEALTH OF NATIONS

First, Adam Smith's *The Wealth of Nations*. This book, published in 1776, founded economic science. It introduced the notion of the "invisible hand" and explained how free trade could produce cooperation among people in achieving economic productivity. It remains a book well worth reading, full of wonderful comments to warm a libertarian's heart.

MILL'S *ESSAY ON LIBERTY*

Second, John Stuart Mill's *Essay on Liberty*. The most concise and clearest statement of the fundamental libertarian principle, "The only purpose for which power can be rightfully exercised over any member of a civilized community, against his will, is to prevent harm to others. . . ."

DICEY'S *LECTURES* ON LAW
AND PUBLIC OPINION

Third, A. V. Dicey's *Lectures on the Relation between Law and Public Opinion in England during the Nineteenth Century*. A remarkable work initially presented as lectures at Harvard in the 1890's and reprinted with a new and very important preface in 1914. Dicey saw clearly the ultimate outcome of initial social welfare measures in the first decade of the twentieth century. He essentially predicted the emergence of the full-fledged welfare state. More than a century ago, Dicey explained why the rhetoric in terms of the general interest is so persuasive: "The beneficial effect of state intervention, especially in the form of legislation, is direct, immediate, and so to speak, visible while its evil effects are gradual and indirect and lying out of sight. . . . Hence the majority of mankind must almost of necessity look with undue favor upon governmental intervention."

HAYEK'S *THE ROAD TO SERFDOM*

Fourth, F. A. Hayek's *The Road to Serfdom*. This profound book was highly influential in the immediate post-World War II period when it was a lone voice presenting the case for libertarian philosophy and pointing out the consequences of an increase in the role of the state. It was certainly one of the most effective works leading people to take libertarian principles seriously.

MY OWN FAVORITE: *CAPITALISM AND FREEDOM* OR *FREE TO CHOOSE?*

Fifth, I have been asked to include one of my own books. I am torn between *Capitalism and Freedom*, published in 1962 with the assistance of Rose D. Friedman, and *Free to Choose*, published in 1980 jointly with Rose D. Friedman. Both present the same philosophy and cover many of the same topics. *Capitalism and Freedom* is more succinct, scholarly, and abstract; it was a product of a series of lectures that I gave in June 1956 at a conference at Wabash College directed by John Van Sickle and Benjamin Rogge [a long-time FEE trustee] and sponsored by the Volker Foundation.

Free to Choose, based on the television program of the same title, is more popular, less abstract, more concrete. It presents a fuller development of the philosophy that permeates both books; it has more nuts and bolts, less theoretical framework. The TV program on which *Free to Choose* is based is available in videocassette and, if I were to consider it as a book, would clearly be my favorite.

SCHOOL CHOICE: A PERSONAL RETROSPECTIVE*

2006

Little did I know when I published an article in 1955 on "The Role of Government in Education" that it would lead to my becoming an activist for a major reform in the organization of schooling, and indeed that my wife and I would be led to establish a foundation to promote parental choice. The original article was not a reaction to a perceived deficiency in schooling. The quality of schooling in the United States then was far better than it is now, and both my wife and I were satisfied with the public schools we had attended. My interest was in the philosophy of a free society. Education was the area that I happened to write on early. I then went on to consider other areas as well. The end result was *Capitalism and Freedom*, published seven years later with the education article as one chapter.

---

* A slightly different version of this essay appeared in the *Wall Street Journal* on June 9, 2005, under the headline "Free to Choose" as well as in the *School Choice Advocate*, June 2005, under the title "A Personal Retrospective."

With respect to education, I pointed out that government was playing three major roles: (1) legislating compulsory schooling, (2) financing schooling, and (3) administering schools. I concluded that there was some justification for compulsory schooling and the financing of schooling, but "the actual administration of educational institutions by the government, the 'nationalization,' as it were, of the bulk of the 'education industry' is much more difficult to justify on free-market or, so far as I can see, on any other grounds." Yet finance and administration "could readily be separated. Governments could require a minimum of schooling financed by giving the parents vouchers redeemable for a given sum per child per year to be spent on purely educational services. . . . Denationalizing schooling," I went on, "would widen the range of choice available to parents. . . . If present public expenditure were made available to parents regardless of where they send their children, a wide variety of schools would spring up to meet the demand. . . . Here, as in other fields, competitive enterprise is likely to be far more efficient in meeting consumer demand than either nationalized enterprises or enterprises run to serve other purposes."

Though the article, and then *Capitalism and Freedom*, generated some academic and popular attention at the time, so far as we know no attempts were made to introduce a system of educational vouchers until the Nixon administration, when the Office of Economic Opportunity took up the idea and offered to finance actual experiments. One result of that initiative was an ambitious attempt to introduce vouchers in the large cities of New Hampshire, which appeared to be headed for success until it was aborted by the opposition of the teachers' unions and the educational administrators—one of the first instances of the oppositional role they were destined to play in subsequent decades. Another result was an experiment in the Alum Rock school system involving a choice of schools within a public system.

What really led to increased interest in vouchers was the deterioration of schooling, dating in particular from 1965 when the National Education Association converted itself from a professional association to a trade union.

Concern about the quality of education led to the establishment of the National Commission on Excellence in Education, whose final report "A Nation at Risk" was published in 1983. It used the following quote from Paul Copperman to dramatize its own conclusion:

> Each generation of Americans has outstripped its parents in education, in literacy, and in economic attainment. For the first time in the history of our country, the educational skills of one generation will not surpass, will not equal, will not even approach, those of their parents.

"A Nation at Risk" stimulated much soul-searching and a whole series of major attempts to reform the government educational system. Those reforms, however extensive or bold, have, it is widely agreed, had a negligible effect on the quality of the public school system. Though spending per pupil has more than doubled since 1970, after allowing for inflation, students continue to rank low in international comparisons, dropout rates are high, and scores on SATs and the like have fallen and remain flat. Simple literacy, let alone functional literacy, in the United States is almost surely lower at the beginning of the twenty-first century than it was a century earlier. And all this is despite a major increase in real spending per student since "A Nation at Risk" was published.

One result has been experimentation with such alternatives as vouchers, tax credits, and charter schools. Government voucher programs are in effect in a few places (Wisconsin, Ohio, Florida, the District of Columbia); private voucher programs are widespread; tax credits for educational expenses have been adopted in at least three states; and tax credit vouchers (tax credits for gifts to scholarship-granting organizations) have been adopted in three states. In addition, a major legal obstacle to the adoption of vouchers was removed when the Supreme Court affirmed the legality of the Cleveland voucher program in 2002. However, all of those programs are limited; taken together, they cover only a small fraction of all children in the country.

Throughout this long period, we have been repeatedly frustrated by the gulf between the clear and present need, the burning desire of parents to have more control over the schooling of their children, on the one hand, and the adamant and effective opposition of trade union leaders and educational administrators to any change that would in any way reduce their control of the educational system.

We have been involved in two initiatives in California to enact a statewide voucher system (in 1993 and 2000). In both cases, the initiatives were carefully drawn up and the voucher sums moderate. In both cases, nine months or so before the election, public opinion polls recorded a sizable majority in favor of the initiative. In addition, of course, there was a sizable group of fervent supporters, whose hopes of finally getting control of their children's schooling ran high. In each case, about six months before the election, opponents of vouchers launched a well-financed and thoroughly unscrupulous campaign against the initiative. Television ads blared that vouchers would break the budget, whereas in fact they would reduce spending since the proposed voucher was to be only a fraction of what government was spending per student. Teachers were induced to send home with their students misleading propaganda against the initiative. Dirty tricks of every variety were financed from a very deep purse. The result was to convert the initial majority into a landslide defeat. That has also occurred in Washington State, Colorado, and Michigan. Opposition like this explains why progress has been so slow in such a good cause.

The good news is that, despite the setbacks, public interest in and support for vouchers and tax credits continues to grow. Legislative proposals to channel government funds directly to students rather than to schools are under consideration in something like twenty states. Sooner or later there will be a breakthrough; we shall get a universal voucher plan in one or more states. When we do, a competitive private educational market serving parents who are free to choose the school they believe best for each child will demonstrate how it can revolutionize schooling.

PART TWO

ECONOMICS

WESLEY C. MITCHELL AS AN ECONOMIC THEORIST[1]

1950

Wesley C. Mitchell is generally considered primarily an empirical scientist rather than a theorist. In my opinion, this judgment is valid; yet it can easily be misunderstood. The ultimate goal of science in any field is a theory—an integrated "explanation" of observed phenomena that can be used to make valid predictions about phenomena not yet observed. Many kinds of work can contribute to this ultimate goal and are essential for its attainment: the collection of observations about the phenomena in question; the organization and arrangement of observations and the extraction of empirical generalizations from them; the development of improved methods of measuring or analyzing observations; the formulation of partial or complete theories to integrate existing evidence.

In this sense, Wesley Mitchell's empirical work is itself a contribution to economic theory—and a contribution of the first magnitude. His work on prices and on business cycles provides an invaluable body of tested knowledge about these phenomena for the formulation of new theories and the testing of old theories; his work on the construction of index numbers and on statistical techniques for analyzing data on business cycles furthers the accumulation of additional tested knowledge. These contributions are so important and far reaching that they have tended to obscure the significance of the work with which this paper is concerned—Mitchell's contribution to economic theory in the narrower sense of the explicit formulation of theory.

There is of course no sharp line between the empirical scientist and the theorist—we are dealing with a continuum, with mixtures in all proportions, not with a dichotomy. "The most reckless and treacherous of all theorists is he who professes to let facts and figures speak for themselves."[2] And, one might add, the most reckless and treacherous of all empirical workers is he who formulates theories to explain observations that are the product of careless and inaccurate empirical work. A so-called "empirical generalization" may integrate many narrower generalizations; it may have great predictive power. A so-called "theory" may integrate little and have small predictive power. Yet there is a distinction worth drawing between work that is concerned primarily with the description of phenomena and the discovery of empirical regularities and work that is concerned primarily with the integration of empirical knowledge through the abstraction of supposedly essential features and their formulation into a coherent system of relationships.

The absence of a sharp line between empirical and theoretical work is particularly evident in Mitchell's work. His empirical work is throughout shaped by a thorough knowledge of existing theory and directed toward the construction of a better theory. It is always analytical, never aridly descriptive. His theoretical work is throughout interwoven with his empirical work and made a part of an "analytic description" of the phenomena under study.[3] Even in the most explicitly theoretical parts of his major writings—Part III of the 1913 *Business Cycles* and Chapter II of the 1927 *Business Cycles*[4]—Mitchell did not state baldly the bare bones of his theoretical structure; they are concealed in a summary of descriptive evidence and an elaboration of qualifications to the theoretical core or deviations from it.

Any attempt to make a thoroughgoing separation of Mitchell's theoretical from his empirical work would be artificial and would yield parts whose sum would be less than the whole from which they were extracted. In consequence, I have not attempted such a separation. Instead, with one important exception, I have selected for discussion a few theoretical formulations that seem to me important and that happen to be relatively easily separable without distortion (Sec. II). The one exception is Mitchell's theory of business cycles. This is clearly his most important theoretical contribution. At the same time, it is so deeply imbedded in a summary of the empirical characteristics of business cycles as to make any attempt at separation subject to serious error. Accordingly, I have adopted the device of displaying this contribution indirectly. Section III presents a business-cycle theory compounded entirely out of elements to be found in his work yet in a synthesis that I cannot confidently say he would have accepted as his own.

The form and the direction of Mitchell's work reflect in some measure his conception of economic theory and of the kind of work currently most important for its further development. They reflect, too, the kind of work in which his own comparative advantage was the greatest as well as his own standards of workmanship. These factors, discussed in Section I as a prelude to an examination of his theoretical formulations, do not of course provide a complete explanation; nothing short of an understanding of the whole man could do so.

I. FACTORS BEARING ON THE FORM AND DIRECTION OF MITCHELL'S WORK

"Economic theory" is often taken to be a label for an existing body of doctrine concerned primarily with the allocation of resources among alternative ends and the division of the product among the co-operating resources, and based on the hypothesis that economic events can be "explained" and "predicted" by supposing men to behave as if they sought single-mindedly and successfully to pursue their own interests and as if their interests were predominantly to maximize the money income they could wring from a hostile environment. Mitchell consistently designated this concept "orthodox economic theory. He recognized its value as part of economic theory and made extensive use of it. Yet he was wholly convinced that orthodox economic theory was too narrow and that preoccupation with its improvement impeded progress in the area of what to him were the (currently) important problems.

To Mitchell, economic theory was more than orthodox economic theory. It was a set of hypotheses explaining economic behavior in all its leading manifestations, and he was himself almost exclusively concerned with a part of economic theory that was largely outside the main stream of economic thought when he began his scientific work and that even today is least developed and least satisfactory—the dynamic adjustment of the economic system as a whole. Because we know so little about this part of economic theory, we tend to neglect it in thinking about economic theory, to use the term to cover what we have, rather than what we ought to have. This circumstance, I think, partly accounts for the widespread illusion that Mitchell was anti-theoretical, or at least not concerned with "economic theory"; for Mitchell's work was consistently and almost exclusively devoted to the development of a theory of economic change.

Mitchell's emphasis on "process," on dynamic change, is already clearly evident in his *History of the Greenbacks*,[5] and more explicitly in a 1904 article on "The Real Issues in the Quantity Theory Controversy,"[6] in which he listed as one of the real issues: "How does the quantity of money exert its effect on prices?" and went on to say, "Adherents of the quantity theory . . . have usually neglected to trace the process by which a change in the supply of money affects prices with the care required by the subject."[7]

Thorstein Veblen, who was at the University of Chicago during Mitchell's period there, doubtless had much to do with stimulating Mitchell's interest in process and dynamic change. One of Veblen's chief criticisms of "orthodox" economics was that it was not an "evolutionary science," that it did not deal with the problem of "cumulative change."

Mitchell's experience in working on the *History of the Greenbacks* and its sequel, *Gold, Prices, and Wages under the Greenback Standard*,[8] must have reinforced Veblen's teachings and given them vitality. For here he found that existing theory, while helpful in organizing material and in suggesting explanations, was unable to explain some of the most striking features of the price revolution during and after the Civil War. He found a rough correspondence between the premium on gold and the average level of prices— a correspondence that he attributed primarily to the influence of trade with foreign countries that were on a gold standard. But what explained the behavior of the premium on gold? Its broad movements might conceivably be explained by changes in the quantity of money—though Mitchell was unable to satisfy himself about even this point because of the absence of reasonably satisfactory data on the quantity of money. But it was clear that detailed movements could not be so explained—they were too rapid and violent and corresponded too closely with the changing fortunes of the Northern armies. The proximate cause was better described by saying that "the quantity of the greenbacks influenced their specie value rather by affecting the credit of the government than by altering the volume of the circulating medium."[9] But this was no final answer: "The problems remain to be discussed," he wrote in the final chapter of *Gold, Prices, and Wages*, "What factors controlled the premium on gold? Were the fluctuations both of the premium and of prices a consequence of some common cause, such as the changes in the quantity of money?"[10]

Mitchell also found systematic and important differences in the behavior of different classes of prices. Wholesale prices tended to change more sluggishly and later than the premium on gold, retail prices than wholesale, cost of living than retail prices, and wages than the cost of living. Mitchell found a proximate explanation of these differences in the organization of the markets, the growing importance of "friction" and "custom" as one moved from the market for gold to the wholesale market, the retail market, the housing market, and the market for labor—factors that orthodox price theory treated as peripheral. The explanation of these phenomena required an understanding of process, of different capacities for adaptation; it could not be wrung from a theory of comparative statics. So the importance of the phenomena left unexplained by the theories he had studied must have impressed him forcibly and made him receptive to Veblen's message. The quantity theory of money and orthodox price theory explain a wide-range of important phenomena, but they are incomplete and need to be extended and revised to explain other phenomena equally important and not less puzzling.

Mitchell might have approached his objective of broadening economic theory by accepting the phenomena themselves as largely known and devoting his efforts to the excogitation of plausible hypotheses that would account for them. And Arthur F. Burns tells us that, in fact, Mitchell started on this route by beginning in 1907 "a theoretical treatise on money—a study in which he at first saw no place for statistics."[11] But in a little over two years he had left it and turned to the kind of work that was to dominate his scientific activities—the large-scale collection, organization, and interpretation of empirical evidence on business cycles, whether from historical research, contemporary judgments, or quantitative records.

This shift and Mitchell's continued emphasis on providing an "analytic description"[12] of economic phenomena reflect in part his judgment about the kind of work that would contribute most to the development of a satisfactory theory of economic change. In concluding a summary of the existing theories of business cycles in his 1913 *Business Cycles*, Mitchell wrote:

> One seeking to understand the recurrent ebb and flow of economic activity characteristic of the present day finds these numerous explanations both suggestive and perplexing. All are plausible, but which is valid? None necessarily excludes all the

others, but which is the most important? Each may account for certain phenomena; does any one account for all the phenomena? Or can these rival explanations be combined in such a fashion as to make a consistent theory which is wholly adequate? ... It is by study of the facts which they purport to interpret that the theories must be tested (p. 19).

If I understand Mitchell rightly, he was saying something like this: Granted that our objective is a theory of economic change that will explain observed phenomena and correctly predict phenomena not yet observed; granted, too, that, when attained, such a theory will abstract essential elements from the complex of economic phenomena and in that sense will be "unrealistic"; it does not follow that the best way to derive such a theory is to proceed directly to its formulation. In the study of any class of phenomena, it is necessary first to examine the phenomena themselves, to describe them, and to find empirical regularities, in order to provide a basis for generalization and abstraction; and at this stage the orderly organization of empirical data is more important than the elaboration and refinement of abstract hypotheses. In his judgment the theory of economic change was at this stage; yet he felt that economists were treating it as if it were not, as if the phenomena were already sufficiently well known to provide a basis for generalization. In consequence, they were excogitating numerous theories "both suggestive and perplexing." He would be better occupied, he felt, in using these theories to suggest the empirical phenomena to be investigated, and then devoting the major part of his attention to describing these phenomena, only afterward formulating a rationalization of them.

On the whole, I think, Mitchell's judgment about the state of the theory of economic change at the time he began his work was thoroughly sound. Indeed, if we are at a somewhat more advanced stage today, it is in no small measure because of his work in adding to the body of tested knowledge about economic change. And, even so, we still seem to know so little about the empirical phenomena to be explained by a theory of economic change that we cannot adequately choose between widely divergent theories. If Mitchell erred at all in his judgment, it was in occasionally applying it too broadly—to economic theory as a whole rather than to the theory of economic change alone. I do not think the same judgment is valid for orthodox relative price theory, as Mitchell recognized on occasion.[13]

Mitchell's emphasis on "analytic description" probably reflected also his own comparative advantage. His great genius was in an unparalleled capacity for bringing together an enormous mass of material, putting it into systematic form, and giving an orderly, lucid, and meaningful account of it. This capacity is demonstrated in every one of Mitchell's major works. Its finest and fullest expression is in the 1913 *Business Cycles*, particularly in Part II, whose 356 pages contain a brilliant presentation of "Statistical Data concerning the Business Cycles of 1890–1911 in the United States, England, France and Germany." Though his subsequent work would alone suffice to give him an unquestioned place in the front ranks of economists, none of it, in my view, rivals in quality or significance the 1913 volume. This volume treats the phenomenon that has come to occupy perhaps the major place in the work and strivings of economists. It describes this phenomenon with a completeness that has rarely if ever been equaled; and it presents hypotheses to explain the phenomenon that still provide the inspiration for much of the current work on business cycles. Its nice balance between breadth of conception and precision of detail is matched in none of Mitchell's other work, perhaps because of the narrowness of scope of his earlier work, the comprehensiveness of his later work.

Mitchell believed that economics could become a cumulative science only if each worker could build on what earlier workers had done, that there was no hope of constructing an adequate theory on a foundation of careless and inaccurate empirical work. So despite the magnitude of the task he undertook—the breathtaking variety of phenomena and evidence he considered relevant to his problem—he sought unceasingly for accuracy and exactness. A single example from the 1913 volume will illustrate the meticulous attention to detail that marks his work. While Mitchell was working on this book, A. Piatt Andrew published *Statistics for the United States,*

1867–1909, for the National Monetary Commission.[14] This volume contains a detailed and excellent presentation of monetary and banking statistics, compiled directly from official sources. Yet Mitchell was not content simply to take them over. He discovered that Andrew had not taken account of revisions in the estimated gold stock made by the Director of the Mint; so he corrected Andrew's figures to incorporate these revisions. He was dissatisfied with Andrew's estimates of the amount of money held by banks. Irving Fisher had independently made similar estimates, but new data had since become available. So he rejected both Andrew's and Fisher's estimates and proceeded to construct independent estimates of his own. But he did not neglect to compare his estimates with the others, to point out the reasons for the differences, and to adduce evidence to support the superiority of his procedures. Similarly, he was unwilling to accept Irving Fisher's earlier estimates of the volume of deposit currency in the United States, again because additional data had become available. So again he made his own estimates, carefully comparing them with Fisher's. The final figures he compiled were better than anything else then available, and at least some of them are probably superior to the figures contained in the most recent compilation of banking and monetary statistics.[15]

Mitchell's high standard of workmanship and meticulous attention to detail help to explain why in every field he touched—whether economic history, business cycles, prices, or statistical technique—his work has tended to become authoritative. His work stands up to exacting scrutiny; it does not fall to pieces as does much shoddy work that passes for scientific. I think it also helps to explain why his theoretical insights are so deeply imbedded in his descriptive work, so frequently qualified by his empirical instincts and knowledge. He could not put to one side phenomena he knew existed, even in order to throw into sharp relief features he considered basic.

Even in his *Lecture Notes on Types of Economic Theory,* recently made readily available in mimeographed form, Mitchell does not concern himself primarily with technical economic theory. Instead, he takes the development of economic theory as itself a process to be described, interpreted, and explained. Even here his emphasis on process, on "analytic description," is evident. In consequence, the *Lecture Notes*, particularly Volume I, which ends with John Stuart Mill, are an absorbing essay in the sociology of knowledge organized about the great economists of the period much more than a critical examination of alternative theoretical formulations.

II. SOME OF MITCHELL'S THEORETICAL FORMULATIONS

a) The influence of "money" on economic practice and thinking.—To Mitchell, "money" was a symbol for a much broader range of problems than is ordinarily treated under that heading. It stood for the whole complex of modern pecuniary institutions, not for technical monetary and banking arrangements alone. His use of the word in this sense, reflected one of the central hypotheses that emerged from his work—that the use of money was the dominant characteristic distinguishing modern systems of economic organization from earlier ones. "The money economy," he wrote, "is in fact one of the most potent institutions in our whole culture. In sober truth it stamps its pattern upon wayward human nature, makes us all react in standard ways to the standard stimuli it offers, and affects our very ideals of what is good, beautiful, and true."[16]

This hypothesis recurs repeatedly in Mitchell's writing. It is a leading theme of his 1910 article on "The Rationality of Activity,"[17] the basis of his interpretation of current developments in economic theory in his 1916 article "The Role of Money in Economic Theory,"[18] and an important part of his interpretation of earlier classical writers in his *Lecture Notes*. It is most completely formulated in one of his last papers, "The Role of Money in Economic History,"[19] a beautiful essay that summarizes the thoughts of a lifetime on "how monetary forms have infiltrated one human relation after another, and their effects upon men's practices and habits of thought."[20]

"The use of money," Mitchell argues, "gives society the technical machinery of exchange, the opportunity to combine personal freedom with orderly co-operation on a grand scale. . . . It is the foundation of that complex system of prices to which the individual must adjust his behavior in getting a living."[21] But while it enlarged man's freedom, it also required him to become

> more calculating, more self-reliant, and more provident. . . . Individuals who possessed superior aptitude for making money came to the fore in all walks of life. . . . The new leaders found many chances to exploit others and took advantage of them; but, broadly speaking, men who are trying to make money are the servants of consumers—that is, of the whole society. . . . In this sense, the money economy gradually put the task of making goods under the direction of men who provided most efficiently what solvent consumers wished to buy, and whose continued leadership depended on maintaining their efficiency.[22]

It thereby accelerated changes in methods of production and distribution of goods and in the character of production, but at the expense of exposing nations "to a novel set of dangers arising from the technical exigencies of monetary systems. . . . I think," Mitchell wrote, "money economy is responsible also for business cycles."[23]

Since money molds man's "objective behavior, it becomes part of his subjective life, giving him a method and an instrument for the difficult task of assessing the relative importance of dissimilar goods in varying quantities, and affecting the interests in terms of which he makes his valuations."[24] In this way, men's minds become obsessed by monetary illusions. An objective counterpart is that "production in a money economy is directed toward wares that promise a profit to the makers, not toward goods that will be most beneficial to the consumers, whatever that should be taken to mean. Money economy fosters inequality in the distribution of income, and where inequality is marked no one contends that what pays best is what the community needs most."[25] A subtler counterpart is that "we are prone to pay far more attention to the relatively few factors that influence our money incomes in a way we can readily trace than to the host of factors that influence our money expenditures,"[26] which, among other effects, makes us receptive to protectionist devices that promise to raise money incomes despite the losses they entail on the side of consumption.

Mitchell argues also that the use of money is a key to understanding both the development of orthodox economic theory and its range of usefulness.

> Because it thus rationalizes economic life itself, the use of money lays the foundation for a rational theory of that life. Money may not be the root of *all* evil, but it is the root of economic science.[27]
>
> It is the habit of mind begotten by the use of money that makes the pleasure-pain calculus plausible as an account of our own functioning. Thus the use of money lays the psychological basis for that philosophy of human behavior which Bentham and Mill, Marshall and Clark, represent. . . . Economic theory written from the private and acquisitive viewpoint becomes a system of pecuniary logic that exaggerates the importance of one institutional factor in behavior to the neglect of others.[28]
>
> Pecuniary logic is such a momentous factor in the economic situation, that a clear working-out of theorems along its lines of logical development is illuminating.[29]
>
> The assumption of economic rationality is not so much mistaken as inadequate. It applies to the work of the captains but not to the work of the rank and file in industry and business; it does not explain the activities of consumption; and it betrays the economist into neglect of his chief problem, [which is how economic rationality itself arose].[30]
>
> A man who realizes that he is studying an institution keeps his work in historical perspective, even when he confines himself to analyzing the form that the institution has assumed at a particular stage of its evolution. By so doing he opens vistas

enticing to future exploration . . . [and is] eager to profit by any light shed upon his problem by any branch of learning.[31]

One need not agree with every detail of this sketch to recognize its value. Mitchell here offers a simple yet subtle and fruitful hypothesis to integrate a wide range of seemingly unrelated phenomena. In his celebrated article, "The Backward Art of Spending Money," published in 1912, Mitchell illustrated his general hypothesis by elaborating its bearing on consumption. The backwardness of the art of spending money, he argued, reflects both failure and the success of the money economy in extending its sway over the household. Our retention of the family as the basic unit for spending money sets narrow limits to the standardization of function, the division of labor, and the extensive use of labor-saving machinery in consumption—the means whereby the money economy revolutionized production. In consequence, "housewives still face essentially the same problems of ways and means as did their colonial grandmothers."[32] But while the money economy failed to alter means fundamentally, it succeeded in shaping the ends of consumption in a way that is

> subversive of economical management. . . . The money economy forms in us the habit of extravagant expenditure for the unacknowledged purpose of impressing both ourselves and our neighbors with an adequate sense of our standing. . . . The housewife . . . must buy not only gratifications for the appetites and the aesthetic senses, but also social consideration and the pleasant consciousness of possessing it. The cost of the latter is an air of disregarding cost.[33]

Mitchell completes his explanation of the backwardness of the art of spending money by adding three other factors to these divergent effects of the development of the money economy: (1) the backwardness of "physiology and functional psychology," "the sciences of fundamental importance" for the art of spending money, by comparison with physics and chemistry, the most important sciences for industry;[34] (2) the absence of a common denominator like the dollar to value costs and gains; and (3) the indefiniteness of ultimate ends.

A more important application of Mitchell's broad hypothesis on the role of money, and something of a test of its validity, is contained in his discussion of the origin of business cycles. The three pages devoted to this subject in the 1913 *Business Cycles* are obviously a concentrated summary of a good deal of thought and study. His empirical generalization is that "business cycles are much later in appearing than economic, or even strictly financial crises. In England itself they seem not to have begun before the close of the eighteenth century…. In proportion as the Industrial Revolution and its concomitant changes in the organization of commerce and transportation spread to other countries, the latter began to develop the phenomena of business cycles already familiar in England." His hypothesis to explain this generalization is that "business cycles…make their appearance at that stage of economic history when the process of making and distributing goods is organized chiefly in the form of business enterprises conducted for profit."[35]

This subject receives somewhat fuller treatment in the 1927 volume. The empirical generalization is repeated, tested with more adequate data, and retained essentially unchanged. The hypothesis to explain generalization is stated more fully and linked more closely to the broader hypothesis of which it is a part.

> Communities slowly become subject to recurrent alternations of prosperity and depression as a large proportion of the people begin to rely upon making and spending money in a large proportion of their activities…. To suggest the differentiating features of that highly developed form of money economy within which business cycles occur…perhaps the combination "profits economy" or "business economy" is most suggestive and least

misleading.... What seems to count in producing business cycles is the common practice of money-making and money-spending by the population as a whole, not merely by a limited class of businessmen.[36]

NOTES

1. I am deeply indebted to Dorothy S. Brady, Arthur F. Burns, Earl J. Hamilton, Lloyd A. Metzler, and George J. Stigler for helpful comments, suggestions, and criticisms. I owe a very different kind of debt to Wesley C. Mitchell for his part, as teacher, colleague, and friend, in my intellectual development in general, and in my understanding of his own scientific creed in particular.

2. Alfred Marshall, "The Present Position of Economics" (1885), in *Memorials of Alfred Marshall*, ed. A. C. Pigou (Macmillan & Co., 1925), p. 168.

3. Quoted phrase from the Preface to *Business Cycles* (1913), p. vii.

4. *Business Cycles: The Problem and Its Setting* (1927).

5. University of Chicago Press, 1903.

6. *Journal of Political Economy*, June 1904, pp. 403–8.

7. *Ibid.*, p. 407.

8. The University Press, Berkeley, 1908.

9. *History of the Greenbacks*, p. 208.

10. *Ibid.*, p. 272.

11. [Arthur S. Burns, ed., *Wesley Clair Mitchell: The Economic Scientist* (New York: National Bureau of Economic Research, 1952), p. 20.]

12. Preface to *Business Cycles*, p. vii.

13. "The Rationality of Economic Activity," *Journal of Political Economy*, March 1910, p. 215; "The Prospects of Economics," reprinted in Wesley C. Mitchell, *The Backward Art of Spending Money and Other Essays*, p. 371; *Lecture Notes on Types of Economic Theory* (Augustus M. Kelley, 1949), Vol. I, pp. 11–15 (mimeographed).

14. Senate Doc. No. 570 (61st Cong., 2d sess.).

15. In particular, the figures on currency in circulation in *Banking and Monetary Statistics* (Board of Governors of the Federal Reserve System, 1943), p. 408, are identical with Andrew's, except for the addition of minor coin, and do not include the correction in the estimated gold stock made by the Director of the Mint.

16. "The Prospects of Economics," in *The Backward Art*, p. 371.

17. *Journal of Political Economy*, February and March 1910, pp. 97–113, 197–216.

18. Reprinted in *The Backward Art*, pp. 149–76.

19. *Journal of Economic History*, Supplement IV, December 1944, pp. 61–67.

20. *Ibid.*, p. 61.

21. *The Backward Art*, pp. 170–71.

22. "The Role of Money in Economic History," *op. cit.*, p. 62.

23. *Ibid.*, pp. 63–64.

24. *The Backward Art*, p. 171.

25. "The Role of Money in Economic History," *op. cit.*, pp. 63–64.

26. *Ibid.*, p. 64.

27. *The Backward Art*, p. 171.

28. *Ibid.*, p. 306.

29. "The Rationality of Economic Activity," *op. cit.*, p. 215.

30. *Ibid.*, p. 201.

31. *The Backward Art*, p. 256.

32. *Ibid.*, 5.

33. *Ibid.*, pp. 15–16.

34. *Ibid.*, p. 11.

35. *Business Cycles*, pp. 584–85.

36. *Business Cycles: The Problem and Its Setting*, pp. 62–63. See also Arthur F. Burns and Wesley C. Mitchell, *Measuring Business Cycles*, pp. 3, 5, and 113.

LEON WALRAS AND HIS ECONOMIC SYSTEM

1955

"Thus the system of the economic universe reveals itself, at last, in all its grandeur and complexity: a system at once vast and simple, which, for sheer beauty, resembles the astronomic universe."
—*Leon Walras.*[1]

The appearance of William Jaffé's loving translation of Leon Walras' *Elements of Pure Economics* offers an excuse for re-examining that great work some eighty odd years after its original publication. Though in so far as this is a review, it is a review of Walras and not of Jaffé, I cannot refrain from prefacing it with a word of thanks to Jaffé for his translation, which is a model of its kind: careful; accurate, and marked throughout by an unobtrusive attention to detail. His notes on the collation of editions are an important aid to research; his translator's notes illuminate many points of the text as well as directing the reader's attention to much recent writing that is relevant to its interpretation.

Though I regard as somewhat extravagant Schumpeter's judgment that, "so far as pure theory is concerned, Walras is . . . the greatest of all economists,"[2] there can be no doubt that the *Elements* is a great work which marked an important step forward in the development of economics as a science, and which still plays an important role in economic thinking. It is well worth having a translation even at this late date in order to make it more readily accessible both to the profession at large and particularly to students learning to become economists: it belongs on their "five foot shelf." The comments that follow deal with the book in this context, as a piece of living literature, rather than with its role in the history of economic thought.

On the broadest level of generality, there are two main themes in the *Elements*: the analysis of *rareté*, or marginal utility; and the theory of general equilibrium. Walras regarded the two as fitting together in one harmonious whole, which is certainly tenable; he also viewed the marginal utility analysis as indispensable for the study of general equilibrium, which seems much more dubious. The marginal utility analysis impresses the modern reader as "dated," as important primarily in understanding the development of economic ideas rather than in directly extending his horizons as a scientist. For this reason I shall discuss the marginal utility analysis first, in order to clear the ground for the theory of general equilibrium.

I. RARETÉ

Walras essentially completes his analysis of the "'Theory of Exchange of Two Commodities for Each Other," the title of Part 2 of the *Elements*, before he introduces utility analysis at all. Prior to that point, he has derived demand curves and offer curves, discussed their typical shapes, and considered the meaning of their points of intersection, distinguishing stable from unstable equilibria. These topics are described as revealing the "nature of exchange"; and utility curves are then introduced in order to examine "the cause" of exchange. Similarly, at each successive stage in the analysis— the extension of the theory of exchange of two commodities to several commodities, and the expansion of the system to include successively production, capital formation and credit,[3] and circulation and money—utility considerations strike the reader as something introduced rather artificially, as being on a different level from the rest of the analysis and capable of being extracted from it bodily without in any way altering its essence—a step that Cassel took in his reformulation of the Walrasian system.

Yet this is clearly not the way it seemed to Walras or to his contemporaries, Jevons and Menger. Today, Walras' primary contribution would surely be regarded as general equilibrium theory, of which at best only pale reflections can be found in Jevons or Menger; yet the three linked themselves together and were linked together by others as the pioneers of "marginal utility." Walras writes as an italicized theorem, "The exchange of two commodities for each other in a perfectly competitive market is an operation by which all holders of either one, or of both, of the two commodities can obtain the greatest possible satisfaction of their wants consistent with the condition that the two commodities are bought and sold at one and the same rate of exchange throughout the market," and goes on to say, "The main object of the theory of social wealth is to generalize this proposition.... We may say ... that this proposition embraces the whole of pure and applied economics" (p. 143).

It is hard now for us to understand why this marginal utility analysis should have been regarded as so vital and revolutionary. We can repeat the formulae of the histories of economic thought that it gave a meaningful solution to the diamond-water paradox and so permitted demand to be assigned its proper role and the shackles of the cost of production or, even worse, labor theory of value to be overthrown. But I do not believe that such formulae carry real conviction or understanding. Partly, this is for the usual reason that an error, once pointed out, seems obvious to those who never held it, though it may have taken a real stroke of genius to discover the error and though simply pointing it out did not make it obvious to those who had the error imbedded in the fabric of their thought. But I suspect the main reason is quite different, namely, the change in our general philosophical and methodological outlook that has been wrought, though by no means directly, by the developments in physical science, in particular, by the replacement of the physics of Newton by the physics of Einstein. Surely this is why a chapter title like that of Lesson 10, "*Rareté*, the Cause of Value in Exchange," strikes us as an anachronism.

The almost purely metaphysical role of *rareté* in Walras is brought out very well by his discussion of measurement

> The above analysis is incomplete; and it seems impossible, at first glance, to pursue it further, because intensive utility, considered absolutely, is so elusive, since it has no direct or measurable relation to space or time, as do extensive utility [the quantity that will be taken at a price zero] and the quantity of a commodity possessed. Still, this difficulty is not insurmountable. We need only assume that such a direct and measurable relationship does exist, and we shall find ourselves in a position to give an exact, mathematical account of the respective influences on prices of extensive utility, intensive utility and the initial stock possessed. I shall, therefore, assume the existence of a standard measure of intensity of wants or intensive utility . . . (p. 117).

In a modern writer, one would expect this to be followed by a statement that such an assumption, combined presumably with others, has observable implications of a kind that will enable utility, though "it has no direct or measurable relation to space or time," to be assigned numerical values that are inferred from what are regarded as its manifestations. Walras, of course, does not take this line. He says nothing more on the subject and simply proceeds to take for granted that there is something called *rareté* which has numerical values that can be plotted, averaged, and so on, and can be identified with "satisfaction" in a sense that is relevant for welfare purposes.

In a way, Walras' ready acceptance of the nonmeasurability by physical operations of his *rareté* is somewhat ironical. For, like the other pioneers of marginal utility, he made a subsidiary assumption about utility functions that, if accepted, gives a relatively straightforward method of assigning numbers to utility. Walras throughout assumes that the total utility of a collection of commodities can be written as the sum of functions, each containing as a variable the quantity of only one commodity. Indeed, one gets the impression that it may well have been this feature of his utility function that was to him the main justification for regarding *rareté* as *the* cause of value in exchange; for *rareté* was "absolute," depending only on the quantity of the one commodity itself, whereas value in exchange was "relative," the ratio of two such absolutes; and along the same lines, the utility curve for a particular commodity was more fundamental, because a function of only one variable, than the demand function which had to be regarded as depending on several. However, if a consumer's preferences can be validly represented by a sum of one-variable functions, a convenient measuring rod for utility is at hand; one need only take the utility added by some specified unit of one commodity, say the utility added by the tenth slice of bread, as the basic unit, and the utility of all other commodities can be expressed in terms of it—essentially the procedure that both Fisher and Frisch experimented with at a later date.

The reason why this method of measuring utility has not been adopted is, of course, because a utility function consisting of a sum of one-variable functions has implications for consumer behavior that are contradicted by observation, the most striking, perhaps being the implication that the higher the income of a consumer, the more he will consume of every commodity separately, *i.e.*, that there are no inferior goods. Needless to say, Walras does not explore such implications, though he does record the corresponding implication that a demand curve for one commodity is always negatively sloped for given amounts possessed of other commodities (which is equivalent to given money income and other prices). However, he asserts this (on p. 91) prior to introducing his marginal utility analysis, giving little justification for it, apparently because he regarded it as obvious.

One must conclude, I think, that this part of Walras' book has interest almost solely for the student of economic thought. In so far as utility theory plays a role in modern economic analysis, it does so in a more sophisticated, albeit empirically emptier, form than in Walras, though it should perhaps be recorded that there is much current literature that has not advanced beyond Walras in its understanding of the meaning and role of the measurability of utility.

II. THE THEORY OF GENERAL EQUILIBRIUM

Cournot writes in Chapter 11 of his *Researches*,

> So far we have studied how, for each commodity by itself, the law of demand in connection with the conditions of production of that commodity, determines the price of it and regulates the incomes of its producers. We considered as given and invariable the prices of other commodities and the incomes of other producers; but in reality the economic system is a whole of which all the parts are connected and react on each other. An increase in the income of the producers of commodity A will affect the demand for commodities B, C, etc., and the incomes of their producers, and, by its reaction, will involve a change in the demand for commodity A. It seems, therefore, as if, for a complete and rigorous solution of the problems relative to some parts of the economic system, it were indispensable to take the entire system into consideration. But this would surpass the powers of mathematical analysis and of our practical methods of calculation, even if the values of all the constants could be assigned to them numerically.[4]

It is Walras' great and living achievement to have constructed a mathematical system displaying in considerable detail precisely the interrelationships emphasized by Cournot. Did he thereby show Cournot to be wrong in supposing that the task surpassed the powers of mathematical analysis? I believe not. For there is a fundamental, if subtle, difference between the task Cournot outlined and the task Walras accomplished; an understanding of this difference is essential to an assessment of both the positive contribution of Walras and the limitations to that contribution; and failure to recognize the difference seems to me a primary source of methodological confusion in economics. It is clear from Cournot's references to "practical methods of calculation" and to the assignment of numerical values to constants that the "rigorous solution" he had in mind was not a solution "in principle," but a numerical solution to a specific problem. His goal was an analysis that would, given the relevant statistical material, yield specific answers to specific empirical questions, such as the effects of a specified tax on a specified product; answers that could be confronted by observation and confirmed or contradicted. And surely there can be little doubt that a "complete and rigorous solution" of this kind does "surpass the powers of mathematical analysis and of our practical methods of calculation" even today despite the enormous advances in methods of calculation. Cournot was quite right that *for his problem* a "complete and rigorous" solution was out of the question, that the thing to do was, "while maintaining a certain kind of approximation ... to carry on ... a useful analysis."[5]

Walras solved a different, though no less important, problem. He emptied Cournot's problem of its empirical content and produced a "complete and rigorous" solution "in principle," making no pretense that it could be used directly in numerical calculations. His problem is the problem of form, not of content: of displaying an idealized picture of the economic system, not of constructing an engine for analyzing concrete problems.[6] His achievement cannot but impress the reader with its beauty, its grandeur, its architectonic structure; it would verge on the ludicrous to describe it as a demonstration how to calculate the numerical solution to a numerically specified set of equations. The difference is brought out clearly by the further developments along Walras' line that have been—and rightly—regarded as improvements in his system. These have all consisted in making the system still more general and elegant, in eliminating empirically specializing assumptions. The clearest example is, of course, in the theory of production: Walras assumed constant coefficients of production recognizing that this was an "approximation" and in later editions suggesting the route to generalize the analysis. Pareto generalized Walras' solution to cover variable as well as constant coefficients of production. The recent reintroduction of the assumption of constant coefficients of production in connection with input-output analysis has not been a further development of Walras' pure theory. It has rather been an attempt—so far largely unsuccessful—to use Walrasian constructs in solving Cournot's problem.

Emphasis on pure form has an important role to play in economics in two rather different respects. One, the easier to specify, is the role of mathematics or pure logic in general, namely, to help us to avoid contradictory statements—to avoid mistakes in arithmetic, as it were. This role is immediately recognized and granted, and for that reason tends to be passed over rapidly; yet it deserves to be emphasized how many, how important, and sometimes how difficult to detect, are the fallacies in economics of this kind; fallacies that consist in the assertion that contradictory statements are simultaneously valid, that we can have our cake and eat it too. The ability to think clearly and exactly is a scarce resource for which, unfortunately, there seems no adequate substitute. Walras' discussion of bimetallism (Lessons 31 and 32) and of Ricardo's and Mill's theories of rent and wages (Lessons 39 and 40) are excellent examples, largely peripheral to his own general equilibrium theory, of how useful emphasis on pure form can be. By translating vague statements into symbolic form and using very elementary mathematics indeed, Walras is able to clear away much irrelevant material, show that some widely accepted statements are mutually contradictory, and specify the conditions under which others are valid.

The other respect in which emphasis on pure form has an important role to play is in providing a language, a classificatory scheme to use in organizing materials—labels, as it were, for the compartments of our analytical filing box. This is Walras' great contribution. His general equilibrium system gives a bird's-eye view of the economic system as a whole, which has not only an extraordinary aesthetic appeal as a beautifully articulated abstraction but also a utilitarian appeal as providing relevant, meaningful, and mutually exhaustive categories. This bird's-eye view rests fundamentally on two dichotomies: between services and sources of services or between income and capital; and between the markets for consumer services or goods and for productive services or goods. A third dichotomy might almost be added: between entrepreneurs and consumer units, though this seems somewhat less fundamental. Each consumer unit and entrepreneur is conceived as operating in both markets: in terms of markets for services, a consumer unit sells productive services of the capital sources he owns in the resource market and buys consumer services in the consumption market; an entrepreneur buys productive services in the resource market and sells consumer services in the consumption market either directly or indirectly. The distinction between markets thus leads naturally and directly to the distinction between demand and supply.

This classificatory scheme is developed in considerable detail, with extraordinary skill and ingenuity, great attention being devoted to showing, or attempting to show, that it is internally consistent and exhaustive (*i.e.*, that the system of equations has a solution that tends to be attained and maintained by the operation of market forces). I have described this analysis as involving emphasis on pure form, which I think in a meaningful way it does. Yet I do not mean thereby to imply either that it lacks importance for economics as a substantive science, or that empirical considerations play no role in its construction and use. Quite to the contrary. Walras' picture is not pure mathematics but economics precisely because it was constructed to provide a framework for organizing substantive material of an economic character; the classifications it employs reflect a judgment about the empirically important characteristics of the economic structure, the usefulness of the picture, though not its logical coherence, depends on the extent to which this judgment is confirmed by experience. One cannot read Walras, it seems to me, without recognizing that he was an economist first and a mathematician and logician second; he accomplished what he did not because he was a mathematical genius but despite inferior mathematical equipment—reading the *Elements* gives no reason to doubt the fairness of the examiners who failed him twice in the mathematics examination for entry to the École Polytechnique.[7] In some ways, indeed, "despite" might perhaps be replaced by "because." Walras' necessity to work things out rather cumbrously, from the simplest cases to the more complicated, must have forced him to give much more attention to the economic significance and meaning of his categories than he would have if he had been able to proceed on a still higher level of abstraction. I hasten to add that I do not mean to be urging that bad mathematics is better than good but only that each task requires its own tools. A hand spade may well be better than a modern steam shovel for some kinds of work; pure mathematicians are notoriously bad at simple arithmetic.

Though emphasis on form can and does play a vital role in economic analysis, it can also be mischievous if it is not illuminated by empirical judgment and understanding. An excellent example is Walras' utility analysis of savings. This analysis was first introduced into the fourth edition, which appeared in 1900, about a quarter of a century after the first edition. In this edition, Walras yielded to the temptation, which has claimed so many lesser men, of treating "savings" like a consumer good and simply carrying over mechanically the formal analysis applicable to consumer goods. So he defines a commodity (E) consisting of a perpetual net income stream, a unit of (E) being one unit of *numeraire* per unit of time indefinitely, writes down for each individual a marginal utility function for (E), and regards him as possessing a certain quantity of (E) and maximizing his utility subject to a budget constraint which includes expenditures on (E) along with expenditures on other commodities. He regards this process as yielding a demand function for (E) like other demand functions (pp. 274 and 275).

In symbols, this looks like a simple extension of Walras' general analysis and one is led to ask why it was that he did not discover this obvious yet important extension for a quarter of a century. But the moment one digs beneath the symbols and asks why, as economists, we regard it as important to distinguish savings from current consumption, it becomes clear that Walras' procedure is fallacious and involves precisely the kind of confusion between stocks and flows that Walras elsewhere so carefully avoids and indeed underlines. I can perhaps illustrate this best by Walras' utility function for (E) which, in deriving the demand curve, he writes as

$$\Phi_e(q_e + d_e),$$

where q_e is the initial quantity of (E) possessed, d_e, the quantity purchased or sold during the time unit in question. Now q_e and d_e are of different dimensions and cannot be added: q_e is the number of units of (E) that the individual possesses, *i.e.*, the number of units of *numeraire* per unit of time that the individual can receive indefinitely if he so chooses—for simplicity, let us say the number of dollars per year that is yielded by his existing stock of wealth; d_e is the number of dollars per year that he is going to add to this flow as income on the savings he accumulates during the time period in question (see p. 117), say a year, so that savings during that period are $p_e d_e$, where p_e is the price of a dollar a year indefinitely. In other words, q_e is of the dimension of dollars per year; d_e, of the dimension of dollars per year. Let the time period in question be half a year instead of a year; the same numerical value of d_e means that he saves twice as large a fraction of his income. q_e and d_e simply cannot be added: an individual will not be indifferent, as Walras' equation implies that he is, between a situation in which he starts with an income of $10,000 a year and adds $100 a year income to it by saving $2,000 during the year in question, which means that the rate of interest is 5 percent, and a situation in which he starts with an income of $9,700 a year and adds $400 a year to it by saving $8,000 during the year in question. Savings cannot be assimilated directly to current consumption, precisely because their whole function is to provide a stream of consumer services.

In the earlier editions of the *Elements*, Walras made no attempt to derive the demand for savings from utility analysis. He simply wrote down as an empirical datum an individual savings function, and noted, quite correctly, that in order to derive it from utility considerations it would be necessary "to consider utility under a new aspect, distinguishing present utility from future utility."[8] This was no oversight and the change in the fourth edition no belated discovery of a neglected truth. Surely, the explanation must be that when Walras made the change in the fourth edition, he no longer had his system and its meaning and its role in his bones the way he did when he developed it; he was taken in by considerations of pure form; the substance which the form was to represent was no longer part of him. It would be hard to find a better example of the nonsense to which even a great economist can be led by the divorce of form from substance.

III. CONCLUSION

Walras has done more than perhaps any other economist to give us a framework for organizing our ideas, a way of looking at the economic system and describing it that facilitates the avoidance of mistakes in logic. It is no derogation of this contribution to emphasize that it is not by itself enough for a fruitful and meaningful economic theory; division of labor is appropriate in economic theory too. Economics not only requires a framework for organizing our ideas, it requires also ideas to be organized. We need the right kind of language; we also need something to say. Substantive hypotheses about economic phenomena of the kind that were the goal of Cournot are an essential ingredient of a fruitful and meaningful economic theory. Walras has little to contribute in this direction; for this we must turn to other economists, notably, of course, to Alfred Marshall.

The large and substantial immediate rewards from Walras' concentration on form; the prestige and intellectual appeal of mathematics; the difficulty of making experiments in economics and the consequent laboriousness and seeming unproductiveness of substantive work devoted to filling in our analytical filing boxes—all these have combined to favor the Walrasian emphasis on form, to make it seem not only an essential part of a full-blown economic theory, but that economic theory itself. This conception—or misconception—of economic theory has helped to produce an economics that is far better equipped in respect of form than of substance. In consequence, the major work that needs now to be done is Marshallian rather than Walrasian in character—itself a tribute to Walras' impact.

I am tempted, in concluding this rather discursive commentary, to paraphrase Mill's comment that "A person is not likely to be a good economist who is nothing else."[9] A person is not likely to be a good economist who does not have a firm command of Walrasian economics; equally, he is not likely to be a good economist if he knows nothing else.

NOTES

1.   *Elements of Pure Economics*, translated by William Jaffé, published for The American Economic Association and the Royal Economic Society. (Homewood, Ill.: Richard Irwin, 1954, p. 374.) All subsequent page references not otherwise identified are to this volume.

2.   J. Schumpeter, *History of Economic Analysis* (New York, 1954), p. 827.

3.   As Jaffé remarks the analysis of utility considerations in connection with the theory of capital formation and credit is in parts "obscure to the point of almost complete incomprehensibility." Jaffé gives an extensive reconstruction in an attempt to render the argument intelligible in his translator's note [2] to Lesson 27 (pp. 536–39). I find it difficult to accept this reconstruction in one important respect, namely, Jaffé's interpretation of the argument as applying to a stationary state and his resulting assignment of an essential role to expenditures on the replacement of capital goods. I am inclined to go to the opposite extreme. It seems to me that Walras here, as elsewhere, thought initially in terms of capital

goods that were permanent, required no maintenance or replacement, and gave rise to a permanent flow of services. The question he seems to me to be asking in the section at issue is: given a certain amount of productive power to be used in producing an additional set of permanent capital goods of this kind, what bundle of capital goods will produce the additional stream of consumer goods having the greatest utility. His proof is correct, provided one consistently treats the capital goods as permanent and interprets his differential coefficient or ratios between them as rates of substitution—which seems to me also required in Lesson 26 and to explain what puzzles Jaffé in his translator's note [1] to that lesson (p. 533). The equations labeled [e] at the bottom of p. 297 are not simultaneously valid; they are alternatives, showing that if (A) is substituted for (T), and all other quantities are unchanged, the quantity of (A) acquired must equal in value the quantity of (T) given up; and so on for every possible pair. That this is intended seems to me even clearer from the wording of earlier editions.

The tendency for Walras to work his argument out initially in terms of permanent capital goods requiring no replacement seems to me to explain also how the difficulty arose which Jaffé deals with in his translator's note [31] to Lesson 27 (pp. 530–41). Having arrived at a result for this case, Walras generalized it without full proof to the case of nonpermanent capital goods, in the process making what Jaffé terms—correctly, I believe—a "slip."

4.   Augustin Cournot, *Researches into the Mathematical Principles of the Theory of Wealth* (1838), transl. by Nathaniel T. Bacon (New York, 1897), p. 127.

5.   *Ibid.*, pp. 127–28.

6.   Walras comments that "when we pass from the realm of pure theory to that of applied theory or to actual practice,... the variations in the unknown quantities will be effects of either the first or the second order, that is to say, effects which need or need not be taken into consideration, according as they arise from variations in the special or the general data" (pp. 307–8; see also similar comment on p. 431). In a translator's note, Jaffé cites this sentence as evidence that I "drew too sharp a contrast between Marshall and Walras" in my article "The Marshallian Demand Curve," *Jour. Pol. Econ.* Dec., 1949, LVII, 463–95; reprinted in my *Essays in Positive Economics* (Chicago, 1953), pp. 47–99. He goes on to say, "There one gets the impression that Walras's sole preoccupation was the achievement of 'abstractness, generality and mathematical elegance' (p. 490), while Marshall sought 'an engine for the discovery of concrete truth.' A more valid and important distinction between Walras and Marshall resides in the fact that the former always took great care not to confuse pure theory with applied theory, while the latter gloried in fusing the two" (p. 542).

In his final sentence, Jaffé speaks like a true Walrasian in methodology. One first constructs a pure theory, somehow on purely formal considerations without introducing any empirical content; one then turns to the "real" world, fills in the empty boxes, assigns numerical values to constants, and neglects "second-order" effects at this stage. As I have argued extensively elsewhere [particularly in "The Methodology of Positive Economics" and "Lange on Price Flexibility and Employment: A Methodological Criticism," both in my *Essays*, pp. 3–43, 277–300, the latter reprinted from this *Review*, Sept., 1946, XXXVI, pp. 613–31], this seems to me a basically false view. Without denying the importance of what Jaffé and Walras call "pure theory" (see my comments below), I deny that it is the whole of "pure theory." More important in the present context, two largely parenthetical comments in the *Elements* to the effect that second-order effects will have to be or can be neglected in application seem a rather thin basis on which to claim that Walras was concerned with the construction of "an engine for the discovery of concrete truth." As I argue in the text, I retain of my original opinion; indeed, I am confirmed therein by the careful rereading of Walras to which I was led by the request to write this article, by Jaffé's critical comment, and by similar comments in reviews of my *Essays*.

7. I am indebted for this tidbit to Richard S. Howey, *The Rise of the Marginal Utility School, 1870-1889*, unpublished Ph.D. dissertation at the University of Chicago, 1955.

8. Jaffé's Collation of Editions, note [*h*] to Lesson 23, p. 587; my translation from Jaffé's quotation in French.

9. From *On Comte*, p. 82, as quoted by Alfred Marshall, *Principles of Economics*, 8th ed., (London, 1920), pp. 771.

THE MONETARY THEORY AND POLICY OF HENRY SIMONS

1967

I t is a great honor for me to give the Henry Simons Lecture. He was my teacher and my friend—and above all, a shaper of my ideas. No man can say precisely whence his beliefs and his values come—but there is no doubt that mine would be very different than they are if I had not had the good fortune to be exposed to Henry Simons. If, in this lecture, I express much disagreement with him, that, too, bespeaks his influence. He taught us that an objective, critical examination of a man's ideas is a truer tribute than slavish repetition of his formulas.

I am especially pleased to be giving this lecture under the auspices of the Law School. One of the unique advantages of the University of Chicago for economists has always been the close cooperation and interchange between economists and lawyers. Henry Simons was for many years on the Law School faculty, and Aaron Director and Ronald Coase have continued that fine tradition. *The Journal of Law and Economics* has set the seal on a happy affair.

On re-reading Henry Simons' work in preparation for this lecture, I was struck by the contrast between my reaction to his discussion of monetary theory, on the one hand, and to his proposals for monetary reform, on the other. The monetary theory impressed me as sophisticated and correct; the proposals for reform as largely irrelevant and wrong. This contrast and how it can be explained are the themes of this lecture.

Though Simons nowhere set forth a consistent and comprehensive statement of his monetary theory, his views are implicit in his discussion of policy proposals, and explicit in many parenthetical remarks in his often lengthy and always penetrating footnotes.[1] I find myself, not only in full agreement with the views so revealed, but more important, enlightened by them and impressed by their sophistication.

Simons wrote on money mostly during the dozen years from 1933 to 1945. That was a period when, thanks to the Keynesian Revolution, the economics profession came to regard money—in the sense of currency, deposits, banking, and allied issues—as an unimportant and uninteresting subject. The fraction of the profession's attention devoted to this area probably reached an all time low from the late 'thirties to the early 'fifties. Since then there has been a tremendous revival of interest in this area, so that monetary theory is at the moment a dramatic growth industry. Recent developments have deepened and widened our understanding but they have cast no doubt on Simons' basic analysis of how money enters into the economic system or of the influence it exerts. Quite the contrary. These developments have produced a return to Simons' view that the quantity of money and its behavior play a central role in affecting the course of prices and of economic activity; that monetary stability is an essential prerequisite for economic stability.

Simons' policy proposals are a very different matter. They consist of two separable elements: (1) proposals for reforming the banking and financial structure—as he put it "transition to a less preposterous structure of private money contracts" (at 170), (2) proposals for "establishment of a simple, mechanical rule of monetary policy" (at 170). In his role as a monetary theorist, he clearly found the second much more intriguing and interesting. Yet he regarded it as the less important. The urgent and immediate task, the essential precondition for the satisfactory operation of any monetary rule, was, he believed, financial reform.

In Simons' view, the "financial good society" (at 239) required "financial reform . . . aiming at sharp differentiation between money and private obligations" (at 79). He viewed his well-known proposal for 100 percent reserve banking "only as the proper first step toward reconstruction of our whole financial organization. Standing by itself, as an isolated measure, it would promise little but evasion . . . and would deserve classification as merely another crank scheme" (at 331 n.17).[2] In addition to 100 percent reserve banking, "Narrow limitation of the formal borrowing powers of other corporations would obviously be necessary. . . . Further limitations might also be necessary with respect to financing via the open account (book credit) and installment sales" (at 171). For government, the debt structure should be drastically simplified, with all government obligations taking the form either of non-interest bearing money or very long-term securities, ideally perpetuities (consols).

On monetary policy, Simons vacillated between favoring a rule expressed in terms of the quantity of money—for example, that the quantity of money be kept constant—and a rule expressed in terms of a price index—for example, that the authorities be instructed to keep the wholesale price index stable. His final position was, roughly, that the price-index rule was the only feasible rule pending a closer approximation to the "financial good society," but that the quantity of money rule was much preferable, when and if the "financial good society" was attained.

I would myself be inclined precisely to reverse Simons' priorities—and so, I believe would most other modern students of money, even those of us who share most completely Simons' basic objectives of social policy. Financial reform along his lines seems not only unnecessary but in the wrong direction.[3] Why should we not have variety and diversity in the market for borrowing and lending as in other markets? Is it not desirable that borrowers tailor their obligations to the demands of lenders? Is it not a sign of the ingenuity and efficiency of the free market that financial intermediaries develop which reconcile the needs of borrowers and lenders—providing funds on terms desired by borrowers and borrowing on terms desired by lenders? This simultaneously lowers the cost of capital to borrowers and raises the effective return on capital to lenders—thereby fostering a higher level of capital formation than would otherwise occur.

I agree with Simons on the desirability of 100 percent reserve banking—but I regard it as less important and basic than he did and favor it in some ways for almost the opposite reasons. He viewed it as a step toward simplifying the structure of financial claims, as a step toward making effective the legislative limitations he favored on the terms on which people could borrow and lend. I view it as a step toward reducing government interference with lending and borrowing in order to permit a greater degree of freedom and variety in the arrangements for borrowing and lending.

Even on monetary policy, where the passage of time has only strengthened my belief in the lesson he taught me—that rules are greatly to be preferred to authorities, I am inclined to reverse his emphasis. A rule in terms of the quantity of money seems to me far superior, for both the short and the long-run, than a rule in terms of price-level stabilization.

What explains this contrast? How is it that I can admire so greatly Simons' grasp of monetary theory and disagree so completely with his proposals for reform?

We have all of us in our personal lives had the experience of coming on a fact that suddenly illuminated an issue in a flash, showing us how wrong we had been and leading us to a fresh and very different opinion. It is something of an oversimplification, but only a slight one, I believe, to say that that is the explanation of the contrast I have been stressing. A few facts, which we now know and he did not, have made all the difference.

The facts have to do primarily with the Great Depression of 1929–1933. Were I to interpret that episode as Simons did, I would agree with his recommendations. Had he interpreted that episode as I do, he would not have made the policy recommendations he did. And our differences of interpretation is not simply a difference of personality or taste. It reflects—or so I would like to believe—the accumulation of evidence through scientific study.

Needless to say, Simons' interpretation was not unique to him. On the contrary, it was widely shared by his contemporaries. In particular, I have been struck that the statements I have been making about Simons apply almost verbatim to John Maynard Keynes. He, too, was led to make policy recommendations that seem wrong now—and in his case that differed drastically from his own earlier views—because he accepted the same interpretation of 1929–1933 as did Henry Simons. In his case, too, I find his monetary theory sophisticated and modern, yet his policy recommendations unacceptable. As we shall see later, though some of his policy recommendations parallel Simons', in other respects they differ drastically. But they differ not because of a difference in monetary theory or a different interpretation of 1929–1933 but because of a different basic attitude toward social policy—Keynes was a reformer, Simons, a radical.

In exploring this thesis further, I shall outline Simons' interpretation of the 1930's and similar episodes, show how his policy recommendations follow from that interpretation, and contrast his policy recommendations with Keynes'. I shall then indicate what our current interpretation of this episode is and suggest what policy views derive from that interpretation.

1. *Simons' Interpretation of Business Cycles in General and the Great Depression in Particular.* "The problem of synchronous industrial . . . fluctuations," wrote Simons, "is a problem (a) of rigidities in crucial areas of the price structure . . . and (b) of perverse flexibility in the total turnover (quantity and velocity) of effective money" (at 165).

The perverse flexibility in "total turnover"—Keynes' aggregate demand—was reinforced, Simons thought, but not essentially produced, by changes in the quantity of money. It reflected rather changes in "the speculative temper of the community."[4] Such changes, he argued, produce changes in velocity that can develop into "catastrophic disturbances as soon as short-term borrowing develops on a large scale. . . . Short-term obligations provide abundant money substitutes during booms, thus releasing money from cash reserves [that is, raising velocity]; and they precipitate hopeless efforts at liquidation during depressions [that is, lowering velocity]" (at 166).

These "cumulative maladjustments are likely to be peculiarly severe" "in an economy where most of the effective money is provided by private banks" because "the quantity of effective money, as well as its velocity, responds promptly and markedly to changes of business earnings."[5]

Widespread borrowing on short-term in order to finance long-term obligations is the key to instability because, in Simons' view, it makes the economy vulnerable to changes in confidence and hence in the desire for liquidity. Each individual separately may be in a position to convert his assets into cash but the economy as a whole is not. There is "shiftability" but not "liquidity." The commercial banking system makes this problem more serious not primarily as a creator of money, but because it fosters more widespread and extensive borrowing on demand and lending on time.

This vision undoubtedly was derived largely from the 1929–33 crash. Hence, Simons put special emphasis on the potentialities in such a system for deflation. ". . . [W]e evolved a fantastic financial structure and collections of enterprises for money-bootlegging, whose sanctimonious respectability and marble solidity only concealed a mass of current obligations and a shoestring of equity that would have been scandalous in any other type of business. . . . [W]e evaded long term deflation by "continuously courting deflation catastrophe" (at 198–99).

Or again, "once a crisis has developed, and once earnings have begun to decline, the process is even more chaotic. Each bank seeks to contract its loans; but none augments its reserves unless it contracts more rapidly than the rest. Every reduction in bank loans means reduction in the community's effective money; and this in turn means lower prices, smaller volume of business, and still lower earnings.

"It is more than an incidental aggravation that practically all the banks of necessity become insolvent in the process, and that large numbers are actually forced to close."[6]

For our purposes, the key feature of this interpretation is that the channel of influence runs from changes in business confidence to changes in velocity to changes in the quantity of money. For the depression, it is the collapse of confidence (Keynes' collapse of the marginal efficiency of investment) that sets off a demand for liquidity. This demand cannot be met but the attempt to meet it forces widespread liquidation, including the liquidation of bank loans with a resultant decline in the quantity of money and runs on banks.

Simons implicitly regarded the Great Depression as occurring despite not because of governmental monetary policy. Though he made no explicit statement to this effect, Simons' quite clearly accepted the official apologia of the Federal Reserve System—it had done its best but was powerless to stop the collapse, once private confidence was sapped, as it was by the stock-market crash. "Reflect casually," says Simons, "on what the thirties might have been if only we had not permitted the stock-market crash to initiate a long and precipitous deflation in the United States. . . ." (at 272).

2. *Simons' Theory of Cycles and His Policy Proposals*. It is clear how Simons' policy proposals derive from his interpretation of the Great Depression. It is the rigidity of prices that converts fluctuations in aggregate demand into fluctuations in output and employment. Hence, greater flexibility of prices is highly desirable, whatever else is done. This is the link between Simons' views on money, on the one hand, and on monopoly in industry and labor and government price-fixing, on the other. The way to make prices less rigid was by measures that are desirable in any event in order to make the economy more competitive. Hence, in his monetary writings, he only stated the objective of price flexibility, without a bill of particulars.

Since the inherent instability of the financial structure is the source of cumulative maladjustments, the *sine qua non* of stability in a free market economy is an improved financial structure. The "approximately ideal condition" would be one in which "there were no fixed money contracts at all—if all property were held in a residual-equity or common-stock form. With such a financial structure, no one would be in a position either to create effective money substitutes (whether for circulation or for hoarding) or to force enterprises into wholesale efforts at liquidation. Hoarding and dishoarding (changes in velocity) would, to be sure, still occur; but the dangers of cumulative maladjustment would be minimized" (at 165).

In the absence of such financial reform, "The obvious weakness of fixed quantity [of money], as a sole rule of monetary policy, lies in the danger of sharp changes on the velocity side.... The fixing of the quantity of circulating media might merely serve to increase the perverse variability in the amounts of 'near moneys' and in the degree of their general acceptability...." (at 164).

Hence, pending such financial reform, the theoretically attractive quantity of money criterion had to be relegated to the "more distant future" (at 183) despite its unique advantage of providing an objective rule and minimizing the role of discretion by monetary authorities. "For the present, we obviously must rely on a large measure of discretionary money management . . ." (at 170). But this discretion should be guided by some definite policy objective, not be ". . . merely the composite of the uncertain daily actions of an indefinite number of agencies, governmental and private" (at 174). Simons was led by this route to endorse reluctantly the stabilization of a price index as the only feasible means of ". . . bringing the totality of monetary measures under the discipline of some rule...." (at 174—75). "If price-level stabilization is a poor system," he wrote, "it is, still from a liberal viewpoint, infinitely better than no system at all. And it seems now highly questionable whether any better system is feasible or possible at all within the significant future" (at 174).

Finally, if, in the existing financial structure, the fluctuations in aggregate demand originate in the private sector and in turn affect the commercial banking system; if a major problem is the ease with which non-banks can create and destroy near-moneys, then the banking authorities, strictly interpreted, operate on too narrow a base to be able to control the price level. "Banking," Simons said, "is a pervasive phenomenon, not something to be dealt with merely by legislation directed at what we call banks" (at 172). Hence, "The task [of stabilizing the price level] is certainly not one to be entrusted to banking authorities, with their limited powers and restricted techniques, as should be abundantly evident from recent experience. Ultimate control over the value of money lies in fiscal practices—in the spending, lazing, and borrowing operations of the central government" (at 175).

3. *Simons and Keynes.* There is clearly great similarity between the views expressed by Simons and by Keynes—as to the causes of the Great Depression, the impotence of monetary policy, and the need to rely extensively on fiscal policy. Both men placed great emphasis on the state of business expectations and assigned a critical role to the desire for liquidity. Indeed, in many ways, the key novelty of Keynes' *General Theory* was the role he assigned to "absolute" liquidity preference under conditions of deep depression. It was this, in his view, that made it impossible for the monetary authorities to influence interest rates. It was this that meant that changes in the quantity of money produced by the monetary authorities would simply be reflected in opposite movements in velocity and have no effect on income or employment.

Keynes had earlier been a strong champion of relying primarily on orthodox monetary policy to promote economic stability. He abandoned this position when he concluded that liquidity preference could frustrate central bank attempts to alter long-term interest rates. Like Simons, be turned instead to fiscal policy—changes in government expenditures and taxes—as his primary reliance.[7]

Despite the similarity between the views held by Simons and Keynes, Simons, as best I can determine, arrived at his views independently. My earlier quotation from Simons that "ultimate control over the value of money lies in fiscal practices" comes from an article published in February, 1936, or at roughly the same time as Keynes' *General Theory*. (The preface is dated December, 1935, and the book bears the publication date of 1936.)

More important yet, Simons' basic ideas on both theory and policy are all contained in an unpublished mimeographed memorandum dated November, 1933. Already in that memorandum, Simons had written "at the present time, increase of expenditures or reduction of taxes would be far more immediately effective toward raising prices than conversion of the federal debt into the non-interest bearing form."[8] Indeed, I have always thought that it was because such ideas as these, and the earlier ones I have summarized, were in the air at the University of Chicago in the early and mid-1930's that the Chicago students were so much less susceptible to the Keynesian virus than their contemporaries in London, England, and Cambridge, Massachusetts, who were taught, that the Great Depression was a necessary and ultimately healthy purgative.

The major differences between Keynes and Simons on policy reflected their difference in temperament. To both, the financial structure threatened instability. To Keynes the reformer, with his emphasis on short-run problems—it was he, after all, who said, "in the long-run we are all dead," with his confidence in civil servants to control and regulate—he was himself, after all; in and out of the civil service, with his belief that we had seen "the end of laissez-faire," as he entitled a famous article, the solution was to substitute government intervention for market adjustment, to replace where necessary private investment by government spending. To Simons the radical, who always took the long view, who had the mid-westerner's suspicion of the bureaucrats in Washington, who regarded a large measure of laissez-faire as an essential requisite for the preservation of political liberty, the solution was to go to the root of the problem by reforming drastically the financial structure.

4. *The Key Facts as We Now Know Them.* The keystone of Simons' interpretation of 1929–1933 was that the trouble originated with business earnings and the shock to business confidence, documented or perhaps initiated by the stock-market crash. The subsequent widespread pressure for liquidation, on his interpretation, left the monetary authorities, narrowly defined, largely powerless. Once the scramble for liquidity was on, there was no way

they could prevent a decline in the value of private claims and debts, which in turn rendered banks insolvent, and induced their depositors to try to withdraw deposits.

We now know that the critical relations ran precisely the other way. Beginning in mid-1928, the Federal Reserve System, concerned about stock market speculation, adopted a monetary policy of nearly continuous restraint, despite its desire to foster business expansion. The result was a policy that was ". . . not restrictive enough to halt the bull market yet too restrictive to foster vigorous business expansion."[9] The stock of money failed to rise and even fell slightly during most of the cyclical expansion from November, 1927 to August, 1920—a phenomenon not matched in any prior or subsequent cyclical expansion.

Cyclical contraction began in August, 1929, well before the stock-market crash in October, 1929. That crash no doubt did shake business confidence and may well have produced a rise in liquidity preference (that is, a decline in velocity). But there is no sign that it produced any panicky pressure for liquidation, any tendency for bankers to call loans, any concern about the safety of banks, or any widespread deterioration in the value of bank assets—on the contrary, the prices of the kinds of bonds banks held initially went up rather than down.

The downward pressure on velocity produced by the reaction to the stock-market crash was strongly reinforced by the behavior of the quantity of money, which fell by 2.6 percent from August, 1929 to October, 1930. This may seem like a small decline—and it is, compared to the total decline of over 30 percent that occurred before the depression was over. But the decline should be interpreted in the light of prior and subsequent experience. Because of the long-term growth in the quantity of money, there are only four earlier cyclical contractions and no later ones in which the quantity of money declined as much—and all of these earlier exceptions were also unusually severe contractions.

For our purposes, the source of the decline in the quantity of money is even more important than its magnitude. It was produced entirely by a decline in Federal Reserve credit outstanding. No part whatever was played by weakness in the banking structure, attempted liquidation of loans by banks, or an attempt by depositors to convert deposits to currency. On the contrary, the banks' willingness to reduce reserves and the public's willingness to hold more deposits relative to currency offset half of the decline in Federal Reserve credit. The monetary authorities, not the private economy, were the major source of deflationary pressure.

The character of the contraction changed drastically in December, 1930 when a series of scattered bank failures culminated in the dramatic failure of the Bank of the United States in New York—the largest single bank failure in the United States up to that time. For the first time, there was widespread distrust of banks and runs on banks. But again the sequence was the opposite of that which Simons postulated. The runs on banks produced pressure on banks to liquidate. This did lower the market value of their assets and so gave substance to the initially unfounded fears of the safety of the banks. But their position was not weakened by declines in the value of their assets originating in the rest of the financial structure.

A major objective in establishing the Federal Reserve System in 1913 was to meet precisely this kind of situation—to serve as a "lender of last resort" in order to enable banks to meet the demands of depositors without having to dump assets. In the immediate month of December, 1930, the Reserve System behaved to some extent as initially intended. But no sooner was the immediate crisis over than it retreated back to its earlier position and renewed its deflationary pressure on the money supply.

When a second banking crisis began in March, 1931, the Reserve System did not even temporarily step in to ease the situation. The only relief came from gold imports. The Reserve System renounced its heritage and treated the banking crisis as something outside its sphere of competence.

But worse was yet to come. When Britain left gold in September, 1931, the Reserve System embarked on an active deflationary policy—taking the most extreme deflationary measures in its history before or since. The result was to turn a crisis into a catastrophe. The quantity of money had fallen at an annual rate of 13 percent from March, 1931 to August, 1931. It fell at the incredible annual rate of 31 percent in the five months from August, 1931 to January, 1932.

One fact during this episode highlights the error in Simons' interpretation. The chief problem confronting banks was not the collectibility of their commercial loans but the decline in the prices of the bonds they held in their portfolios. Among the prices that declined was the price of U.S. government bonds, which fell by 10 percent. This price decline clearly did not reflect a scramble for liquidity on the part of the community at large or the decline in earnings of business enterprises or a fear about the safety of the bonds. Like the accompanying decline of 20 percent in the price of high grade corporate bonds, it reflected the inevitable effect of the dumping of bonds by banks which was enforced by the failure of the Federal Reserve System to provide sufficient liquidity to enable banks to meet the demands of their customers.

In our *Monetary History*, Anna Schwartz and I summarized the role of the Reserve System in the great contraction from 1929–1933 as follows:

"The System pleaded impotence, arguing explicitly that the non-monetary forces making for contraction were so strong and violent that it was powerless to stem the tide, and implicitly that the depth of the decline in the money stock was due to the depth of the decline in business activity, rather than . . . the reverse. Many others, recognizing the good intentions of the monetary authorities and the ability of many individuals in the System, while independently holding a wide variety of views about the role of money in economic affairs, accepted the System's plea"—as we have seen, Simons and Keynes were in this company.

Evaluating the claim of impotence, we concluded that "At all times throughout the 1929–33 contraction, alternative policies were available to the System by which it could have kept the stock of money from falling, and indeed could have increased it at almost any desired rate. These policies did not involve radical innovations. They involved measures of a kind the System had taken in earlier years, of a kind explicitly contemplated by the founders of the System to meet precisely the kind of banking crisis that developed in late 1930 and persisted thereafter. They involved measures that were actually proposed and very likely would have been adopted under a slightly different bureaucratic structure or distribution of power, or even if the men in power had had somewhat different personalities. Until late 1931—and we believe not even then—the alternative policies involved no conflict with the maintenance of the gold standard. Until September, 1931, the problem that recurrently troubled the System was how to keep the gold inflows under control, not the reverse."[10]

I have stressed the Great Depression because this climactic episode clearly played a key role in leading Simons—and also Keynes—to believe that the orthodox powers of the monetary authorities were too weak to cope with disorders arising in the private financial markets. In fact, as I have emphasized, the private financial markets displayed extraordinary resilience and stability—but not enough to cope with the disorders arising from the actions—and inaction—of the monetary authorities.

An enormous amount of evidence has accumulated since Simons wrote that bears not only on these few years but also on a far wider range of economic history. This evidence, too, contradicts Simons' interpretation of the source of instability. It turns out that the rate of growth of the quantity of money has systematically tapered off well before the economy in general slows down, and has speeded up well before the economy speeds up. The movements in velocity—which Simons took as an independent source of instability—come later than the movements in the quantity of money and are mild when the movements in the quantity of money are mild. They have been sharp only when there have been sharp movements in the quantity of money. There is no evidence to support Simons' fear that a fixed quantity of money might involve "the danger of sharp changes on the velocity side." On the contrary, the evidence is precisely the reverse—that it would lessen the danger of sharp changes in velocity.

5. *Policy Implications.* Had Simons known the facts as we now know them, he would, I believe, have been confirmed in "his earlier persuasion

as to the merits of the rule of a fixed quantity of money. . . ." (at 170)[11] rather than have accepted, albeit with great reluctance, stabilization of a price level as at least a temporary objective pending the establishment of the "financial good society." He would not have felt constrained to denigrate monetary powers narrowly conceived and to elevate fiscal powers to the forefront as the major weapon of monetary policy.

In short, as it happens, a correct view of the facts would have strengthened his basic intuitions, would have reinforced his confidence in policies fully consistent with his central belief in laissez-faire for the private economy and the rule of law for governmental bodies.

Instead, because of a misconception of the facts, he was led to compromise for the short run and to propose radical reform for the long-run.

Is it just a happy accident that a fuller study of the facts would have led Henry Simons to compromise less with his basic intuitions, would have supported the conclusions to which he was drawn by his economic theorizing? I believe not. Those intuitions, those conclusions were derived from a sophisticated body of economic theory that had developed over centuries. Such a body of theory has implicit in it a set of empirical judgments about the character of the world. It survives if and only if those implicit judgments are vindicated by experience. It may go into temporary eclipse when casual empiricism seems to run counter to it. That is what happened during the 'thirties. But the sign that it is a good theory is that it will revive and be restored to grace as emerging evidence vindicates it. That is what has been happening in the past decade. That is why Simons' keen theoretical understanding has proved more permanent than his empirical compromises.

NOTES

1.   One partial exception to the statement that Simons nowhere set forth a consistent statement of his theory is an Appendix on Banking and Business Cycles in an unpublished and unsigned memorandum dated November, 1933, Banking and Currency Reform. In a footnote, Simons describes this memorandum as

having been "prepared and circulated by several Chicago economists" but, according to Aaron Director, one of the group, it was written primarily by Simons. See *Henry Simons, Economic Policy for a Free Society* 326 n.2 (1943). All subsequent page references in the text are to this book.

2.   His proposal involved separating existing commercial banks into two sets of institutions. One would be essentially a warehouse for money. It would accept demand deposits transferable by check but be required to keep a reserve in cash (or deposits at the Federal Reserve) of 100% of such deposits, and would get its income from service charges paid by depositors. The other would be an investment trust which would take over the lending activities of commercial banks, getting its capital by issuing securities to the public.

3.   Emphasis on this type of reform has almost disappeared from the literature. Its only counterpart was a temporary flurry of interest in non-bank financial intermediaries a few years ago.

4.   Appendix to Banking and Currency Reform, *supra* note 1, at 2.

5.   *Id.* at 3.

6.   *Id.* at 5.

7.   In a letter commenting on this lecture, Friedrich A. Hayek writes: "I believe you are wrong in suggesting that the common element in the doctrines of Simons and Keynes was the influence of the Great Depression. We all held similar ideas in the 1920's. They had been most fully elaborated by R. G. Hawtrey who was all the time talking about the 'inherent instability of credit' but he was by no means the only one. . . . It seems to me that all the elements of the theories which were applied to the Great Depression had been developed during that great enthusiasm for 'business cycle theory' which preceded it."

No doubt the elements of the theories were all present and Hayek may be right that the Great Depression did not have the effect on Keynes' views that I attributed to it. However, the Great Depression surely produced a different emphasis. More important, my impression is that the Great Depression also produced an important difference in substance. Hawtrey and others emphasized the inherent instability of banking credit proper; their stress was on the forces that Simons described as explaining why these "cumulative maladjustments are likely to be peculiarly severe" "in an economy where most of the effective money is provided by private banks," not on the earlier effects to which Simons attributed the cumulative maladjustments themselves. The Great Depression led, I believe, Keynes and Simons to emphasize the inherent instability of the financial structure more generally—the effect of near-moneys rather than of money itself.

Unfortunately, I have not had the opportunity to investigate this point at all fully, so this reaction to Hayek's comment is a tentative impression, not a documented conclusion.

8. *Supra* note 4, at 13.

9. M. Friedman and A. Schwartz, *A Monetary History of the United States, 1867–1960*, 298 (1963).

10. *Supra* note 8, at 691, 693.

11. To avoid misunderstanding, I should note explicitly that Simons' rule is not identical with the rule I have come to favor. Simons proposed that the quantity of money be held constant in amount. I propose that it grow at a fixed rate year after year, the rate of growth being designed to produce roughly stable final product prices.

Simons explicitly rejected the rule of a constant rate of growth. He recognized that his rule of a constant money supply involved a secular decline in final product prices. His basic reason for favoring it nonetheless was that the sticky and inflexible prices were factor prices, especially wages, and that a constant quantity of money would (aside from growth of population, which he thought would decline and might disappear, and aside from secular changes in velocity, which he ignored) mean stability in these prices and hence would minimize the necessity for changes in the sticky prices. Supplementary reasons were the greater ease of public understanding of a constant quantity of money than of a necessarily arbitrary rate of growth and the greater pressure for fiscal discipline it would impose on legislators.

THE COUNTER-REVOLUTION IN MONETARY THEORY[1]

1970

It was a great pleasure to be honoured with being the first of the Harold Wincott lecturers, partly because economics owes so much to the work that has been done on this island. Coming back to Britain, as I am fortunate enough to be able to do from time to time, always means coming back to a warm circle of friends or friendly enemies.

I am going to discuss primarily a scientific development that has little ideological or political content. This development nonetheless has great relevance to governmental policy because it bears on the likely effects of particular kinds of governmental policy regardless of what party conducts the policy and for what purpose.

A counter-revolution must be preceded by two stages: an initial position from which there was a revolution, and the revolution. In order to set the stage, I would like first to make a few remarks about the initial position and the revolution.

It is convenient to have names to describe these positions. The initial position I shall call the quantity theory of money and associate it largely with the name of an American economist, Irving Fisher, although it is a doctrine to which many prominent English economists also made contributions. The revolution was made by Keynes in the 1930s. Keynes himself was a quantity theorist, so that his revolution was from, as it were, within the governing body. Keynes's name is the obvious name to attach to the revolution. The counter-revolution also needs a name and perhaps the one most widely used in referring to it is 'the Chicago School.' More recently, however, it has been given a name which is less lovely but which has become so attached to it that I find it hard to avoid using it. That name is 'monetarism' because of the renewed emphasis on the role of the quantity of money.

A counter-revolution, whether in politics or in science, never restores the initial situation. It always produces a situation that has some similarity to the initial one but is also strongly influenced by the intervening revolution. That is certainly true of monetarism, which has benefited much from Keynes's work. Indeed I may say, as have so many others since there is no way of contradicting it, that if Keynes were alive today he would no doubt be at the forefront of the counter-revolution. You must never judge a master by his disciples.

IRVING FISHER AND THE QUANTITY THEORY

Let me then start briefly to set the stage with the initial position, the quantity theory of money as developed primarily by Irving Fisher who is to my mind by far the greatest American economist. He was also an extraordinarily interesting and eccentric man. Indeed, I suspect that his professional reputation suffered during his life because he was not only an economist but also involved in many other activities, including being one of the leading members of the American prohibitionist party. He interviewed all potential presidential candidates for something like thirty years to find out what their position was on the subject of alcohol. His best-selling book, which has been translated into the largest number of

languages, is not about economics at all but about health. It is about how
to eat and keep healthy and is entitled *How to Live* (written jointly with Dr.
E. L. Fisk). But even that book is a tribute to his science. When he was a
young man in his early thirties, he contracted tuberculosis, was given a year
to live by his physicians, went out to the Far West where the air was good
and proceeded to immerse himself in the study of health and methods of
eating and so on. If we may judge the success of his scientific work by its
results, he lived to the age of eighty. He was also a leading statistician, developed the theory of index numbers, worked in mathematics, economics and
utility theory and had time enough besides to invent the Kardex filing
system, the familiar system in which one little envelope flaps on another, so
you can pull out a flat drawer to see what is in it. He founded what is now
Remington-Rand Corporation in order to produce and distribute his invention. As you can see, he was a man of very wide interests and ability.

$MV = PT$

The basic idea of the quantity theory, that there is a relation between
the quantity of money on the one hand and prices on the other, is surely
one of the oldest ideas in economics. It goes back thousands of years. But
it is one thing to express this idea in general terms. It is another thing to
introduce system into the relation between money on the one hand and
prices and other magnitudes on the other. What Irving Fisher did was to
analyse the relationship in far greater detail than had ever been done earlier.
He developed and popularised what has come to be known as the quantity
equation; $MV = PT$, money multiplied by velocity equals prices multiplied
by the volume of transactions. This is an equation that every college student
of economics used to have to learn, then for a time did not and now, as the
counter-revolution has progressed, must again learn. Fisher not only presented this equation, he also applied it in a variety of contexts. He once
wrote a famous article interpreting the business cycle as the 'dance of the
dollar', in which he argued that fluctuations in economic activity were
primarily a reflection of changes in the quantity of money. Perhaps even

more pertinent to the present day, he analyzed in detail the relation between inflation on the one hand and interest rates on the other. His first book on this subject, *Appreciation and Interest*, published in 1896, can be read today with profit and is immediately applicable to today's conditions.

In that work, Fisher made a distinction which again is something that went out of favour and has now come back into common use, namely the distinction between the nominal interest rate in pounds per year per hundred pounds and the real interest rate, i.e. corrected for the effect of changing prices. If you lend someone £100 today and in twelve months receive back £106, and if in the meantime prices rise by 6 percent then your £106 will be worth no more than your £100 today. The nominal interest rate is 6 percent, but the real interest rate is zero. This distinction between the nominal interest rate and the real interest rate is of the utmost importance in understanding the effects of monetary policy as well as the behavior of interest rates. Fisher also distinguished sharply between the actual rate, the rate realized after the event, and the anticipated real rate that lenders expected to receive or borrowers expected to pay. No one would lend money at 6 percent if he expected prices to rise by 6 percent during the year. If he did lend at 6 percent, it must have been because he expected prices to rise by less than 6 percent: the realized real rate was less than the anticipated real rate. This distinction between the actual real rate and the anticipated real rate is of the greatest importance today in understanding the course of events. It explains why inflation is so stubborn once it has become embedded, because as inflation accelerates, people come to expect it. They come to build the expected inflation into the interest rates that they are willing to pay as borrowers or that they demand as lenders.

Wide Consensus

Up to, let us say, the year 1930, Irving Fisher's analysis was widely accepted. In monetary theory, that analysis was taken to mean that in the quantity equation $MV = PT$ the term for velocity could be regarded as highly stable, that it could be taken as determined independently of the other terms in the equation, and that as a result changes in the quantity of money would be reflected either in prices or in output. It was also widely taken for granted that short-term fluctuations in the economy reflected changes in the quantity of money, or in the terms and conditions under which credit was available. It was taken for granted that the trend of prices over any considerable period reflected the behavior of the quantity of money over that period.

In economic policy, it was widely accepted that monetary policy was the primary instrument available for stabilizing the economy. Moreover, it was accepted that monetary policy should be operated largely through a combination of two blades of a scissors, the one blade being what in the USA is called 'discount rate' and in Britain is called 'Bank rate', the other blade being open-market operations the purchase and sale of government securities.

That was more or less the initial doctrinal position prior to the Keynesian revolution. It was a position that was widely shared. Keynes's *A Tract on Monetary Reform*,[2] which I believe remains to this day one of his best books, reflects the consensus just described.

THE KEYNESIAN REVOLUTION

Then came the Keynesian revolution. What produced that revolution was the course of events. My colleague, George Stigler, in discussing the history of thought, has often argued that major changes within a discipline come from inside the discipline and are not produced by the impact of outside events. He may well be right in general. But in this particular instance I believe the basic source of the revolution and of the reaction against the quantity theory of money was a historical event, namely the great contraction or depression. In the United Kingdom, the contraction started in 1925 when Britain went back on gold at the prewar parity and ended in 1931 when Britain went off gold. In the United States, the contraction started in 1929 and ended when the USA went off gold in early 1933.

In both countries, economic conditions were depressed for years after the contraction itself had ended and an expansion had begun.

Wrong Lessons from the Great Depression

The Great Depression shattered the acceptance of the quantity theory of money because it was widely interpreted as demonstrating that monetary policy was ineffective, at least against a decline in business. All sort of aphorisms were coined that are still with us, to indicate why it was that providing monetary ease would not necessarily lead to economic expansion, such as 'You can lead a horse to water but you can't make him drink' or 'Monetary policy is like a string: you can pull on it but you can't push on it', and doubtless there are many more.

As it happens, this interpretation of the depression was completely wrong. It turns out, as I shall point out more fully below, that on re-examination, the depression is a tragic testament to the effectiveness of monetary policy, not a demonstration of its impotence. But what mattered for the world of ideas was not what was true but what was believed to be true. And it was believed at the time that monetary policy had been tried and had been found wanting.

In part that view reflected the natural tendency for the monetary authorities to blame other forces for the terrible economic events that were occurring. The people who run monetary policy are human beings, even as you and I, and a common human characteristic is that if anything had happens it is somebody else's fault. In the course of collaborating on a book on the monetary history of the United States, I had the dismal task of reading through fifty years of annual reports of the Federal Reserve Board. The only element that lightened that dreary task was the cyclical oscillation in the power attributed to monetary policy by the system. In good years the report would read 'Thanks to the excellent monetary policy of the Federal Reserve. . .'. In bad years the report would read 'Despite the excellent policy of the Federal Reserve . . .', and it would go on to point out that monetary policy really was, after all, very weak and other forces so much stronger.

The monetary authorities proclaimed that they were pursuing easy money policies when in fact they were not and their protestations were largely accepted. Hence Keynes, along with many others, concluded that monetary policy had been tried and found wanting. In contrast to most others, he offered an alternative analysis to explain why the depression had occurred and to indicate a way of ameliorating the situation.

Keynes's Critique of the Quantity Theory

Keynes did not deny Irving Fisher's quantity equation. What Keynes said was something different. He said that, while of course MV equals PT, velocity, instead of being highly stable, is highly adaptable. If the quantity of money goes up, he said, what will happen is simply that the velocity of circulation of money will go down and nothing will happen on the other side of the equation to either prices or output. Correspondingly, if something pushes the right-hand side of the equation, PT or income, up without an increase in the quantity of money, all that will happen will be that velocity will rise. In other words, he said, velocity is a will-of-the-wisp. It can move one way or the other in response to changes either in the quantity of money or in income. The quantity of money is therefore of minor importance. (Since I am trying to cover highly technical material very briefly, I am leaving out many qualifications that are required for a full understanding of either Fisher or Keynes. I do want to stress that the statements I am making are simplifications and are not to be taken as a full exposition of any of the theories.)

What matters, said Keynes, is not the quantity of money. What matters is the part of total spending which is independent of current income, what has come to be called autonomous spending and to be identified in practice largely with investment by business and expenditures by government.

Keynes thereby directed attention away from the role of money and its relation to the flow of income and toward the relation between two flows of income, that which corresponds to autonomous spending and that which corresponds to induced spending. Moreover, he said, in the modern world, prices are highly rigid while quantities can change readily. When for whatever reason autonomous spending changes, the resulting change in income will manifest itself primarily in output and only secondarily and only after long lags in prices. Prices are determined by costs consisting mostly of wages, and wages are determined by the accident of past history.

The great contraction, he said, was the result of a collapse of demand for investment which in turn reflected a collapse of productive opportunities to use capital. Thus the engine and the motor of the great contraction was a collapse of investment transformed into a collapse of income by the multiplier process.

The Implications for Policy

This doctrine had far-reaching implications for economic policy. It meant that monetary policy was of little importance. Its only role was to keep interest rates down, both to reduce pressure on the government budget in paying interest on its debts, and also because it might have a tiny bit of stimulating effect on investment. From this implication of the doctrine came the cheap money policy which was tried in country after country following the Second World War.

A second implication of the doctrine was that the major reliance for economic stabilization could not be on monetary policy, as the quantity theorists had thought, but must be on fiscal policy, that is, on varying the rate of government spending and taxing.

A third implication was that inflation is largely to be interpreted as a cost-push phenomenon. It follows, although Keynes himself did not draw this conclusion from his doctrine, that the way to counteract inflation is through an incomes policy. If costs determine prices and costs are historically determined, then the way to stop any rise in prices is to stop the rise in costs.

These views became widely accepted by economists at large both as theory and as implications for policy. It is hard now at this distance in time to recognize how widely they were accepted. Let me just give you one quotation which could be multiplied many-fold, to give you the flavor of the views at the end of the Second World War. Parenthetically, acceptance of these views continued until more recently in Britain than in the United States. I quote from John H. Williams, who was a Professor of Economics at Harvard University, a principal advisor to the Federal Reserve Bank of New York, and widely regarded as an anti-Keynesian. In 1945 he wrote: 'I have long believed that the quantity of money by itself has a permissive rather than a positive effect on prices and production'. And in the sentence I want to stress he wrote: 'I can see no prospect of a revival of general monetary control in the post-war period'. That was a very sweeping statement, and one that obviously proved very far indeed from the mark.

The high point in the United States of the application of Keynesian ideas to economic policy probably came with the new economists of the Kennedy administration. Their finest hour was the tax cut of 1964 which was premised entirely on the principles that I have been describing.

Having sketched briefly the initial stage of the quantity theory, and the revolutionary stage of the Keynesian theory, I come now to the monetarist counter-revolution.

THE COUNTER-REVOLUTION

As so often happens, just about the time that Keynes's ideas were being triumphant in practice, they were losing their hold on the minds of scholars in the academies. A number of factors contributed to a change of attitude towards the Keynesian doctrine. One was the experience immediately after the Second World War. On the basis of the Keynesian analysis, economists and others expected the war to be followed for another great depression. With our present experience of over two decades of inflation behind us it is hard to recognize that this was the sentiment of the times. But alike in the United States, in Great Britain and in many other countries, the dominant view was that, once the Second World War ended, once the pump-priming and government spending for military purposes ended, there would be an enormous economic collapse because of the scarcity of investment opportunities that had been given the blame for the Great Depression. Massive unemployment and massive deflation were the buga-boos of the time. As you all know, that did not happen. The problem after the war turned out to be inflation rather than deflation.

A second postwar experience that was important was the failure of cheap money policies. In Britain, Chancellor Dalton tried to follow the Keynesian policy of keeping interest rates very low. As you all know, he was unable to do so and had to give up. The same thing happened in the United States. The Federal Reserve System followed a policy of pegging bond prices, trying to keep interest rates down. It finally gave up in 1953 after the Trea-sury–Federal Reserve Accord of 1951 laid the groundwork for setting inter-est rates free. In country after country, wherever the cheap money policy was tried, it led to inflation and had to be abandoned. In no country was inflation contained until orthodox monetary policy was employed. Ger-many was one example in 1948; Italy shortly after; Britain and the United States later yet.

Reconsideration of the Great Depression

Another important element that contributed to a questioning of the Keynesian doctrine was a re-examination of monetary history and par-ticularly of the Great Depression. When the evidence was examined in detail it turned out that bad monetary policy had to be given a very large share of the blame. In the United States, there a reduction in the quantity of money by a third from 1929 to 1933. This reduction in the quantity of money clearly made the depression much longer and more severe than it otherwise would have been. Moreover, and equally important, it turned out that the reduction in the quantity of money was not a consequence of the unwilling-ness of horses to drink. It was not a consequence of being unable to push on a string. It was a direct consequence of the policies followed by the Federal Reserve system.

From 1930 to 1933, a series of bank runs and bank failure were permitted to run their course because the Federal Reserve failed to provide liquidity for the banking system, which was one of the main functions the designers of the Federal Reserve system intended it to perform. Banks failed because the public at large, fearful for the safety of their deposits, tried to convert their deposits into currency. In a fractional reserve system, it is literally impossible for all depositors to do that unless there is some source of additional currency. The Federal Reserve system was established in 1913 in response to the banking panic of 1907 primarily to provide additional liquidity at a time of pressure on banks. In 1930–33, the system failed to do so and it failed to do so despite the fact that there were many people in the system who were calling upon it to do so and who recognized that this was its correct function.

It was widely asserted at the time that the decline in the quantity of money was a consequence of the lack of willing borrowers. Perhaps the most decisive bit of evidence against that interpretation is that many banks failed because of a decline in the price of government securities. Indeed, it turned out that many banks that had made bad private loans came through much better than banks that had been cautious and had bought large amounts of Treasury and municipal securities for secondary liquidity. The reason was that there was a market for the government securities and hence when bank examiners came around to check on the banks, they had to mark down the price of the governments to the market value. However, there was no market for bad loans, and therefore they were carried on the books at face value. As a result, many careful, conservative banks failed.

The quantity of money fell by a third and roughly a third of all banks failed. This is itself a fascinating story and one that I can only touch on. The important point for our purposes is that it is crystal clear that at all times during the contraction, the Federal Reserve had it within its power to prevent the decline in the quantity of money and to produce an increase. Monetary policy had not been tried and found wanting. It had not been tried. Or, alternatively, it had been tried perversely. It had been used to force an incredible deflation on the American economy and on the rest of the world. If Keynes had known the facts about the Great Depression as we now know them, he could not have interpreted that episode as he did.

Wider Evidence

Another scholarly element that contributed to a reaction against the Keynesian doctrine and to the emergence of the new doctrine was extensive empirical analysis of the relation between the quantity of money on the one hand, and income, prices and interest rates on the other. Perhaps the simplest way for me to suggest why this was relevant is to recall that an essential element of the Keynesian doctrine was the passivity of velocity. If money rose, velocity would decline. Empirically, however, it turns out that the movements of velocity tend to reinforce those of money instead of to offset them. When the quantity of money declined by a third from 1929 to 1933 in the United States, velocity declined also. When the quantity of money rises rapidly in almost any country, velocity also rises rapidly. Far from velocity offsetting the movements of the quantity of money, it reinforces them.

I cannot go into the whole body of scientific work that has been done. I can only say that there has arisen an extensive literature concerned with exploring these relations which has demonstrated very clearly the existence of a consistent relation between changes in the quantity of money and changes in other economic magnitudes of a very different kind from that which Keynes assumed to exist.

The final blow, at least in the United States, to the Keynesian orthodoxy was a number of dramatic episodes in our recent domestic experience. These episodes centered on two key issues. The first was whether the behavior of the quantity of money or rates of interest is a better criterion to use in conducting monetary policy. You have had a curious combination in this area of central bankers harking back to the real bills doctrine of the early nineteenth century on the one hand, and Keynesians on the other, who alike agreed that the behavior of interest rates was the relevant criterion for the conduct of monetary policy. By contrast, the new interpretation is that interest rates are a misleading index of policy and that central bankers should look rather at the quantity of money. The second key issue was the relative role of fiscal policy and of monetary policy. By fiscal policy, I mean changes in government spending and taxing, holding the quantity of money constant. By monetary policy, I mean changes in the quantity of money, holding government spending and taxing constant.

Fiscal versus Monetary Policy

The problem in discussing the relative roles of fiscal policy and monetary policy is primarily to keep them separate, because in practice they operate jointly most of the time. Ordinarily if a government raises its spending without raising taxes, that is, if it incurs a deficit in order to be expansionary, it will finance some of the deficit by printing money. Conversely if it runs a surplus, it will use part of that surplus to retire money. But from an analytical point of view, and from the point of view of getting at the issue that concerns the counter-revolution, it is important to consider fiscal policy and monetary policy separately, to consider each operating by itself. The Keynesians regarded as a clear implication of their position the proposition that fiscal policy by itself is important in affecting the level of income, that a large deficit would have essentially the same expansionary influence on the economy whether it was financed by borrowing from the public or by printing money.

The 'monetarists' rejected this proposition and maintained that fiscal policy by itself is largely ineffective, that what matters is what happens to the quantity of money. Off-hand that seems like an utterly silly idea. It seems absurd to say that if the government increases its expenditures without increasing taxes, that may not by itself be expansionary. Such a policy obviously puts income into the hands of the people to whom the government pays out its expenditures without taking any extra funds out of the hands of the taxpayers. Is that not obviously expansionary or inflationary? Up to that point, yes, but that is only half the story. We have to ask where the government gets the extra funds it spends. If the government prints money to meet its bills, that is monetary policy and we are trying to look at fiscal policy by itself. If the government gets the funds by borrowing from the public, then those people who lend the funds to the government have less to spend or to lend to others. The effect of the higher government expenditures may simply be higher spending by government and those who receive government funds and lower spending by those who lend to government or by those to whom lenders would have loaned the money instead. To discover any net effect on total spending, one must go to a more sophisticated level—to differences in the behaviour of the two groups of people or to effects of government borrowing on interest rates. There is no first-order effect.

Evidence from US 'Experiments'

The critical first test on both these key issues came in the USA in 1966. There was fear of developing inflation and in the spring of 1966 the Federal Reserve Board, belatedly, stepped very hard on the brake. I say 'stepped very hard' because the record on the Federal Reserve over fifty years is that it has almost invariably acted too much too late. Almost always it has waited too long before acting and then acted too strongly. In 1966, the result was a combination of a very tight monetary policy, under which the quantity of money did not grow at all during the final nine months of the year, and a very expansive fiscal policy. So you had a nice experiment. Which was going to dominate? The tight money policy or the easy fiscal policy? The Keynesians in general argued that the easy fiscal policy was going to dominate and therefore predicted continued rapid expansion in 1967. The monetarists argued that monetary policy would dominate, and so it turned out. There was a definite slowing down in the rate of growth of economic activity in the first half of 1967, following the tight money policy of 1966. When, in early 1967, the Federal Reserve reversed its policy and started to print money like mad, about six or nine months later, after the usual lag, income recovered and a rapid expansion in economic activity followed. Quite clearly, monetary policy had dominated fiscal policy in that encounter.

A still more dramatic example came in 1968 and from 1968 to the present. In the summer of 1968, under the influence of the Council of Economic Advisers and at the recommendation of President Johnson, Congress enacted a surtax of 10 percent on income. It was enacted in order to fight the inflation which was then accelerating. The believers in the Keynesian view were so persuaded of the potency of this weapon that they were afraid of 'overkill'. They thought the tax increase might be too much and might stop the economy in its tracks. They persuaded the Federal Reserve system, or I should rather say that the Federal Reserve system was of the same view. Unfortunately for the United States, but fortunately for scientific knowledge, the Federal Reserve accordingly decided that it had best offset the overkill effects of fiscal policy by expanding the quantity of money rapidly. Once again, we had a beautiful controlled experiment with fiscal policy extremely tight and monetary policy extremely easy. Once again, there was a contrast between two sets of predictions. The Keynesians or fiscalists argued that the surtax would produce a sharp slow-down in the first half of 1969 at the latest while the monetarists argued that the rapid growth in the quantity of money would more than offset the fiscal effects, so that there would be a continued inflationary boom in the first half of 1969. Again, the monetarists proved correct. Then, in December 1968, the Federal Reserve Board did move to tighten money in the sense of slowing down the rate of growth of the quantity of money and that was followed after the appropriate interval by a slow-down in the economy. This test, I may say, is still in process, but up to now it again seems to be confirming the greater importance of the monetary than of the fiscal effect.

'This Is Where I Came In'

One swallow does not make a spring. My own belief in the greater importance of monetary policy does not rest on these dramatic episodes. It rests on the experience of hundreds of years and of many countries. These episodes of the past few years illustrate that effect; they do not demonstrate it. Nonetheless, the public at large cannot be expected to follow the great masses of statistics. One dramatic episode is far more potent in influencing public opinion than a pile of well-digested, but less dramatic, episodes. The result in the USA at any rate has been a drastic shift in opinion, both professional and lay.

This shift, so far as I can detect, has been greater in the United States than in the United Kingdom. As a result, I have had in the UK the sensation that one has in a continuous cinema at the point where one says 'Oh, this is where I came in'. The debate about monetary effects in Britain is pursuing the identical course that it pursued in the United States about five or so years ago. I am sure that the same thing must have happened in the 1930s. When the British economists wandered over to the farther shores among their less cultivated American brethren, bringing to them the message of Keynes, they must have felt, as I have felt coming to these shores in the opposite direction, that this was where they came in. I am sure they then encountered the same objections that they had encountered in Britain five years earlier. And so it is today. Criticism of the monetary doctrines in this country today is at the naive, unsophisticated level we encountered in the USA about five or more years ago.

Thanks to the very able and active group of economists in this country who are currently working on the monetary statistics, and perhaps even more to the effect which the course of events will have, I suspect that the developments in this country will continue to imitate those in the United States. Not only in this area, but in other areas as well, I have had the experience of initially being in a small minority and have had the opportunity to observe the scenario that unfolds as an idea gains wider acceptance. There is a standard pattern. When anybody threatens an orthodox position, the first reaction is to ignore the interloper. The less said about him the better. But if he begins to win a hearing and gets annoying, the second reaction is to ridicule him, make fun of him as an extremist, a foolish fellow who has these silly ideas. After that stage passes the next, and the most important, stage is to put on his clothes. You adopt for your own his views, and then attribute to him a caricature of those views saying, 'He's an extremist, one of those fellows who says only money matters—everybody knows that sort. Of course money does matter, but.... '

KEY PROPOSITIONS OF MONETARISM

Let me finally describe the state to which the counter-revolution has come by listing systematically the central propositions of monetarism.

1. There is a consistent though not precise relation between the rate of growth of the quantity of money and the rate of growth of nominal income. (By nominal income, I mean income measured in pounds sterling or in dollars or in francs, not real income, income measured in real goods.) That is, whether the amount of money in existence is growing by 3 percent a year, 5 percent a year or 10 percent a year will have a significant effect on how fast nominal income grows. If the quantity of money grows rapidly, so will nominal income; and conversely.

2. This relation is not obvious to the naked eye largely because it takes time for changes in monetary growth to affect income and how long it takes is itself variable. The rate of monetary growth today is not very closely related to the rate of income growth today. Today's income growth depends on what has been happening to money in the past. What happens to money today affects what is going to happen to income in the future.

3. On the average, a change, in the rate of monetary growth, produces a change in the rate of growth of nominal income about a six to nine months later. This is an average that does not hold in every individual case. Sometimes the delay is longer, sometimes shorter. But I have been astounded at how regularly an average delay of six to nine months is found under widely different conditions. I have studied the data for Japan, for India, for Israel, for the United States. Some of our students have studied it for Canada and for a number of South American countries. Whichever country you take, you generally get a delay of around six to nine months. How

clear-cut the evidence for the delay is depends on how much variation there is in the quantity of money. The Japanese data have been particularly valuable because the Bank of Japan was very obliging for some 15 years from 1948 to 1963 and produced very wide movements in the rate of change in the quantity of money. As a result, there is no ambiguity in dating when it reached the top and when it reached the bottom. Unfortunately for science, in 1963 they discovered monetarism and they started to increase the quantity of money at a fairly stable rate and now we are not able to get much more information from the Japanese experience.

4. The changed rate of growth of nominal income typically shows up first in output and hardly at all in prices. If the rate of monetary growth is reduced, then about six to nine months later the rate of growth of nominal income and also of physical output will decline. However, the rate of price rise will be affected very little. There will be downward pressure on prices only as a gap emerges between actual and potential output.

5. On the average, the effect on prices comes about six to nine months after the effect on income and output, so the total delay between a change in monetary growth and a change in the rate of inflation averages something like twelve–eighteen months. That is why it is a long road to hoe to stop an inflation that has been allowed to start. It cannot be stopped overnight.

6. Even after allowance for the delay in the effect of monetary growth, the relation is far from perfect. There's many a slip 'twixt the monetary change and the income change.

7. In the short run, which may be as much as five or ten years, monetary changes affect primarily output. Over decades, on the other hand, the rate of monetary growth affects primarily prices. What happens to output depends on real factors: the enterprise, ingenuity and industry of the people; the extent of thrift; the structure of industry and government; the relations among nations, and so on.

8. It follows from the propositions I have so far stated that *inflation is always and everywhere a monetary phenomenon* in the sense that it is and can be produced only by a more rapid increase in the quantity of money

than in output. However, there are many different possible reasons for monetary growth, including gold discoveries, financing of government spending, and financing of private spending.

9. Government spending may or may not be inflationary. It clearly will be inflationary if it is financed by creating money, that is, by printing currency or creating bank deposits. If it is financed by taxes by borrowing from the public, the main effect is that the government spends the funds instead of the taxpayer or instead of the lender or instead of the person who would otherwise have borrowed the funds. Fiscal policy is extremely important in determining what fraction of total national income is spent by government and who bears the burden of that expenditure. By itself, it is not important for inflation (This is the proposition about fiscal and monetary policy that I discussed earlier.)

10. One of the most difficult things to explain in simple fashion is the way in which a change in the quantity of money affects income. Generally, the initial effect is not on income at all, but on the prices of existing assets, bonds, equities, houses, and other physical capital. This effect, the liquidity effect stressed by Keynes, is an effect on the balance-sheet, not on the income account. An increased rate of monetary growth, whether produced through open-market operations or in other ways, raises the amount of cash that people and businesses have relative to other assets. The holders of the now excess cash will try to adjust their portfolios by buying other assets. But one man's spending is another man's receipts. All the people together cannot change the amount of cash all hold—only the monetary authorities can do that. However, as people *attempt* to change their cash balances, the effect spreads from one asset to another. This tends to raise the prices of assets and to reduce interest rates, which encourages spending to produce new assets and also encourages spending on current services rather than on purchasing existing assets. That is how the initial effect on balance-sheets gets translated into an effect on income and spending. The difference in this area between the monetarists and the Keynesians is not on the nature of the process, but on the range of assets considered. The Keynesians tend

to concentrate on a narrow range of marketable assets and recorded interest rates. The monetarists insist that a far wider range of assets and of interest rates must be taken into account. They give importance to such assets as durable and even semidurable consumer goods, structures and other real property. As a result, they regard the market interest rates stressed by the Keynesians as only a small part of the total spectrum of rates that are relevant.

11. One important feature of this mechanism is that a change in monetary growth affects interest rates in one direction at first but in the opposite direction later on. More rapid monetary growth at first tends to lower interest rates. But later on, as it raises spending and stimulates price inflation, it also produces a rise in the demand for loans which will tend to raise interest rates. In addition, rising prices introduce a discrepancy between real and nominal interest rates. That is why world-wide interest rates are highest in the countries that have had the most rapid rise in the quantity of money and also in prices—countries like Brazil, Chile or Korea. In the opposite direction, a slower rate of monetary growth at first raises interest rates but later on, as it reduces spending and price inflation, lowers interest rates. That is why world-wide interest rates are lowest in countries that *have had* the slowest rate of growth in quantity of money—countries like Switzerland and Germany.

This two-edged relation between money and interest rates explains why monetarists insist that interest rates are a highly misleading guide to monetary policy. This is one respect in which the monetarist doctrines have already had a significant effect on US policy. The Federal Reserve in January 1970 shifted from primary reliance on 'money market conditions' (i.e. interest rates) as a criterion of policy to primary reliance on 'monetary aggregates' (i.e. the quantity of money).

The relations between money and yields on assets (interest rates and stock market earnings—price ratios) are even lower than between money and nominal income. Apparently, factors other than monetary growth play an extremely important part. Needless to say, we do not know in detail what they are, but that they are important we know from the many movements in interest rates and stock market prices which cannot readily be connected with movements in the quantity of money.

CONCLUDING CAUTIONS

These propositions clearly imply both that monetary policy is important and that the important feature of monetary policy is its effect on the quantity of money rather than on bank credit or total credit or interest rates. They also imply that wide swings in the rate of change of the quantity of money are destabilizing and should be avoided. But beyond this, differing implications are drawn.

Some monetarists conclude that deliberate changes in the rate of monetary growth by the authorities can be useful to offset other forces making for instability, provided they are gradual and take into account the lags involved. They favor fine tuning using changes in the quantity of money as the instrument of policy. Other monetarists, including myself, conclude that our present understanding of the relation between money, prices and output is so meager, that there is so much leeway in these relations, that such discretionary changes do more harm than good. We believe that an automatic policy under which the quantity of money would grow at a steady rate—month-in, month-out, year-in, year-out—would provide a stable monetary framework for economic growth without itself being a source of instability and disturbance.

One of the most widespread misunderstandings of the monetarist position is the belief that this prescription of a stable rate of growth in the quantity of money derives from our confidence in a rigid connection between monetary change and economic change. The situation is quite the opposite. If I really believed in a precise, rigid, mechanical connection between money and income, if also I thought that I knew what it was and if I thought that the central bank shared that knowledge with me, which is an even larger 'if', I would then say that we should use the knowledge to offset other forces making for instability. However, I do not believe any of these 'ifs' to be true. On the average, there is a close relation between changes in the quantity of money and the subsequent course of national income. But economic policy must deal with the individual case, not the average. In any one case, there is much slippage. It is precisely this leeway, this looseness in the relation, this lack of a mechanical one-to-one correspondence between changes in money and in income that is the primary reason why I have long favored for the USA a quasi-automatic monetary policy under which the quantity of money would grow at a steady rate of 4 or 5 percent per year, month-in, month-out. (The desirable rate of growth will differ from country to country depending on the trends in output and money-holding propensities.)

There is a great deal of evidence from the past of attempts by monetary authorities to do better. The verdict is very clear. The attempts by monetary authorities to do better have done far more harm than good. The actions by the monetary authorities have been an important source of instability. As I have already indicated, the actions of the US monetary authorities were responsible for the 1929—33 catastrophe. They were responsible equally for the recent acceleration of inflation in the USA. That is why I have been and remain strongly opposed to discretionary monetary policy—at least until such time as we demonstrably know enough to limit discretion by more sophisticated rules than the steady-rate-of-growth rule I have suggested. That is why I have come to stress the danger of assigning too much weight to monetary policy. Just as I believe that Keynes disciples went further than he himself would have gone, so I think there is a danger that people who find that a few good predictions have been made by using monetary aggregates will try to carry that relationship further than it can go. In 1967 I wrote:

We are in danger of assigning to monetary policy a larger role than it can perform, in danger of asking it to accomplish tasks that it cannot achieve and, as a result, in danger of preventing it from making the contribution that it is capable of making.[3]

A steady rate of monetary growth at a moderate level can provide a framework under which a country can have little inflation and much growth. It will not produce perfect stability; it will not produce heaven on earth; but it can make an important contribution to a stable economic society.

NOTES

1.   I chose this title because I once used it for a talk at the London School of Economics. At that time, I was predicting. Now, I am reporting.
2.   Macmillan, London, 1923.
3.   Milton Friedman, "The Role of Monetary Policy", Presidential Address to the American Economic Association, 29 December, 1967: *American Economic Review*, March 1968 (reprinted in *The Optimum Quantity of Money and Other Essays*, Aldine Publishing, New York, 1969, pp. 95–110—quotation from p. 99).

HOMER JONES: A PERSONAL REMINISCENCE

1976

When I first met Homer Jones, he was a third older than I, a mature man of the world in my eyes—though, as I now look back, I realize that he was only a callow youth of twenty-four, in his second year of teaching. Yet, in the nearly half-century since, that original image has seemed to me to remain valid: in one sense, Homer matured early; in another sense, Homer never matured.

I met Homer when I was a junior at Rutgers University, where he had just arrived as an instructor, having gone from graduate work with Frank Knight at Chicago to teach at the University of Pittsburgh for one year, and then on to Rutgers—if I recall rightly mainly in order to coordinate better with the professional activity of his wife, Alice Hanson. As low man on the academic totem pole, Homer was stuck with teaching, among other courses, insurance and statistics—two subjects that I doubt he had been exposed to before. At the time, I was planning to become an actuary, so naturally I took both these subjects. Only later did I realize how fortunate I was. Insurance would hardly seem a subject of far-ranging significance, yet Homer made it one. His quizzical mind, his theoretical bent, yet withal his Iowa farmer interest in down-to-earth practical matters, combined to lead us far beyond the dry, matter-of-fact textbook into the much more fundamental issues of *Risk, uncertainty, and profit*.

In statistics, Homer was clearly learning along with us, and that experience has always persuaded me that the blind can in fact lead the blind—or is the right aphorism that in the country of the blind, the one-eyed man is king. Because he was just learning, Homer could recognize the points of difficulty. Because he was so mature despite his chronological youth, he had neither false pride nor false modesty. He did not try to hide his limited knowledge of mathematics and statistics, but neither was there any question, on his part or ours, that he was the teacher and we the students.

The pattern of that course has characterized Homer ever since, with far less objective justification. Homer's shrewd questions and critical evaluations belie the profession of ignorance and puzzlement. But the tactic is extremely effective in leading others to examine more carefully their premises, improve their argument, and understand more deeply their conclusions.

Chronological maturity which can bring wisdom and self-confidence and, less often, modesty, also often brings a dulling of the inquisitive sense, of the feeling of wonder, of the openness to new ideas that is the pearl of youth. It is in this sense that Homer has never matured. Today, as when I first met him, Homer's great forte is asking interesting and probing questions, not accepting superficial answers, and retaining the attitude that we all have a great deal to learn. He combines with this a great belief in the persuasive power of hard facts and an unusual patience in pressing his views.

Homer's inquisitiveness, his hunger for information and understanding, rested, even when I first knew him, on a bed-rock of strong values and firmly held principles. He first introduced me to what was even then known as the Chicago view. A disciple of Frank Knight, and like him a product of the rural midwest, he put major stress on individual freedom, was cynical and skeptical about attempts to interfere with the exercise of individual freedom in the name of social planning or collective values, yet was by no means a nihilist. It has always seemed to me a paradox in Frank Knight, to a lesser extent in Homer—and I can believe that others say the same about me—that they could be at once so cynical, realistic, and negative about the effects of reform measures and yet at the same time such ardent proponents of the 'right' reform measures.

The paradox is perhaps brought out best by an episode in which Homer was not involved. One evening in the early 1950s, a group of us were discussing various economic issues at Frank Knight's house, with much of the discussion consisting of Charles Hardy opposing one proposed change after another. Finally, Frank Knight said, 'Hardy, is there anything wrong in the world?' Quick as a flash, Hardy retorted, 'Yes, there are too damn many reformers.' How strange and yet how correct that Knight should be labeled a 'reformer.'

Homer, along with Arthur Burns, another of my teachers at Rutgers, was primarily responsible for my going on in economics—rather than in actuarial work or mathematics—both by opening my eyes to the broader reaches of economics and to the beauties and intricacies of economic theory, and, on a more practical level, by getting me a scholarship to Chicago. Until that time, I had never been west of the Delaware River—except perhaps to Philadelphia—and without Homer's advice and encouragement, it would never have occurred to me to take graduate work in Chicago.

From Rutgers, Homer returned to graduate work at Chicago, then joined the New Deal migration of economists to Washington, where, after a year at Brookings, he settled in for a decade at the then recently established Federal Deposit Insurance Corporation. Before our marriage, my wife worked for him as a research assistant for a time. Her fondest memory is of Homer's daily greeting—his 'good morning' was always accompanied by either a nugget of freshly acquired information or a question that had been nagging him, that he could not answer, but always asked as if she obviously could. Also, the never-ending files—the reams of clippings and other odds and ends that piqued Homer's curiosity and that he wanted to squirrel away because he was sure that they would sometime be useful.

My own contacts with Homer were rather limited during this decade or the succeeding decade when he was at the Board of Governors of the Federal Reserve System. We were personal friends, part of the Chicago circle and more particularly the group that regarded themselves as students of Frank Knight—including as key figures Lloyd Mints, Henry Simons, Aaron Director, Russell Nichols, Allen Wallis, and George Stigler. Already in the early thirties, Homer had joined with Allen, George, and me to edit *The Ethics of Competition* as an offering for Knight's 50th birthday. But beyond these personal and ideological connections, we had little professional interaction. While Homer was at the FDIC, I was not working primarily in the monetary area. After the war, when I was, and Homer was at the Federal Reserve Board, he came to be primarily responsible for the liquid assets survey, which the Fed conducted jointly with the Michigan Survey Research Center.

Throughout this period most of Homer's friends, and certainly my wife and I, believed that his talents were being grossly underutilized—and that remains my opinion today. But finally in 1958 when by some strange chance he was called and that is the proper word in this context—to the Federal Reserve Bank of St. Louis, propensity, capacity, and opportunity coalesced.

Homer was in his element as Director of Research and then Senior Vice President of the St. Louis Bank. He was at home again in the Midwest, in a bank that had always had a reputation for independence and iconoclasm (I once teased William McChesney Martin Jr. at a Federal Reserve meeting by referring to some critical remarks that his father had made at an open market meeting in 1930 or so when his father was Governor of the St. Louis Bank, remarking, 'You see, Bill, St. Louis was a maverick even then.'), and with a President, Darryl Francis, who shared his basic values, as well as his integrity and independence of character, and had a properly high regard for his abilities.

Between them, Homer and Darryl Francis converted the St. Louis Bank into by far the most important unit in the System. For the first time since the days of Walter Stewart, Winfield Riefler, and Randolph Burgess in the 1920s, monetary research from within the System began to influence academic research and thinking. For the first time, a bank publication, *The Review of the Federal Reserve Bank of St. Louis*, began to be cited regularly in the academic journals. This academic revival was joined with a similar penetration into practical affairs. Homer's insatiable curiosity about the facts, and his belief in the power of repeated exposure to the facts to erode illusion, led to the publication by the Bank of its now famed series of weekly and monthly collections of statistics. These preached no explicit doctrine. They simply presented numbers. Yet the appearance week after week of those clearly drawn charts of the money supply, did more than any other single thing, in my opinion, to bring about the change that has occurred from almost exclusive concentration in monetary policy on interest rates and on the esoteric 'tone and feel of the market' to stress on the quantity of money. The shift is not yet complete but without Homer, I doubt that it would have occurred to anything like the extent it has.

Homer's influence is not to be looked for primarily or even largely in publications over his name. His influence is manifest rather in the whole output of the Federal Reserve Bank of St. Louis, from its great contribution to the improvement of current monetary statistics, to the series of important and wide-ranging articles in its *Review*, to the speeches of its senior officials, to the positions taken at the Open Market Committee and before Congress by its President. It is to be found also in the people whom Homer searched out, attracted to St. Louis, taught and influenced, and who are now spread far and wide. The hallmark of his contribution is throughout those same traits that exerted so great an influence on me in my teens: complete intellectual honesty; insistence on rigor of analysis; concern with facts; a drive for practical relevance; and, finally, perpetual questioning and reexamination of conventional wisdom.

THE KEYNES CENTENARY: A MONETARIST REFLECTS

1983

J ohn Maynard Keynes was born 100 years ago this month. His economic views have been more influential than any other economist of his time, perhaps of all time. To commemorate the centenary of his birth, we asked four Nobel-prize-winning economists to write an essay on Keynes, assessing his contribution to economics and the way his ideas have been used in practice. Our four essayists are Professor Milton Friedman, Professor Friedrich Hayek, Professor Sir John Hicks, and Professor Paul Samuelson. Some are more sympathetic to Keynesian economics than others, but none doubts its significance. We start this week with Professor Milton Friedman, for many years at the University of Chicago and now at the Hoover Institution. He won the Nobel prize in 1976.

Some years ago, in replying to criticisms of my work mostly from a "Keynesian" point of view, I wrote:

> One reward from writing this reply has been the necessity of rereading earlier work, in particular [Keynes's] ... General Theory.

The General Theory is a great book, at once more naïve and more profound than the 'Keynesian economics' that Leijonhufvud contrasts with the 'economics of Keynes.' . . .

I believe that Keynes's theory is the right kind of theory in its simplicity, its concentration on a few key magnitudes, its potential fruitfulness. I have been led to reject it, not on these grounds, but because I believe that it has been contradicted by evidence: its predictions have not been confirmed by experience. This failure suggests that it has not isolated what are 'really' the key factors in short-run economic change.

The General Theory is profound in the wide range of problems to which Keynes applies his hypothesis, in the interpretations of the operation of the operation of modern economies and, particularly, of capital markets that are strewn throughout the book, and in the shrewd and incisive comments on the theories of his predecessors. These clothe the bare bones of his theory with an economic understanding that is the true mark of his greatness.

Rereading the General Theory has not only reinforced my confidence in the validity of the interpretation [of the 'Keynesian challenge to the quantity theory'] in my article; much more important, it has also reminded me what a great economist Keynes was and how much more I sympathies with his approach and aims than with those of many of his followers.

While the General Theory is a great book, I do not regard it as Keynes's best, precisely because, despite its brilliance, it records an unsuccessful experiment. Had the General Theory never been written, Keynes would nevertheless have deservedly been regarded as one of the great economists of all time—to be listed in the pantheon of great British economists along with Adam Smith, David Ricardo, John Stuart Mill, William Stanley Jevons, and Alfred Marshall.

His best book, in my no doubt jaundiced opinion, is his much briefer, more popular, less technical A Tract on Monetary Reform, published in 1923. That book was stimulated by the post-first-world-war inflations that ravaged so many European countries, and by what Keynes termed "the new ideas, now developing in many quarters" about monetary policy.

It was in considerable measure an outgrowth of his far more famous Economic Consequences of the Peace, published in 1919, in which he remarked: "There is no subtler, no surer means of overturning the existing basis of society than to debauch the currency. The process engages all the hidden forces of economic law on the side of destruction, and does it in a manner which not one man in a million is able to diagnose."

INFLATION WORRIED HIM

The concern with inflation dominates Monetary Reform, the contents of which are aptly summarized by the titles of its five chapters: " The Consequences to Society of Changes in the Value of Money"; "Public Finance and Changes in the Value of Money"; "The Theory of Money and of the Foreign Exchanges"; "Alternative Aims in Monetary Policy"; "Positive Suggestions for the Future Regulation of Money."

The book is strictly in the quantity-theory tradition as developed to Keynes's teacher Alfred Marshall, to whom he pays repeated tribute. At one point, in expanding on a quotation from Marshall. Keynes sets out to explain the "error often made by careless adherents of the quantity theory, which may partly explain why it is not universally accepted". In the course of this discussion, he made his famous and much-quoted remark, "*In the long run* we are all dead" (italics in Keynes's original).

The context was a discussion of how changes in the quantity of money would, in the short run, affect velocity and output as well as prices, though "in the long run" the whole effect would be on prices. "But," Keynes then went on, "this long run is a misleading guided to current affairs. In the long run we are all dead. Economists set themselves too easy, too useless a task if in tempestuous seasons they can only tell us that when the storm is long past the ocean is flat again."

THE ADAPTABLE THEORIST

As someone who has spent much of his professional life studying and trying to understand those short-run storms, I am wholly in accord with the substance of Keynes's comment. Yet his abrupt dismissal of "the long run" reflects an important facet of Keynes's character.

Keynes was unusually quick and flexible—both in his mental reactions and in the policy positions he adopted. He was attuned far more closely to the "tempestuous seasons" than to the dead calm, and could adapt his views to the tempest as it raged. The best example is with respect to his brief flirtation with protectionism in 1931. Britain, along with other countries on the gold standard, was experiencing sharp deflation, thanks (as Anna Schwartz and I show in our Monetary History) to the decline in the quantity of money in the United States. It was clear to Keynes that the best solution was for Britain to devalue. However, regarding devaluation as politically not feasible, he was led "somewhat in desperation", as he noted in reprinting his article "Proposals for a Revenue Tariff," to suggest "a tariff combined, if possible, with a bounty to exports"—or, in other words, a concealed devaluation.

As has occurred repeatedly with economists, his political judgment was highly defective. Six months later, on September 21, 1931, Britain devalued and left the gold standard. Within a week, in a letter of September 28, 1931, to The Times, Keynes wrote "the immediate question for attention is not a tariff but the currency question." In reprinting this letter in his Essays in Persuasion, he added a most revealing footnote: "Not all my Free Trade friends proved to be so prejudiced as I had thought. For after a tariff was no longer necessary, many of them were found voting for it."

As this episode reveals, Keynes's flexibility was both a virtue and a vice. It enabled him to adapt his ideas and proposals promptly to changing circumstances. But it also meant that he was something of a fine-tuner, that he tended to neglect the cumulative effect of short-run policies. The truth that in the long run we are all dead needs to be balanced by the equally relevant truth that the long run consists of a succession of short runs.

Keynes's flexibility and fine-tuning propensities were in accord with his elitist political philosophy, his conception of a society run by an able corps of public-spirited intellectuals entitled to power that they could be counted on to exercise in the interest of the masses. They may also have been related to an excessive confidence in his ability to shape public opinion. As Roy Harrod noted, in commenting on the tariff episode, "It seemed to me ... that he was relying too much on public opinion being amenable to his reasoning ... in holding that ... it would be at all easy to remove Protection when revival came."

Keynes's flexibility and his attribution to others of his own capacity to adapt his views to changing circumstances led him astray in matters far removed from economic policy. In a forthcoming review in the Journal of Economic Literature of the volume of his writings dealing with his activities from 1931 to 1939, Anna Schwartz refers to

> his statement in a conversation with Kingsley Martin ... that he liked and respected "the post-war generation of intellectual Communists under thirty-five," and while sympathizing with "Mr. Bevin in fighting shy of contact with the professional Communists, regarding their body as a Trojan horse and their overtures in doubtful faith ... But I would risk the contact all the same, so as not to lose touch with the splendid material of the young amateur Communists. For with them in their ultimate maturity lies the future."

Schwartz goes on to say "The 'splendid material' in the event turned out to include the duplicitous spies for Russia—Anthony Blunt, Guy Burgess,

Donald McLean, Kim Philby, and Michael Straight—some if not all of whom Keynes certainly knew at Cambridge."

PERMANENT TRUTHS

Another example, of a very different kind, of Keynes's flexibility is contained in his final article—one that was published posthumously—dealing with international trade. " I find myself moved," he wrote,

> not for the first time, to remind contemporary economists that the classical teaching embodied some permanent truths of great significance, which we are liable today to overlook because we associate them with other doctrines which we cannot now accept without much qualification. There are in these matters deep undercurrents at work, natural forces, we can call them, or even the invisible hand, which are operating toward equilibrium.

A bit later, he referred to the "modernist stuff, gone wrong and turned sour and silly, [that] is circulating in our system."

I have always regarded it as a tragedy—for Britain and the world—that Keynes's life was cut so short. He was the only person in postwar Britain who had the prestige, the intellectual force, and the persuasive power to have prevented his disciples from carrying his ideas to extremes that he would have avoided and applying them under conditions very different from those that they were constructed to explain. The posthumous article suggests, I have always believed, the direction in which he would have moved if he had lived a few years longer.

Keynes's concern with inflation, expressed in the Economic Consequences and in Monetary Reform, did not disappear when the key problem in Britain became unemployment rather than inflation. It was simply put on the back burner for the time being. The second world war brought it back to the fore, which led Keynes to write his important pamphlet How to Pay for the War, in which he proposed a programme of compulsory savings in order to avoid the inflationary financing of the war, "the worst possible solution."

Inflation, not unemployment, continued to be the major economic problem after the war, as it was during the war. Keynes's sensitivity to the problems of the day, his emphasis on the short run, his flexibility would have led him to turn his attention increasingly to the policy themes of Monetary Reform, which were far more relevant to the postwar decades than those of the General Theory.

POLICY FIRST

Though Keynes was a great theorist, his interest in theory was not for its own sake but as a basis for designing policy. In Monetary Reform, his conclusions about "the evil consequences of instability in the standard of value" led him to examine "the theory of money and of the foreign exchanges" in order to "lay the theoretical foundations for the practical suggestions of the concluding chapters."

His most original contribution, in my opinion, was his emphasis on the conflict between stability of prices and stability of exchange:

> If . . . the external price level lies outside our control, we must submit either to our own internal price level or to our exchange being pulled about by external influences. If the external price level is unstable, we cannot keep both our own price level and our exchanges stable. And we are compelled to choose.

As an aside, Keynes could state the issue as a dilemma because he implicitly assumed away the possibility of foreign exchange control as an alternative to a variable exchange rate for disconnecting the internal price level from the external price level. Hjalmar Schacht's invention (or perfection) of detailed exchange control in 1934 for a very different purpose (to despoil the Jews and other refugees) has forced those of us who have written on this subject more recently to expand Keynes's dilemma to a trilemma. A country is compelled to choose two of the following three desirable objectives: stable prices (or, more generally, an independent monetary policy), a stable exchange rate (or, more generally, a predetermined path of exchange rates), freedom from exchange controls.

Keynes had no doubt about his own choice; he was unequivocally for giving internal price stability priority over stability in exchange rates, and certainly over a pre-first-world-war gold standard. "In truth, the gold standard is already a barbarous relic"—another of those memorable phrases that seemed to come effortlessly from his, if I may say so, golden pen. "Advocates of the ancient standard do not observe how remote if now is from the spirit and the requirements of the age. A regulated non-metallic standard has slipped in unnoticed. It exists."

I have long shared Keynes's view on this subject, simply expanding it to include the rejection of exchange control as a device for disconnecting the internal from the external price level. And clearly, actual policy in the major countries of the world has moved slowly and at long last in the same direction—not, indeed, in the sense of achieving stable prices, but of accepting flexible exchange rates and, for the most part, rejecting exchange controls in order to preserve independence in domestic monetary policy.

MANAGEMENT BENIGN?

Where I have disagreed with the views Keynes expressed in Monetary Reform and subsequently is with respect to the appropriate method for achieving a stable price level. Keynes favored managed money and managed exchange rates—that is, discretionary control by monetary authorities (the Bank of England in Britain, the Federal Reserve System in the United States) over the "supply of currency and credit with a view to maintaining, so far as possible, the stability of the internal price level"; and "over the supply of foreign exchange so as to avoid purely temporary fluctuations . . . in the relation between the internal and external price level." He was confident that the authorities had—or could have—sufficient knowledge to achieve these objectives and that, given the power, they would use it for that purpose.

Discretion in the hands of public-spirited and competent civil servants fitted in well with Keynes's elitist political philosophy. But it must also be granted that, at the time he wrote, little or no experience existed to judge how such a method of regulating the supply of money would work in practice.

The situation is very different today. Since 1931 in Britain, since 1933 in America, both countries have had precisely the kind of managed systems that Keynes advocated and, since 1971, they have not even paid token obeisance to the "barbarous relic." The results have been anything but the achievement of either stable prices or stable exchange rates. The era of managed money has also been an era of greater and more widespread instability in both prices and exchange rates than any earlier period, except only the immediate period after the first world war which stimulated Monetary Reform.

Unfortunately, the available knowledge (including Monetary Reform) has either not been adequate to enable the monetary authorities to achieve Keynes's objectives or has been overwhelmed by the political and institutional pressures on the authorities to use their powers for very different purposes. My own conclusion, to paraphrase Clemenceau's remark about war, is that money is much too serious a matter to be left to the central bankers—or, for that matter, to economists.

It is impossible to judge how Keynes himself would have reacted to the actual experience with managed money. One thing alone is certain; he would have adjusted his theory to that experience and have come forward with a changed set of policies. It is no tribute to this genius to treat his specific proposals developed for specific problems as if they were engraved in stone and applicable for all time.

CREATIVE FROM THE START

I cannot close this comment on Keynes without at least noting an expression of his creative originality in a field outside of economics: namely, this Treatise on Probability, a rewritten version of his fellowship dissertation at King's College (1909) which was not published until 1921. Just as much recent economic thought has returned to the themes of Monetary Reform, so much recent work in statistics has returned to the themes of the Treatise on Probability. Both L. J. Savage and Bruno de Finetti, two of the pioneers of the Bayesian revolution in statistics, linked their own concept of personal probability to a concept of subjective probability such as that which Keynes developed in his Treatise.

Keynes was truly a remarkable scientist, even if, to use the words that William Stanley Jevons applied to an earlier brilliant economist, David Ricardo, he "shunted the car of economics on to a wrong line" for some decades.

FREEZING
HIGH-POWERED
MONEY

1984

T he final proposal combines features from most of the preceding. It is radical and far-reaching, yet simple.

The proposal is that, after a transition period, the quantity of high-powered money—non-interest-bearing obligations of the U.S. government—be frozen at a fixed amount. These non-interest-bearing obligations now take two forms: currency and deposits at the Federal Reserve System. The simplest way to envisage the change is to suppose that Federal Reserve deposit liabilities were replaced dollar for dollar by currency notes, which were turned over to the owners of those deposits. Thereafter, the government's monetary role would be limited to keeping the amount constant by replacing worn-out currency. In effect, a monetary rule of zero growth in high-powered money would be adopted. (In practice, it would not be necessary to replace deposits at the Federal Reserve with currency; they could be retained as book entries, so long as the total of such book entries plus currency notes was kept constant.)

As noted above, the Fed currently has two roles: determining the quantity of money; and regulating banking institutions and providing such services as collateralized loans, check-clearing, wire transfers, and the like. Under this proposal its first role would be eliminated. In this sense, the proposal would end the independence of the Federal Reserve System. Its second role could, if desired, be continued, preferably by combining it with the similar roles of the FDIC, the FSLIC, and the comptroller of the currency, as suggested earlier.

The proposal would be consistent with, indeed require, the continued existence of private institutions issuing claims to government currency. These could be regulated as now, with the whole paraphernalia of required reserves, bank examinations, limitations on lending, and the like. However, they could also be freed from all or most such regulations. In particular, the need for reserve requirements to enable the Fed to control the quantity of money would disappear.

Reserve requirements might still be desirable for a different though related reason. The new monetary economists argue that only the existence of such government regulations as reserve requirements and prohibition of the private issuance of currency explains the relatively stable demand for high-powered money. In the absence of such regulations, they contend, non-interest-bearing assets, or, at the very least, the demand for such money would be rendered highly unstable.

I am far from persuaded by this contention. It supposes a closer approach to a frictionless world with minimal transaction costs than seems to me a useful approximation to the actual world. Nonetheless, it is arguable that the elimination of reserve requirements would introduce an unpredictable and erratic element into the demand for high-powered money. For that reason, although personally I would favor the deregulation of financial institutions, thereby incorporating a major element of Hayek's proposed competitive financial system, it would seem prudent to proceed in stages: first, freeze high-powered money; then, after a period, eliminate reserve requirements and other remaining regulations, including the prohibition on the issuance of hand-to-hand currency by private institutions.

Why zero growth? Zero has a special appeal on political grounds that is not shared by any other number. If 3 percent, why not 4 percent? It is hard, as it were, to go to the political barricades to defend 3 rather than 4, or 4 rather than 5. But zero is—as a psychological matter—qualitatively different. It is what has come to be called a Schelling point—a natural point at which people tend to agree, like "splitting the difference" in a dispute over a monetary sum. Moreover, by removing any power to create money it eliminate institutional arrangements lending themselves to discretionary changes in monetary growth.

Would zero growth in high-powered money be consistent with a healthy economy? In the hypothetical long-long-run stationary economy, when the whole economy had become adjusted to the situation, and population, real output, and so on were all stationary, zero growth in high-powered money would imply zero growth in other monetary aggregates and mean stable velocities for the aggregates. In consequence, the price level would be stable. In a somewhat less than stationary state in which output was rising, if financial innovations kept pace, the money multiplier would tend to rise at the same rate as output and again prices would be stable. If financial innovations ceased but total output continued to rise, prices would decline. If output rose at about 3 percent per year, prices would tend to fall at 3 percent per year. So long as that was known and relatively stable, all contracts could be adjusted to it, and it would cause no problems and indeed would have some advantages.

However, any such outcome is many decades away. The more interesting and important question is not the final stationary-state result but the intermediate dynamic process.

Once the policy was in effect, the actual behavior of nominal income and the price level would depend on what happened to a monetary aggregate like M1 relative to high-powered money and what happened to nominal income relative to M1—that is, on the behavior of the money multiplier (the ratio of M1 to high-powered money) and on the income velocity of M1 (the ratio of nominal income to M1).

Given a loosening of the financial structure through continued deregulation, there would be every reason to expect a continued flow of innovations raising the money multiplier. This process has in fact occurred throughout the past several centuries. For example, in the century from 1870 to 1970, the ratio of the quantity of money, as defined by Anna Schwartz and me in Monetary History, to high-powered rose at the average rate of 1 percent per year. In the post-World War II period, the velocity of M1 has risen at about 3 percent per year, and at a relatively steady rate. The trend cannot of course continue indefinitely. Above, in specifying a desirable target for the Fed, I estimated the rise in velocity would slow to about 1 or 2 percent per year. However, a complete end to the rapid trend in velocity is not in sight.

There is no way to make precise numerical estimates, but there is every reason to anticipate that for decades after the introduction of a freeze on high-powered money, both the money multiplier and velocity would tend to rise at rates in the range of historical experience. Under these circumstances, a zero rate of growth of high-powered money would imply roughly stable prices, though ultimately, perhaps, slightly declining prices.

What of the transition? Over the three years from 1979 to 1982, high-powered money grew an average of 7.0 percent a year. It would be desirable to bring that rate to zero gradually. As for M1 growth, above a five-year period seems appropriate—or a transition that reduces the rate of growth of high-powered money by about 1.5 percentage points a year. The only other transitional problem would be to phase out the Fed's powers to create and destroy high-powered money by open-market operations and discounting. Neither transition offers any special problem. The Fed, or its successor agency, could still use part of the existing stock of high-powered money for similar purposes, particularly for lender of last resort purposes, if that function were retained.

The great advantage of this proposal is that it would end the arbitrary power of the Federal Reserve System to determine the quantity of money and would do so without establishing any comparable locus of power and without introducing any major disturbances into other existing economic and financial institutions.

I have found that few things are harder even for knowledgeable non-experts to accept than the proposition that twelve (or nineteen) people sitting around a table in Washington, subject to neither election nor dismissal nor close administrative or political control, have the power to determine the quantity of money—to permit a reduction by one-third during the Great Depression or a near doubling from 1970 to 1980. That power is too important, too pervasive, to be exercised by a few people, however public-spirited, if there is any feasible alternative.

There is no need for such arbitrary power. In the system I have just described, the total quantity of any monetary aggregate would be determined by the market interactions of many financial institutions and millions of holders of monetary assets. It would be limited by the constant quantity of high-powered money available as ultimate reserves. The ratios of various aggregates to high-powered money would be doubtless change from time to time, but in the absence of rigid government controls—such as those exemplified by Regulation Q, fortunately being phased-out—the ratios would change gradually and only as financial innovations or changes in business and industry altered the proportions in which the public chose to hold various monetary assets. No small number of individuals would be in a position to introduce major changes in the ratios or in the rates of growth of various monetary aggregates—to move, for example, from a 3 percent per year rate of growth in M1 for one six-month period (January to July 1982) to a 13 percent rate of growth for the next six months (July 1982 to January 1983).

GEORGE JOSEPH STIGLER

JANUARY 17, 1911—DECEMBER 1, 1991

1993

I cannot pretend to objectivity in writing about George Stigler. For nearly sixty years he was either my closest friend or one of my closest friends. My debt to him, both personal and professional, is beyond measure. Despite deep sadness at his death, like so many others who knew him, I cannot think of him without an inadvertent smile rising to my lips. He was as quick of wit as of mind, and his wit always had a point. His occasional humorous articles—such as "A Sketch of the History of Truth in Teaching" (Stigler, 1973)—have become classics and demonstrate that had he, like an earlier Chicago Ph.D. in economics, Stephen Leacock, chosen to become a professional humorist as well as an economist, he would have achieved no less fame in the one field than in the other.

George Stigler was one of the great economists of the twentieth—or any other—century, with a gift for writing matched among modern economists only by John Maynard Keynes. Intellectual history was his first field of specialization. It remained a lasting love and provided a rich seedbed for his scientific work. A deep understanding of the ideas of the great economists of the past gave him a strong foundation on which to build an analysis of contemporary issues. Few economists have so consistently and successfully combined economic theory with empirical analysis, or ranged so widely. Stigler regarded economic theory, in the words of Alfred Marshall, as "an engine for the discovery of concrete truth," not as a subject of interest in its own right, a branch of mathematics.

PERSONAL HISTORY

George Stigler was born January 17, 1911, in Renton, Washington, a suburb of Seattle. He was the only child of Joseph and Elizabeth Hungler Stigler, who had separately migrated to the United States at the end of the nineteenth century, his father from Bavaria, his mother from what was then Austria-Hungary. George writes that his "father had been a brewer until prohibition drove that activity underground. Thereafter, he tried a variety of jobs," finally entering the real estate market. "My parents bought run-down places, fixed them up, and sold them. By the time I was sixteen, I had lived in sixteen different places in Seattle. But my parents had a comfortable if nomadic existence" (Stigler, 1988, pp. 9–10).

George went to public schools and then to the University of Washington, all in Seattle, receiving a B.A. in 1931. "An insatiable and utterly indiscriminate reader," he "got lots of good grades" at the University of Washington. He said that, when he graduated from college, he had "no thought of an academic career"; it was the depression and jobs in business were scarce, so he applied for and was awarded a fellowship at Northwestern University for graduate study in the business school, receiving an M.B.A. in 1932 (Stigler, 1988, p. 15). At Northwestern he developed an interest in economics and decided on an academic career. He returned to the University of Washington for one further year of graduate study, and then received a tuition scholarship to study economics at the University of Chicago. There he found an intense intellectual atmosphere that captivated him. Chicago became his intellectual home for the rest of his life, as a student from 1933 to 1936, a faculty member from 1958 to his death in 1991, and a leading member of and contributor to the "Chicago School" throughout. He received his Ph.D. in 1938.

At Chicago, Stigler was particularly influenced by Frank H. Knight, under whom he wrote his dissertation—a noteworthy feat, since only three or four students ever managed to complete a dissertation under Knight in his twenty-eight years on the Chicago faculty. Stimulating and influential in both economic analysis and social philosophy, Knight was a perfectionist and tended to inhibit students who came under his influence. It is a mark of Stigler's character and drive that he never succumbed to that aspect of Knight's influence; rather, he imbibed what he described as Knight's "devotion to the pursuit of knowledge . . . a sense of unreserved commitment to 'truth'" (Stigler, 1988, pp. 17–18).

The other faculty members whose influence George stressed were Jacob Viner, who taught economic theory and international economics; John U. Nef, economic historian; and their younger colleague Henry Simons, who became a close personal friend and whose *A Positive Program for Laissez Faire* greatly influenced Stigler and many of his contemporaries.

"At least as important to me," wrote George, "as the faculty were the remarkable students I met at Chicago," and he goes on to list W. Allen Wallis; the author of this memoir; Kenneth Boulding and Robert Shone from Great Britain; Sune Carlson from Sweden; Paul Samuelson; and Albert G. Hart—all of whom subsequently had distinguished careers (Stigler, 1988, pp. 23–25).

I overlapped George at Chicago for one year, 1934–35, during which he, W. Allen Wallis, and I formed what proved to be a lifelong friendship. As it happened, all three of our future spouses were also students at Chicago. George was to marry Margaret Mack, always known as Chick, who was majoring in social science. Allen would marry Anne Armstrong, an art history major, and I married Rose Director, whose major was economics. We soon formed a sextuple whose lives were intertwined from then on.

In 1936 George accepted an appointment as an assistant professor at Iowa State College (now University), and shortly thereafter was married to Margaret "Chick" Mack. George and Chick had three sons: Stephen, a professor of statistics at the University of Chicago; David, a corporate lawyer; and Joseph, a businessman. The family suffered a tragic loss in 1970, when Chick died unexpectedly, without any advance warning. George never remarried.

George accepted an appointment at the University of Minnesota in 1938 and then went on leave in 1942 to work first at the National Bureau of Economic Research and later at the Statistical Research Group of Columbia University, a group directed by Allen Wallis that was engaged in war research on behalf of the armed services. When the war ended in 1945, George returned to the University of Minnesota, but he remained only one year, leaving in 1946 to accept a professorship at Brown University. That simple statement conceals a traumatic experience. In George's words: "In the spring of 1946 I received the offer of a professorship from the University of Chicago and, of course, was delighted at the prospect. The offer was contingent upon approval by the central administration after a personal interview. I went to Chicago, met with the president, Ernest Colwell—because Robert Hutchins was ill that day—and I was vetoed! I was too empirical, Colwell said, and no doubt that day I was. So the professorship was offered to Milton Friedman, and President Colwell and I had launched the Chicago School" (Stigler, 1988, p. 40). It speaks volumes for George's character that the incident never cast the slightest shadow on our friendship.

In 1946 George and I were two of the thirty-six participants at a conference in Switzerland convened by Friedrich A. Hayek to discuss the dangers to a free society. The Mont Pelerin Society was founded at that conference and has since grown and flourished, providing a forum for members from all over the world to discuss the issues involved in achieving and maintaining political and economic freedom. An active member of the society until his death, George served as its president from 1976 to 1978.

After a year at Brown, George moved to Columbia, where he remained until 1958, despite several attempts by Theodore Schultz, chairman of the Chicago Department of Economics, to bring him to Chicago. In 1958 Allen Wallis, then dean of the University of Chicago business school, persuaded him to accept the Charles R. Walgreen professorship of American institutions. George remained at Chicago for the rest of his life. At Chicago he became an editor of the *Journal of Political Economy;* established the Industrial Organization Workshop, which achieved recognition as the key testing ground for contributions to the field of industrial organization; and in 1977 founded the Center for the Study of the Economy and the State, serving as its director until his death.

In the academic year 1957–58, George was a fellow at the Center for Advanced Study in the Behavioral Sciences at Stanford. From 1971 to his death, George was a fellow at the Hoover Institution at Stanford, and spent part of almost every year at Hoover.

George was president of the American Economic Association in 1964, and of the History of Economics Society in 1977. He was elected to the National Academy of Sciences in 1975. He received the Alfred Nobel Memorial Prize in Economic Science in 1982 "for his seminal studies of industrial structures, functioning of markets and causes and effects of public regulation." He received the National Medal of Science from Ronald Reagan in 1987.

George's governmental activities included service as a member of the attorney general's National Committee to Study the Antitrust Laws, 1954–55; chairman, Federal Price Statistics Review Committee, 1960–61; member, Blue Ribbon Panel of the Department of Defense, 1969–70; vice-chairman, Securities Investor Protection Corporation, 1970–73; co-chairman, Blue Ribbon Telecommunications Task Force, Illinois Commerce Commission, 1990–91.

A word about George as a person: In the nearly six decades of our friendship, I never knew him to do a mean or hurtful or unworthy thing to anyone. An ideal friend in time of trouble, he would go to any lengths to be helpful.

He always appeared casual and unhurried, seeming to have ample time for golf (his favorite sport), tennis, bridge, carpentry, photography (his favorite hobby), casual talk with friends, consultations with students, and constructive and detailed criticisms of the writings of his students and academic friends. Yet, he also was incredibly productive, turning out a steady stream of fundamental contributions. Truly, as his son Stephen said at a memorial service, "My father had phenomenal energy."

One feature of George's personality that he did his best to conceal was his extreme personal sensitivity. His smart cracks were in part a way of covering that sensitivity, as was his half-embarrassed laugh. He was as sensitive to others as to himself. The stiletto concealed in his humor was always meant for ideas or policies, never ad hominem—unless "An Economist Plays with Blocs" (1954), his brilliant title for an article on Galbraith's theory of countervailing power, can be so interpreted.

George was a delightful correspondent. Serious and profound discussion never came without an interlarding of amusing comments. In a letter from London in 1948 when he was giving *Five Lectures on Economic Problems* (1949), after remarking on the inconvertibility of the pound and the inedible, still-rationed food, he concluded, "So here I am losing weight and gaining pounds."

George was an extremely valuable colleague. He provided much of the energy and drive to the interaction among members of the Chicago economics department, business school, and law school that came to be known at the Chicago School. His workshop on industrial organization was an outgrowth of a law school seminar started by Aaron Director, which George cooperated in running when he came to Chicago. His relations were especially close with Aaron, Gary Becker, Richard Posner, Harold Demsetz, and myself, enhancing significantly the scientific productivity of all of us.

STIGLER AS SCIENTIST

History of Thought

Stigler's doctoral dissertation, published as *Production and Distribution Theories* (1941), was a historical survey of neoclassical theories that remains the definitive study of its subject. That book was followed by a steady flow of perceptive, thoughtful, and beautifully written articles and books interpreting the contributions of his predecessors, some of which were collected in *Essays in the History of Economics* (1965).

Throughout, Stigler's interest was in "the essential structure of the . . . analytical system" of the authors whose work he examined (Stigler, 1969, p. 220). In judging that analytical system, he placed great stress on its implications for observable phenomena. "Surprising as it may sound, no previous scholar had ever examined the development of the discipline with anything like the same insistence that intellectual progress had to be measured in terms of its ability to generate empirically refutable propositions" (Rosenberg, 1993, p. 836). Stigler tried not only to identify such propositions but to put them to the test, often with data that would have been available to the author whose work he was examining.

During most of Stigler's professional career, the history of economic thought was in the doldrums as a field of study. His writing played a major role in keeping the field alive and enhancing its attractiveness. By the end of his career, the field was flourishing, thanks in part to the example he set and to the new directions for research that he pioneered.

Price Theory

George's first important publication after his doctoral thesis was a textbook, *The Theory of Competitive Price* (1942), which was followed by revised versions under the title *The Theory of Price* in 1946, 1952, 1966, and 1987. Its systematic linking of highly abstract theory to observable phenomena is unique among intermediate textbooks in price theory, as is its concise yet rigorous exposition. That feature, according to Thomas Sowell, one of his students, "made it probably the least readable thing Stigler ever wrote. It was not a matter of convoluted writing or confused thought—Stigler was never guilty of either of these common academic sins—but of excessive condensation that required painstakingly slow pondering over every concentrated thought. If the book had been three times as long, it could have been read in half the time. Still, it remained something of a classic, though Stigler himself made many a wry joke about its supposedly meager sales. It was the kind of book that teachers of price theory courses read themselves, while they assigned some other text to the class" (Sowell, 1993, pp. 785–86).

The linkage of fact and theory in his textbook foreshadowed his subsequent scientific work. His many contributions to economic theory were all a byproduct of seeking to understand the real world, and nearly all led to an attempt to provide some quantitative evidence to test the theory or to provide empirical counterparts to theoretical concepts.

An early example of the latter is an article on "The Cost of Subsistence" (1945), which starts, "Elaborate investigations have been made of the adequacy of diets at various income levels, and a considerable number of 'low-cost,' 'moderate,' and 'expensive' diets have been recommended to consumers. Yet, so far as I know, no one has determined the minimum cost of obtaining the amounts of calories, proteins, minerals, and vitamins which these studies accept as adequate or optimum." George then set himself to determine the minimum cost diet, in the process producing one of the earliest formulations of a linear programming problem in economics, for which he found an approximate solution, explaining that "there does not appear to be any direct method of finding the minimum of a linear function subject to linear constraints." Two years later George Dantzig provided such a direct method, the simplex method, now widely used in many economic and industrial applications.

George's approximate solution—very close to the best possible one—cost very little, far less than the standard low-cost adequate diet, demonstrating that those diets could not be defended as "scientific" but reflected mainly allowance for taste and variety rather than simply for nutritive adequacy. The estimated cost of such low-cost diets has subsequently become the basis for the widely used poverty levels of income, assuring the continued significance of this finding.

History of thought apart, George's impact was greatest and most lasting in the three fields that were singled out in the Nobel citation, those he labeled the economics of information, the theory of economic regulation, and the organization of industry.

"The Economics of Information" is the title of a seminal article (Stigler, 1961) that gave birth to an essentially new area of study for economists. In his intellectual autobiography, George termed it, "My most important contribution to economic theory" (Stigler, 1988, pp. 79–80). The article begins, "One should hardly have to tell academicians that information is a valuable resource: knowledge is power. And yet it occupies a slum dwelling in the town of economics. Mostly it is ignored." Stigler then proceeded to illustrate the importance of subjecting information to economic analysis with two examples: the dispersion of prices and the role of advertising (Stigler, 1961, pp. 213–25).

This article is a splendid illustration of several of Stigler's signal virtues: creativity (which he defined as consisting "of looking at familiar things or ideas in a new way"), the capacity to extract new insights about those seemingly familiar things, and the ability to state his main points in a provocative and eminently readable way.

As he wrote in his Nobel memorial lecture,

> The proposal to study the economics of information was promptly and widely accepted. Within a decade and a half, the literature had become so extensive and the theorists working in

the field so prominent, that the subject was given a separate classification in the *Index of Economic Articles*, and more than a hundred articles a year are now devoted to the subject.

The absence of controversy was certainly no tribute to the definitiveness of my exposition. . . . The absence of controversy was due instead to the fact that no established scientific theory was being challenged by this work; in fact, all I was challenging was the neglect of a promising subject (Stigler, 1983, p. 539).

The historian of economic thought practicing his craft on himself.

Economic Regulation

Starting from the traditional view that government regulation was instituted for the protection of the public, Stigler was struck by the absence of any quantitative studies of the actual effect of regulation. His first effort to remedy this was directed at the regulation of the prices of public utilities. The result was a 1962 article written jointly with Claire Friedland, his long-time associate, entitled "What Can Regulators Regulate? The Case of Electricity," which concluded that regulation of electric utilities had produced no significant effect on rates charged. This was followed two years later by "Public Regulation of the Securities Market," which concluded that purchasers of new stock issues fared no better (or worse) after the creation of the Securities and Exchange Commission than before.[1] These articles, like "The Economics of Information," opened a floodgate of empirical studies of the effects of economic regulation. Economists could no longer simply take it for granted that the effects of regulation corresponded to the stated intentions.[2]

These essays "also posed a basic problem: If regulation does not generally achieve its stated objectives, why have so many agencies been established and kept in existence?" (Schmalensee, 1987, p. 499). "The Theory of Economic Regulation" (Stigler, 1971) presents Stigler's answer to that question. The "central thesis of the article," Stigler wrote, "is that, as a rule, regulation is acquired by the industry and is designed and operated primarily for its benefit." He notes that two "alternative views of the regulation of industry are widely held. The first is that regulation is instituted primarily for the protection and benefit of the public at large or some large subdivision of the public . . . The second view is essentially that the political process defies rational explanation." He then gives example after example to support his own thesis, which by now has become the orthodox view in the profession, concluding, "The idealistic view of public regulation is deeply imbedded in professional economic thought . . . The fundamental vice of such a [view] is that it misdirects attention"—to preaching to the regulators rather than changing their incentives.

Stigler's analysis fed the emerging field that has since come to be called "public choice" economics: the shift from viewing the political market as not susceptible to economic analysis, as one in which disinterested politicians and bureaucrats pursue the "public interest," to viewing it as one in which the participants are seeking, as in the economic market, to pursue their own interest, and hence subject to analysis with the usual tools of economics. The seminal work that deserves much of the credit for launching public choice, *The Calculus of Consent*, by James Buchanan and Gordon Tullock, appeared in the same year as the Stigler-Friedland article.

"Smith's Travels on the Ship of State," published in the same year as "The Theory of Economic Regulation," raises the same question on a broader scale. Smith gives self-interest pride of place in analyzing the economic market, but he does not give it the same role in analyzing the political market. Smith's failure to do so constitutes Stigler's main—indeed, nearly only—criticism of the *Wealth of Nations*, that "stupendous palace erected upon the granite of self interest" (Rosenberg, 1993, p. 835). The same theme pervades many of Stigler's later publications.

The Organization of Industry (1968) is the title of a book whose "main content," as Stigler says in the preface, "is a reprinting of 17 articles I have written over the past two decades [including "Economics of Information"] in the area of industrial organization ... Although the main topics in industrial organization are touched upon, the touch is often light. The ratio of hypotheses to reasonably persuasive confirmation is distressingly high in all of economic literature, and it must be my chief and meager defense that I am not the worst sinner in the congregation." Stigler's main contribution to the field, both in this book and later writing, was the use of empirical evidence to test hypotheses designed to explain features of industrial organization. Article after article combines subtle theoretical analysis with substantial nuggets of empirical evidence, presented so casually as to conceal the care with which the data were compiled and the effort that was expended to determine what data were both relevant and accessible. These articles record the shift in Stigler's views on antitrust—from initial support of an activist antitrust policy to skepticism about even a minimalist policy—that led up to his path-breaking article on "The Theory of Economic Regulation" (Stigler, 1971).

Two other facets of Stigler's contributions deserve mention. First, his essays written for the general public, collected in three volumes, *The Intellectuals and the Marketplace* (1963), *The Citizen and the State* (1975), and *The Economist as Preacher* (1982). "There he [the intelligent layman] will find a potpourri of wit and seriousness blended with a high writing style" (Demsetz, 1982, p. 656). Second, his role as editor and reviewer. "For 19 years Stigler was a very successful editor of the *Journal of Political Economy*. Under his leadership this journal solidified its high reputation among economists" (Becker, 1993, p. 765). His complete bibliography lists 73 reviews in 24 publications ranging from strictly professional, like the *Journal of Political Economy* (22) and the *American Economic Review* (10), to the popular, like the *Wall Street Journal* (5), and the *New York Times* (3), and dating from 1939 to 1989.

Stigler's last book, his intellectual autobiography, *Memoirs of an Unregulated Economist* (1988), is a delight to read. As I described it at the time:

"Stigler's memoirs are a gem: in style, in wit, and above all, in substance, they reflect accurately his own engaging personality and his extraordinarily diverse contributions to our science."

STIGLER AS TEACHER

Stigler was also a great teacher. Many who knew him only casually, especially in his younger years, were offended by his wit, which could be biting, and his unerring ability to find just the right response to deflate pomposity and pretentiousness. His students never had that reaction. He was uniformly available, tolerant of their lack of understanding of subtle points, and willing to go to any length to help them. He inspired them by his own high standards and instilled a respect for economics as a serious subject concerned with real problems.

As John Lothian, one of my students who took several courses from Stigler, wrote me after Stigler's death: "His lectures taught me how to think about economics . . . His public persona was one of not suffering fools gladly, but that certainly did not come across in the classroom or in his individual meetings with us to talk over what we were doing in our papers for the course . . . He seemed quite willing to put up with foolishness from us as long as it seemed like we might ultimately get somewhere with what we were doing."[3] Another student of Stigler's, Thomas Sowell, wrote: "What Stigler really taught, whether the course was industrial organization or the history of economic thought, was intellectual integrity, analytical rigor, respect for evidence—and skepticism toward the fashions and enthusiasms that come and go" (Sowell, 1993, p. 788).

Stigler supervised many doctoral dissertations at both Columbia and the University of Chicago, a sharp contrast with the record of Frank Knight, under whom Stigler wrote his thesis. His students come close to dominating the field of industrial organization.[4]

FINAL WORD

I give final word on Stigler to his colleague and fellow recipient of the Nobel Memorial Prize in Economic Science, Ronald Coase:

> He is equally at home in the history of ideas, economic theory, and the study of politics. Even more remarkable is the variety of ways in which he handles a problem; he moves from the marshaling of high theory to aphorism to detailed statistical analysis, a mingling of treatments.... It is by a magic of his own that Stigler arrives at conclusions which are both unexpected and important. Even those who have reservations about his conclusions will find that a study of his argument has enlarged their understanding of the problem being discussed and that aspects are revealed which were previously hidden. Stigler never deals with a subject which he does not illuminate. And he expresses his views in a style uniquely Stiglerian, penetrating, lively, and spiced with wit. His writings are easy to admire, a joy to read, and impossible to imitate (Coase, 1991, p. 472).

NOTES

1.   Both essays are reprinted in *The Citizen and the State: Essays on Regulation*, pp. 61–77, 78–100. Chicago: University of Chicago Press, 1975.
2.   Sam Peltzman recalculated the empirical results in the Stigler-Friedland article to correct a mistake in the original. His thoughtful and sophisticated article brings the story up to date (Peltzman, 1993).
3.   Personal letter dated Dec. 3, 1991.
4.   According to Claire Friedland, Stigler's associate for many years, he served on more than forty thesis committees at Chicago, perhaps forty more at Columbia, and chaired a considerable fraction of those committees.

REFERENCES

1. Becker, G. S. 1993. George Joseph Stigler. *J. Polit. Econ.* 101:761–67.
2. Coase, R. 1991. George J. Stigler. In *Remembering the University of Chicago*, ed. E. Shils, pp. 469–78. Chicago: University of Chicago Press.
3. Demsetz, H. 1982. The 1982 Nobel Prize in economics. *Science* 218:655–57.
4. Peltzman, S. 1993. George Stigler's contribution to the economic analysis of regulation. *J. Polit. Econ.* 101:818–32.
5. Rosenberg, N. 1993. George Stigler: Adam Smith's best friend. *J. Polit. Econ.* 101:833–48.
6. Schmalensee, R. 1987. *The New Palgrave: A Dictionary of Economics*, vol. 4, eds. J. Eatwell, M. Milgate, and P. Newman, pp. 499–500. New York: Stockton Press.
7. Sowell, T. 1993. A student's eye view of George Stigler. *J. Polit. Econ.* 101:784–92.
8. Stigler, G. J. 1961. The economics of information. *J. Polit. Econ.* 69:213–25.
9. ———. 1969. Does economics have a useful past? *Hist. Polit. Econ.* 1:217–30.
10. ———. 1971. The theory of economic regulation. *Bell J. Econ. Man. Sci.* 2:3–21.
11. ——— 1973. A sketch of the history of truth in teaching. *J. Polit. Econ.* 81:491–95.
12. ——— 1975. *The Citizen and the State: Essays on Regulation*. Chicago: University of Chicago Press.
13. ——— 1983. Nobel lecture: The process and progress of economics. *J. Polit. Econ.* 91:529–45.
14. ——— 1988. *Memoirs of an Unregulated Economist*. New York: Basic Books.

REFLECTIONS ON
A MONETARY HISTORY

2004

I t is a source of real gratification that Anna Schwartz's and my book should be deemed worthy of a retrospective after forty years. The extensive research of the past forty years plus the additional forty years of history certainly require many modifications in detail in the story as we told it. However, I believe that our major themes have held up remarkably well. The most controversial of those—our attribution to the Federal Reserve of a major share of the responsibility for the 1929–33 contraction—has become almost conventional wisdom. Money does matter.

THE FED'S PERFORMANCE

In an April 15, 1958, *Wall Street Journal* op-ed, I wrote, "No major institution in the U.S. has so poor a record of performance over so long a period as the Federal Reserve, yet so high a public recognition." That conclusion was, I believe, amply justified by our book and experience in the quarter century after its publication. Fortunately, as I wrote in a *Wall*

Street Journal op-ed of August 19, 2003 ("The Fed's Thermostat"), it no longer is.

Since the mid-1980s, central banks around the world have reacted to the mounting evidence of monetary research by accepting the view that their basic responsibility is to produce price stability. More important, they have succeeded to a remarkable extent as they have discovered that, far from there being a tradeoff between price stability and economic stability, they are mutually supporting. The variability of prices is less by an order of magnitude since the mid-1980s than it was before, not only in the United States, but also in New Zealand (the first country to adopt an explicit inflation target), Great Britain, Euroland, Japan, and elsewhere.

Their success in controlling inflation has altered the empirical relation between short-term movements in money and in nominal income. Achieving price stability requires offsetting changes in velocity by opposite changes in the quantity of money, which reduces sharply the correlation between short-term movements in money and short-term movements in nominal income. To put it differently, short-term changes in the quantity of money can no longer be regarded as largely exogenous. They have become largely endogenous. If the central banks continue to be successful in curbing price fluctuations, they will have converted the quantity of money from an unruly master to an obedient servant.

The generalization that long-term changes in the quantity of money are reflected primarily in prices and little if at all in real output remains valid.

THE ROLE OF FRANCE

Reading the English translation of the memoirs of Emile Moreau (Governor of the Bank of France, 1926–28) persuaded me that we understated the role of France in the international transmission of the contraction. As I wrote in a foreword that I contributed to that book,

Had I fully appreciated these subtleties [in the French version of the memoirs] when Anna Schwartz and I were writing our *A Monetary History of the United States*, we would likely have assigned responsibility for the international character of the Great Depression somewhat differently. We attributed responsibility for the initiation of a worldwide contraction to the United States and I would not alter that judgment now. However, we also remarked "The international effects were severe and the transmission rapid, not only because the gold-exchange standard had rendered the international financial system more vulnerable to disturbances, but also because the United States did not follow gold-standard rules." Were I writing the sentence today, I would say, "because the United States and France did not follow gold-standard rules" [Moreau, Stoller, and Trevor 1991: xii].

VELOCITY

On the final text page of our book, we referred to the contrast between the downward secular trend of velocity before World War II, and the upward trend in the postwar period. And went on to say that "we expect the secular decline to be resumed. But . . . we shall have to wait for experience to unfold before discriminating finally among the alternative explanations."

Forty years of additional experience has now unfolded and, instead of declining, velocity has continued to rise at about the same secular rate as in the immediate postwar period. I believe we do not yet have an adequate explanation of why prewar and postwar trends have been in opposite directions.

A FINAL COMMENT

I cannot close without saying what a joy it was to collaborate for more than a quarter of a century with Anna Schwartz. As in all fruitful collaborations, neither of us alone could have produced *A Monetary History*. But the collaboration could have been fruitful without being pleasurable. Fortunately, it was both.

REFERENCES

1.   Moreau, E.; Stoller, S. D.; and Roberts, T. C. (1991) *The Golden Franc*. Boulder, Colo.: Westview Press.

COMMANDING HEIGHTS INTERVIEW

2000

ON FREEDOM AND FREE MARKETS

INTERVIEWER: Why are free markets and freedom inseparable?

MILTON FRIEDMAN: Freedom requires individuals to be free to use their own resources in their own way, and modern society requires cooperation among a large number of people. The question is, how can you have cooperation without coercion? If you have a central direction you inevitably have coercion. The only way that has ever been discovered to have a lot of people cooperate together voluntarily is through the free market. And that's why it's so essential to preserving individual freedom.

INTERVIEWER: Marxists say that property is theft. Why, in your view, is private property so central to freedom?

MILTON FRIEDMAN: Because the only way in which you can be free to bring your knowledge to bear in your particular way is by controlling your property. If you don't control your property, if somebody else controls it, they're going to decide what to do with it, and you have no possibility of exercising influence on it. The interesting thing is that there's a lot of knowledge in this society, but, as Friedrich Hayek emphasized so strongly, that knowledge is divided. I have some knowledge; you have some knowledge; he has some knowledge. How do we bring these scattered bits of knowledge back together? And how do we make it in the self-interest of individuals to use that knowledge efficiently? The key to that is private property, because if it belongs to me, you know, there's an obvious fact. Nobody spends somebody else's money as carefully as he spends his own. Nobody uses somebody else's resources as carefully as he uses his own. So if you want efficiency and effectiveness, if you want knowledge to be properly utilized, you have to do it through the means of private property.

THE ECONOMIC LOGIC
BEHIND BLACK MARKETS

INTERVIEWER: Tell me why you can see the black market as a positive thing.

MILTON FRIEDMAN: Well, the black market was a way of getting around government controls. It was a way of enabling the free market to work. It was a way of opening up, enabling people. You want to trade with me, and the law won't let you. But that trade will be mutually beneficial to both of us. The most important single central fact about a free market is that no exchange takes place unless both parties benefit. The big difference between government coercion and private markets is that government can use coercion to make an exchange in which A benefits and B loses. But in the market, if A and B come to a voluntary agreement, it's because both of them are better off. And that's what the black market does, is to get around these artificial government restrictions. Now, obviously you'd like a world in which you obey the law. The fact that the black market involves breaking the law is something against it. It's an undesirable feature. But this only exists when there are bad laws. And nobody, nobody believes that obeying every law is an ultimate moral principle. There comes a point, if you look back at the history of law obedience—think of conscientious objection during wars—I think you will see that everybody agrees that there is a point at which there is a higher law than the legislative law.

ON FRIEDRICH HAYEK AND THE MONT PELERIN MEETING

INTERVIEWER: Do you remember reading Hayek's *Road to Serfdom*? Did that have an impact on you?

MILTON FRIEDMAN: Yes, it certainly did have an impact. It was a very clear, definite statement of certain fundamental ideas. It was a passionate plea by a passionate man, and so it was very well written, and for those of us who were concerned about these kinds of issues, I think it had a tremendous impact. In fact, I've often gone around and asked people what determined their views. I've asked people who were in favor of free markets and free enterprise, people who formerly had been of a different view, what caused them to change their mind. I'm talking particularly not about economists, not about professionals, but generally ordinary people, most of whom had been socialist or in favor of government control at one time and had come over to free markets. And two names have come up over and over again: Hayek on the one hand, *The Road to Serfdom* from Hayek, and Ayn Rand on the other, *Atlas Shrugged* and her other books.

INTERVIEWER: You were invited to Friedrich Hayek's first Mont Pelerin meeting in 1947. Why?

MILTON FRIEDMAN: Well, I was invited primarily because of my brother-in-law, Aaron Director. He was an economist teaching [at] the University of Chicago, and when Hayek's *Road to Serfdom* was submitted to American publishers, one publisher after another rejected it. He was finally published by the University of Chicago Press, partly because of Aaron Director's intervention. He wasn't at Chicago at the time, he was in Washington, but he knew the director of the press, and he also was very close to

Frank Knight, who was a professor at Chicago. And so Aaron had a considerable role in getting *The Road to Serfdom* published.

Also, he had studied at the London School of Economics and had met Hayek [there] before. One of the people whom Hayek was in touch with when he was exploring the possibilities of having the Mont Pelerin meeting was there. And so Aaron organized a group from the University of Chicago. There was myself, there was George Stigler, there was Frank Knight, and there was Aaron Director.

INTERVIEWER: What kind of people gathered at Mont Pelerin, and what was the point of the meeting?

MILTON FRIEDMAN: The point of the meeting was very clear. It was Hayek's belief, and the belief of other people who joined him there, that freedom was in serious danger. During the war, every country had relied heavily on government to organize the economy, to shift all production toward armaments and military purposes. And you came out of the war with the widespread belief that the war had demonstrated that central planning would work. It reinforced the lesson that had earlier been driven home, supposedly, by Russia. The left in particular, or the intellectuals in general in Britain and the United States, in France, wherever, had interpreted Russia as a successful experiment in central planning. And so there were strong movements everywhere. In Britain a socialist [Clement Attlee] had won the election. In France there was indicative planning that was [in] development. And so everywhere, Hayek and others felt that freedom was very much imperiled, that the world was turning toward planning and that somehow we had to develop an intellectual current that would offset that movement. This was the theme of *The Road to Serfdom*. Essentially, the Mont Pelerin Society was an attempt to offset *The Road to Serfdom*, to start a movement, a road to freedom as it were. Now, who were the people who were there? There were economists, historians, mostly economists and historians, but a few journalists and businessmen, people who, despite the general intellectual current moving towards socialism, had retained the belief in free markets and in political and economic freedom.

They were those people whom Hayek happened to know, or whom he had met, whom he had run into in the course of his travels.

INTERVIEWER: What was Hayek's role at these meetings, and what was he like personally? This must have been the first time you met him.

MILTON FRIEDMAN: No, I had met him before that. I had met him in Chicago when he was in the United States lecturing on *The Road to Serfdom*. Hayek's role? Number one, he was responsible for the meeting. He organized it. He selected the people who were going to be there. He helped to line up some of the money that was used to finance it, though a considerable part of that came from a Swiss source. That's why it was held in Switzerland. So far as his role at the meetings was concerned, he gave a talk at the opening session which set out what he had in mind. Along with several other people, he set up the agenda and presided over some of the sessions, participated in the debates, and was a very effective participant from beginning to end.

INTERVIEWER: Some of those debates became very, very heated. I think [Ludwig] von Mises once stormed out.

MILTON FRIEDMAN: Oh, yes, he did. Yes, in the middle of a debate on the subject of distribution of income, in which you had people who you would hardly call socialist or egalitarian—people like Lionel Robbins, like George Stigler, like Frank Knight, like myself—Mises got up and said, "You're all a bunch of socialists," and walked right out of the room. (laughs) But Mises was a person of very strong views and rather intolerant about any differences of opinion.

INTERVIEWER: What was Hayek's personal style? What was he like personally?

MILTON FRIEDMAN: Oh, personally Hayek was a lovely man, a pure intellectual. He was seriously interested in the truth and in understanding. He differed very much in this way from Mises. There was none of that same kind of manner. He accepted disagreement and wanted to argue, wanted to reason about it and discuss it. He was a very cultured and delightful

companion on any occasion. . . . I must say, he undoubtedly was the dominant figure in all of the Mont Pelerin meetings for many, many years.

ON JOHN MAYNARD KEYNES

INTERVIEWER: What impact did John Maynard Keynes have on you?

MILTON FRIEDMAN: Well, I read his book, of course, *The General Theory of Employment, Interest, and Money*, as everybody else did. I may say I had earlier read a good deal of Keynes. In fact, in my opinion, one of the best books he wrote was published in 1924 I believe, *A Tract on Monetary Reform*, which I think is really, in the long run, fundamentally better than *The General Theory*, which came much later. And so I was exposed to Keynes as a graduate student, and his *General Theory* was in the air. Everybody was talking about it. It was part of the general atmosphere.

It was when I went back and looked at some memos that I had written while I was working at the Treasury that I discovered how much more Keynesian I was than I thought. (amused) So what was his influence on me? It was, as on everybody else, to emphasize fiscal policy as opposed to mon-etary policy, and in particular to pay relatively little attention to the quantity of money as opposed to the interest rate.

INTERVIEWER: On a personal level, what contact did you have with him?

MILTON FRIEDMAN: With Keynes? The only contact I had with him was to submit an article to the *Economic Journal*, which he was editor of, which he refused and rejected. I had no personal contact with him other than that.

INTERVIEWER: What did the rejection say?

MILTON FRIEDMAN: Well, it was an article that was critical of some-thing that A.C. Pigou, a professor in London and at Cambridge, had written. And Keynes wrote back that he had shown my article to Pigou. Pigou did not agree with the criticism, and so he had decided to reject it. The article was subsequently published by the *Quarterly Journal of Economics*, and Pigou wrote a rejoinder to it.

INTERVIEWER: When did you begin to break with Keynes and why? What were the first doubts you had?

MILTON FRIEDMAN: Very shortly after the war, when I came to the University of Chicago and started working on money and its relation to the economic cycle. I cannot tell you exactly when, but very shortly thereafter, as I studied the facts, they seemed to me to contradict what Keynesian theory would call for.

INTERVIEWER: What was it that you studied that made you begin to feel that this didn't add up?

MILTON FRIEDMAN: Let me emphasize [that] I think Keynes was a great economist. I think his particular theory in *The General Theory of Employment, Interest, and Money* is a fascinating theory. It's a right kind of a theory. It's one which says a lot by using only a little. So it's a theory that has great potentiality.

And you know, in all of science, progress comes through people proposing hypotheses which are subject to test and rejected and replaced by better hypotheses. And Keynes's theory, in my opinion, was one of those very productive hypotheses—a very ingenious one, a very intelligent one. It just turned out to be incompatible with the facts when it was put to the test. So I'm not criticizing Keynes. I am a great admirer of Keynes as an economist, much more than on the political level. On the political level, that's a different question, but as an economist, he was brilliant and one of the great economists.

Now the crucial issue is, which is more important in determining the short-run course of the economy? What happens to investment on the one hand, or what happens to the quantity of money on the other hand? What happens to fiscal policy on the one hand, or what happens to monetary policy on the other hand? And the facts that led me to believe that his hypothesis was not correct was that again and again it turned out that what happened to the quantity of money was far more important than what was happening to investments. The essential difference between the Keynesian theory and the pre-Keynesian, or the monetarist theory, as it was developed, is whether what's important to understanding the short-run movements of the economy is the relation between the flow of investments—the amount of money being spent on new investments, on the one hand, or the flow of money, the quantity of money in the economy and what's happening to it. By the quantity of money I just mean the cash that people count, carry around in their pockets and the deposits that they have in banks on which they can write checks. That's the quantity of money. And the quantity of money is controlled by monetary policy. On the investment side the flow of investment is controlled by private individuals, but is also affected by fiscal policy, by government taxing and government spending. The essential Keynesian argument, the basic Keynesian argument, was that the way to affect what happened to the economy as a whole, not to a particular part of it, but to the level of income, of employment and so on, was through fiscal policy, through changing government taxes and spending. The argument from the monetarists' side was that what was more important was what was happening to the quantity of money, monetary policy on that side. And so, as I examined the facts about these phenomena, it more and more became clear that what was important was the flow of money as compared to the flow of government spending, and when fiscal policy and monetary policy went in the same direction, you couldn't tell which was more important. But if you looked at those periods when fiscal policy went in one direction and monetary policy went in another direction, invariably it was what happened to monetary policy that determined matters. The public event that changed the opinion of the profession and of people at large was the stagflation of the 1970s, because under the Keynesian view, that was a period in which you had a very expansive fiscal policy, in which you should have had a great expansion in the economy. And instead you had two things at the same time, which under the Keynesian view would have been impossible: You had stagnation in the economy, a high level of unemployment. You had inflation with prices rising rapidly. We had predicted in advance that that would be what happened, and when it happened, it was very effective in leading people to believe that, maybe, there was something to what before had been regarded as utter nonsense.

INTERVIEWER: Was stagflation the end for Keynesianism?

MILTON FRIEDMAN: Stagflation was the end of naive Keynesianism. Now obviously the term "Keynesian" can mean anything you want it to mean, and so you have new Keynesianism, but this particular feature was put to an end by the stagflation episode.

INTERVIEWER: Talking about Keynesian policies, John Kenneth Galbraith, when we talked to him a few days ago, said that World War II "affirmed Keynes and his policies." Do you agree?

MILTON FRIEDMAN: No, I don't agree at all. World War II affirmed what everybody knew for a long time. If you print enough money and spend it you can create an appearance of activity and prosperity. That's what it confirmed. It did not confirm his theories about how you preserve full employment over a long time.

THE GREAT DEPRESSION

INTERVIEWER: You've written that what really caused the Depression was mistakes by the government. Looking back now, what in your view was the actual cause?

MILTON FRIEDMAN: Well, we have to distinguish between the recession of 1929, the early stages, and the conversion of that recession into a major catastrophe. The recession was an ordinary business cycle. We had repeated recessions over hundreds of years, but what converted [this one] into a major depression was bad monetary policy. The Federal Reserve system had been established to prevent what actually happened. It was set up to avoid a situation in which you would have to close down banks, in which you would have a banking crisis. And yet, under the Federal Reserve system, you had the worst banking crisis in the history of the United States. There's no other example I can think of, of a government measure which produced so clearly the opposite of the results that were intended. And what happened is that [the Federal Reserve] followed policies which led to a decline in the quantity of money by a third. For every $100 in paper money, in deposits, in cash, in currency, in existence in 1929, by the time you got to 1933 there was only about $65, $66 left. And that extraordinary collapse in the banking system, with about a third of the banks failing from beginning to end, with millions of people having their savings essentially washed out, that decline was utterly unnecessary. At all times, the Federal Reserve had the power and the knowledge to have stopped that. And there were people at the time who were all the time urging them to do that. So it was, in my opinion, clearly a mistake of policy that led to the Great Depression.

INTERVIEWER: How did the Depression change your life and your career plans? You started out [with plans] to become an insurance actuary; instead you became an economist.

MILTON FRIEDMAN: Well, I don't think that's very hard to understand. It's 1932. Twenty-five percent of the American working force is unemployed. My major problem with the world is a problem of scarcity in the midst of plenty ... of people starving while there are unused resources ... people having skills which are not being used. If you're a 19-year-old college senior, which is going to be more important to you: figuring out what the right prices ought to be for life insurance, or trying to understand how the world got into that kind of a mess?

WHY ARE YOU NOT, AND WHY HAVE YOU NEVER BEEN, A COMMUNIST?

INTERVIEWER: A lot of people in the '30s were drawn to the left. So why are you not and why have you never been a communist?

MILTON FRIEDMAN: (laughs) No, I've not, never been a communist. Never even been a socialist—[though] it may well be that I harbored socialist thoughts at the time when I was an undergraduate. But undoubtedly [the fact that I'm not a communist] is tied in with the accident that I went to the University of Chicago for graduate study and at the department of economics at the University of Chicago, they were classical liberal economists. Classical economics, which begins with Adam Smith, with his book *The Wealth of Nations*, published in 1776, the same year as the American Revolution and the American Declaration of Independence, emphasizes the individual as the ultimate objective of science. And the question of economic science is how to explain the way in which individuals interact with one another, to use their limited resources to satisfy their alternative ends. The emphasis is on the fact that there are many objectives that people have. There are limited resources to satisfy them. What's the mechanism whereby you decide which ends are to be satisfied for which people in what way? And the emphasis in the classical liberal economists is on doing that through free markets.

DID YOU SUPPORT FRANKLIN ROOSEVELT'S NEW DEAL?

INTERVIEWER: Now at the time of the Depression, did you personally support New Deal policies?

MILTON FRIEDMAN: You're now talking not about the Depression, but the post-Depression. At least the bottom of the Depression was in 1933. You have to distinguish between two classes of New Deal policies. One class of New Deal policies was reform: wage and price control, the Blue Eagle, the national industrial recovery movement. I did not support those. The other part of the new deal policy was relief and recovery . . . providing relief for the unemployed, providing jobs for the unemployed, and motivating the economy to expand . . . an expansive monetary policy. Those parts of the New Deal I did support.

INTERVIEWER: But why did you support those?

MILTON FRIEDMAN: Because it was a very exceptional circumstance. We'd gotten into an extraordinarily difficult situation, unprecedented in the nation's history. You had millions of people out of work. Something had to be done; it was intolerable. And it was a case in which, unlike most cases, the short run deserved to dominate. I want to emphasize that you're talking about a long time ago. I was very young and unsophisticated, inexperienced, and I can't swear to you that what I'm saying now is actually what I believed then. I don't have any record of what my specific attitude was toward the New Deal policies. I must confess that probably I was thinking at that time more about my own interests and position than I was about these broader issues. So I think this is somewhat retrospective thinking rather than thinking at the time.

ON RICHARD NIXON

MILTON FRIEDMAN: Nixon was the most socialist of the presidents of the United States in the 20th century.

INTERVIEWER: I've heard Nixon accused of many things, but never [of being] a socialist before.

MILTON FRIEDMAN: Well, his ideas were not socialist, quite the opposite, but if you look at what happened during his administration, first of all, the number of pages in the Federal Register, which is full of regulations about business, doubled during his regime. During his regime the EPA, the Environmental Protection Agency, was established and the OSHA, the Occupational Safety and Health Administration, the OECA [the Office of Enforcement and Compliance Assurance of the EPA]— about a dozen, a half-dozen alphabetic agencies were established so that you had the biggest increase in government regulation and control of industry during the Nixon administration that you had in the whole postwar period.

INTERVIEWER: Tell us how Nixon decided to adopt wage and price controls.

MILTON FRIEDMAN: Nixon, as you know, had been in the price control organization during World War II and understood that price controls were a very bad idea, and so he was strongly opposed to price controls. And yet, in 1971, August 15, 1971, he adopted wage and price controls. And the reason he did it, in my opinion, was because of something else that was happening, and that had to do with the exchange rate; that had to do with Bretton Woods and the agreement to peg the price of gold. The United States had agreed in 1944, at the Bretton Woods Conference, on an international financial system under which other countries would link their currencies to the U.S. dollar, and the United States would link its currency to gold and keep the price of gold at $35 an ounce. And because of the policies that were followed by the Kennedy and Johnson administrations, it had become very difficult to do that. We had had inflationary policies, which led to a tendency for the gold to flow out, for the price of gold to go above $35 an ounce. And the situation had become very critical in 1971. Nixon had to do something about that. If he had done nothing but close the gold window, if he had said the United States is going off the gold standard and done nothing else, every headline in every newspaper would have been, "That negative Nixon again! Just a negative act." And so instead he dressed it up by making it part of a general economic policy, a recovery policy, in which wage and price controls, which the democrats had been urging all along, became a major element. And by putting together the combination of closing the gold window and at the same time having wage and price controls, he converted what would have been a negative from a political point of view to a political positive. And that was the political reason for which he did it.

INTERVIEWER: There is a photograph of you and George Shultz with Nixon in the Oval Office. What did you say to him on that occasion? What did you tell him?

MILTON FRIEDMAN: Well, I don't know what occasion that particular one was, but the one that's relevant to your question is the last time I saw Nixon in the Oval Office with George Shultz. What we usually discussed when Nixon wanted to talk was the state of the economy: what monetary policy was doing.

Nixon was a very, very smart person. In fact, he had one of the highest IQs of any public official I've met. The problem with Nixon was not intelligence and not prejudices. The problem with him was that he was willing to sacrifice principles too easily for political advantage. But at any rate, as I was getting up to leave, President Nixon said to me, "Don't blame George for this silly business of wage and price controls," meaning George Shultz. And I believe I said to him, I think I said to him, "Oh, no, Mr. President. I don't blame George; I blame you!" (laughs) And that, I think, was the last thing I said to him. Now, the interesting point of that story is that the Nixon tapes are now available, and I have been trying to get that part of the Nixon tapes, but I haven't been able to get them yet. I want to make sure I didn't make this up.

ON RONALD REAGAN

INTERVIEWER: Tell us briefly how Paul Volcker set out to squeeze inflation out of the economy.

MILTON FRIEDMAN: Well, by the time Paul Volcker came along—this was in 1968–69 [Volcker was undersecretary in the Treasury Department from 1969–74, president of the New York Federal Reserve Bank from 1975–79, and appointed chairman of the Board of Governors of the Federal Reserve Board from 1979–87]—inflation had gotten very high and had gone up close to 20 percent. He was at a meeting of the International Monetary Fund in Yugoslavia in 1979, when the U.S. came under great criticism from the other people there for our inflationary policies. And he came back to the United States and had got the open market committee to announce that they would change their policy and shift from controlling interest rates to controlling the quantity of money. Now, this was mostly verbal rhetoric. What he really wanted to do was to have the interest rate go up very high, to reflect the amount of inflation. But he could do it better by professing that he wasn't controlling it and that he was controlling the quantity of money, and the right policy at that time was to limit what was happening to the quantity of money, and that meant the interest rate shot way up. This is a complex story. It isn't all one way, because in early 1980 President Carter introduced controls on installment spending, and that caused a very sharp collapse in the credit market and caused a very sharp downward spiral in the economy. To counter that, the Federal Reserve increased the money supply very rapidly. In the five months before the 1980 election, the money supply went up more rapidly than in any other five-month period in the postwar era. Immediately after him, Reagan was elected, and the money supply started going down. So that was a very political reaction during that period.

INTERVIEWER: How important was President Reagan's support for Volcker's policies?

MILTON FRIEDMAN: Enormously important. There is no other president in the postwar period who would have stood by without trying to interfere, to intervene with the Federal Reserve. The situation was this: The only way you could get the inflation down was by having monetary contraction. There was no way you could do that without having a temporary recession. The great error in the earlier period had been that whenever there was a little contraction there was a tendency to expand the money supply rapidly in order to avoid unemployment. That stop-and-go policy was really what bedeviled the Fed during the '60s and '70s. That was the situation in 1980, in '81 in particular. After Reagan came into office, the Fed did step on the money supply, did hold down its growth, and that did lead to a recession. At that point every other president would have immediately come in and tried to get the Federal Reserve to expand. Reagan knew what was happening. He understood very well that the only way he could get inflation down was by accepting a temporary recession, and he supported Volcker and did not try to intervene. Now, you know, there is a myth that Reagan was somehow simpleminded and didn't understand these things. That's a bunch of nonsense. He understood this issue very well. And I know—I can speak with, I think, authority on this—that he realized what he was doing, and he knew very well that he was risking his political standing in order to achieve a basic economic objective. And, as you know, his poll ratings went way down in 1982, and then, when the inflation seemed to be broken enough, the Fed reversed policy, started to expand the money supply, the economy recovered, and along with it, Reagan's poll ratings went back up.

INTERVIEWER: And the economy has been pretty solid ever since. [As of the year 2000.]

MILTON FRIEDMAN: Yes, absolutely. There is no doubt in my mind that that action of Reagan, plus his emphasis on lowering tax rates, plus his emphasis on deregulating... I mentioned that the regulations had doubled, the number of pages in the Federal Register had doubled, during the Nixon regime; they almost halved during the Reagan regime. So those actions of Reagan unleashed the basic constructive forces of the free market and from 1983 on, it's been almost entirely up.

INTERVIEWER: What Reagan was doing is almost exactly mirrored in Britain by what Mrs. Thatcher was doing at about the same time. Are the two influencing to each other, or is it just a case of ideas coming into their own?

MILTON FRIEDMAN: Both of them faced similar situations. And both of them, fortunately, had exposure to similar ideas. And they reinforced one another. Each saw the success of the other. I think that the coincidence of Thatcher and Reagan having been in office at the same time was enormously important for the public acceptance, worldwide, of a different approach to economic and monetary policy.

ON HIS ROLE IN CHILE UNDER PINOCHET

INTERVIEWER: Tell us about some of the abuse you had to suffer and the degree to which you were seen as a figure out on the fringes.

MILTON FRIEDMAN: Well, I wouldn't call it abuse, really. (laughs) I enjoyed it. The only thing I would call abuse was in connection with the Chilean episode, when Allende was thrown out in Chile, and a new government came in that was headed by Pinochet. At that time, for an accidental reason, the only economists in Chile who were not tainted with the connection to Allende were a group that had been trained at the University of Chicago, who got to be known as the Chicago Boys. And at one stage I went down to Chile and spent five days there with another group—there were three or four of us from Chicago—giving a series of lectures on the Chilean problem, particularly the problem of inflation and how they should proceed to do something about it. The communists were determined to overthrow Pinochet. It was very important to them, because Allende's regime, they thought, was going to bring a communist state in through regular political channels, not by revolution. And here, Pinochet overthrew that. They were determined to discredit Pinochet. As a result, they were going to discredit anybody who had anything to do with him. And in that connection, I was subject to abuse in the sense that there were large demonstrations against me at the Nobel ceremonies in Stockholm. I remember seeing the same faces in the crowd in a talk in Chicago and a talk in Santiago. And there was no doubt that there was a concerted effort to tar and feather me.

INTERVIEWER: It seems to us that Chile deserves a place in history because it's the first country to put Chicago theory into practice. Do you agree?

MILTON FRIEDMAN: No, no, no. Not at all. After all, Great Britain put Chicago theory in practice in the 19th century. (amused) The United States put the Chicago theory in practice in the 19th and 20th century. I don't believe that's right.

INTERVIEWER: You don't see Chile as a small turning point, then?

MILTON FRIEDMAN: It may have been a turning point, but not because it was the first place to put the Chicago theory in practice. It was important on the political side, not so much on the economic side. Here was the first case in which you had a movement toward communism that was replaced by a movement toward free markets. See, the really extraordinary thing about the Chilean case was that a military government followed the opposite of military policies. The military is distinguished from the ordinary economy by the fact that it's a top-down organization. The general tells the colonel, the colonel tells the captain, and so on down, whereas a market is a bottom-up organization. The customer goes into the store and tells the retailer what he wants; the retailer sends it back up the line to the manufacturer and so on. So the basic organizational principles in the military are almost the opposite of the basic organizational principles of a free market and a free society. And the really remarkable thing about Chile is that the military adopted the free-market arrangements instead of the military arrangements.

INTERVIEWER: When you were down in Chile you spoke to some students in Santiago. In your own words, can you tell me about that speech in Santiago?

MILTON FRIEDMAN: Sure. While I was in Santiago, Chile, I gave a talk at the Catholic University of Chile. Now, I should explain that the University of Chicago had had an arrangement for years with the Catholic University of Chile, whereby they send students to us and we send people down there to help them reorganize their economics department. And I gave a talk at the Catholic University of Chile under the title "The Fragility of Freedom." The essence of the talk was that freedom was a very fragile thing and that what destroyed it more than anything else was central control; that in order to maintain freedom, you had to have free markets, and that free markets would work best if you had political freedom. So it was essentially an anti-totalitarian talk. (amused)

INTERVIEWER: So you envisaged, therefore, that the free markets ultimately would undermine Pinochet?

MILTON FRIEDMAN: Oh, absolutely. The emphasis of that talk was that free markets would undermine political centralization and political control. And incidentally, I should say that I was not in Chile as a guest of the government. I was in Chile as the guest of a private organization.

INTERVIEWER: Do you think the Chile affair damaged your reputation, or more importantly, made it harder for you to get your ideas across?

MILTON FRIEDMAN: That's a very hard thing to say, because I think it had effects in both directions. It got a lot of publicity. It made a lot of people familiar with the views who would not otherwise have been. On the other hand, in terms of the political side of it, as you realize, most of the intellectual community, the intellectual elite, as it were, were on the side of Allende, not on the side of Pinochet. And so in a sense they regarded me as a traitor for having been willing to talk in Chile. I must say, it's such a wonderful example of a double standard, because I had spent time in Yugosla-via, which was a communist country. I later gave a series of lectures in China. When I came back from communist China, I wrote a letter to the Stanford Daily newspaper in which I said, "'It's curious. I gave exactly the same lectures in China that I gave in Chile. I have had many demonstrations against me for what I said in Chile. Nobody has made any objections to what I said in China. How come?"

INTERVIEWER: In the end, the Chilean [economy] did quite well, didn't it?

MILTON FRIEDMAN: Oh, very well. Extremely well. The Chilean economy did very well, but more important, in the end the central govern-ment, the military junta, was replaced by a democratic society. So the really important thing about the Chilean business is that free markets did work their way in bringing about a free society.

WHERE WE STAND TODAY

INTERVIEWER: From your apartment, you can almost see Silicon Valley. How do you think information technology, the Internet, and the new economy, will affect the big issues of economics and politics that you've devoted your life to?

MILTON FRIEDMAN: The most important ways in which I think the Internet will affect the big issue is that it will make it more difficult for government to collect taxes. And I think that's a very important factor. Governments can most effectively collect taxes on things that can't move. That's why property taxes are invariably the first tax. People can move, so it's a little more difficult to collect taxes on them. States within the United States find it more difficult to collect taxes on people, but the United States as a whole can collect taxes on people more easily. Now the Internet, by enabling transactions to be made in cyberspace, not recorded, by enabling them to move so that somebody in Britain can order books from Amazon. com in the United States, somebody in the United States can do a deal in

India, I think the cyberspace is going to make it very much more difficult for government to collect taxes, and that will have a very important effect on reducing the role that governments can play.

INTERVIEWER: So we're sort of marching forward to a kind of, the ultimate "Hayekian" state, are we?

MILTON FRIEDMAN: I think we are in that respect. Now, of course it has its advantages and disadvantages. It makes it easier for criminals to conduct their affairs, but, you know, you have to distinguish between criminals and criminals. We have as many criminals as we have because we have as many laws to break as we have. You take the situation in the United States. We have two million people in prison, four million people who are under parole or under supervision. Why? Because of our mistaken attempt to control what people put in their bodies. Prohibition of so-called drugs, of illegal drugs, is a major reason for all of those prisons. And those are victimless crimes, which should not be crimes.

INTERVIEWER: More than half a century after that first meeting in Mont Pelerin, who's won the argument? Who's lost?

MILTON FRIEDMAN: There is no doubt who won the intellectual argument. There is no doubt that the received intellectual opinion of the world today is much less favorable towards central planning and controls than it was in 1947. What's much more dubious is who won the practical argument. The world is more socialist today than it was in 1947. Government spending in almost every Western country is higher today than it was in 1947, as a fraction of income, not simply in dollars. Government regulation of business is larger. There has not been a great deal of nationalization, socialization in that sense, but government intervention in the economy has undoubtedly gone up. The only countries where that is not true are the countries which were formerly part of the communist system. You can see that we won the argument in practice as well as on the intellectual level in Poland, in Czechoslovakia, in Hungary, in Russia, and throughout that part of the world. But in the West, the practical argument is as yet undecided.

INTERVIEWER: Are you hopeful?

MILTON FRIEDMAN: Oh, yes, I'm very hopeful about it. Don't misunderstand me. At the moment we have not won the argument in practice, but I think in the long run ideas will dominate, and I think we will win the argument in practice as well as on the intellectual level.

INTERVIEWER: Central controls have been discredited, the governments seem to have retreated remarkably, but are we becoming increasingly regulated?

MILTON FRIEDMAN: You have to distinguish different areas. Some kinds of regulations have declined. Regulations of prices, particular regulations of industries as a whole have declined. Other kinds of regulations, particularly regulations on personal behavior, have gone up. It's social control that has been taking the place of narrow economic control.

INTERVIEWER: Do you feel some of those regulations are ultimately a threat to the free market?

MILTON FRIEDMAN: They're not a threat to the free market. They're a threat to human freedom.

INTERVIEWER: At the moment, governments everywhere are retreating from the marketplace, or seem to be. Do you think a pendulum could swing back the other way?

MILTON FRIEDMAN: The pendulum easily can swing back the other way. It can swing back the other way, not because anybody wants to do it in a positive sense, but simply because as long as you have governments which control a great deal of power, there always [will be] pressure from special interests to intervene. And once you get something in government, it's very hard to get it out. So I think there is a real danger. I don't think we can regard the war as won by any manner of means. I think it still is true that it takes continued effort to keep a society free. What's the saying? "Eternal vigilance is the price of liberty."

ORIGINAL
PUBLICATION
INFORMATION

1. "Neo-Liberalism and Its Prospects," *Farmand* (Oslo, Norway; February 17, 1951). Reprinted courtesy of the Friedman family.
2. "Liberalism, Old Style," *1955 Collier's Year Book* (New York: P. F. Collier & Son, 1955). Reprinted courtesy of the Friedman family.
3. "Schools at Chicago," *The University of Chicago Magazine* (Autumn 1974); and also *The University of Chicago Record*, 1974. (Remarks at the 54th Annual Board of Trustees' Dinner for the Faculty, University of Chicago, January 9, 1974.) This version appeared in the *University of Chicago Record*, reprinted courtesy of *the Special Collections Research Center, University of Chicago Library*.
4. "Adam Smith's Relevance for 1976," Selected Papers, no. 50, Graduate School of Business, The University of Chicago. (Presented at a meeting of the Mont Pelerin Society, St. Andrews, Scotland, 1976.)
5. "Introduction to Republication of the *New Individualist Review*" (Indianapolis: Liberty Press, 1981). Reprinted courtesy of the *New Individualist Review* and Liberty Fund, Inc.

6.   "The Tide in the Affairs of Men," by Milton Friedman and Rose D. Friedman, in *Thinking about America: The United States in the 1990s*, edited by Annelise Anderson and Dennis L. Bark (Stanford: Hoover Institution Press, 1988).

7.   "An Open Letter to Bill Bennett," *Wall Street Journal* (September 7, 1989). Reprinted from the *Wall Street Journal* © 1989 Dow Jones & Company. All rights reserved. Reprinted courtesy of the Friedman family.

8.   "How to Cure Health Care," *The Public Interest* (Winter 2001). Reprinted courtesy of *National Affairs*.

9.   "Fortieth Anniversary Preface to *Capitalism and Freedom*" (University of Chicago Press, 2002).

10.   "My Five Favorite Libertarian Books," *FEE Today* (April 2002), FEE. Reprinted by permission of FEE (Foundation for Economic Education), www.FEE.org.

11.   "School Choice: A Personal Retrospective," *Wall Street Journal* (June 9, 2005; appeared under the title "Free to Choose"). Also appeared as the Prologue to *Liberty & Learning: Milton Friedman's Voucher Idea at Fifty*, which is the version that appears here. Publication information is as follows: Milton Friedman, "Prologue: A Personal Retrospective," in *Liberty & Learning: Milton Friedman's Voucher Idea at Fifty*, Robert C. Enlow and Lenore T. Ealy (Eds.), pp. vii–x. © 2006 by the Cato Institute. All rights reserved. Reproduced by permission.

12.   "Wesley C. Mitchell as an Economic Theorist," *Journal of Political Economy* (December 1950). Reprinted here with minor changes as "The Economic Theorist," in *Wesley Clair Mitchell: The Economic Scientist*, edited by Arthur F. Burns (New York: National Bureau of Economic Research, 1952), pp. 237–50, copyright, 1952, by National Bureau of Economic Research, Inc., 1819 Broadway, New York 23, All Rights Reserved. Reproduced by permission of the National Bureau of Economic Research.

13. "Leon Walras and His Economic System," *American Economic Review* (December 1955). Reprinted by permission of the *American Economic Review.*

14. "The Monetary Theory and Policy of Henry Simons," *Journal of Law and Economics* (October 1967). The third Henry Simons Lecture, University of Chicago Law School, May 5, 1967.

15. "The Counter-Revolution in Monetary Theory," IEA Occasional Paper no. 33 (London: Institute of Economic Affairs, 1970).

16. "Homer Jones: A Personal Reminiscence," *Journal of Monetary Economics* (November 1976).

17. "The Keynes Centenary: A Monetarist Reflects," *The Economist* (June 4, 1983). © *The Economist* Newspaper Limited, London 1983. Reprinted by permission.

18. "Freezing High-Powered Money," excerpted from "Monetary Policy for the 1980s," in *To Promote Prosperity: U.S. Domestic Policy in the Mid-1980s,* edited by John H. Moore (Stanford: Hoover Institution Press, 1984). Please see original essay for notes.

19. "George Joseph Stigler," *Biographical Memoirs,* v. 76 (National Academy Press, 1999); the original version included a selected bibliography. Previously appeared as "George Stigler: A Personal Reminiscence," *Journal of Political Economy* (October 1993). Reprinted with permission by the National Academy of Sciences, Courtesy of the National Academies Press, Washington, D.C.

20. "Reflections on *A Monetary History,*" *Cato Journal,* Vol. 23, No. 3, Winter 2004, pp. 349–351. © Cato Institute. All rights reserved. Reproduced by permission.

Appendix. *Commanding Heights* Interview (interview conducted on October 1, 2000), available here, http://www.pbs.org/wgbh/commanding heights/shared/minitext/int_miltonfriedman.html. Reprinted courtesy of the Friedman family.